Judge, Please Don't Strike That Gavel ...

On My Marriage

Judith A. Brumbaugh, MBA, MHE

Cover design by Eleet Technologies: www.eleet-tech.com
PO Box 621995, Oviedo, FL 32762
Joshua Strzalko

This book is being distributed through:
RESTORATION OF THE FAMILY, INC.
PO Box 621342
Oviedo, FL 32762-1342 USA

www.RestorationOfTheFamily.com
RFI is a 50l(c)(3), tax-exempt corporation.

ISBN-10: 0-9624603-0-3
ISBN-13: 978-0-9624603-0-2

Nothing in this book is meant to imply or give legal advice. The author
is not an attorney and is not engaged in rendering legal advice.

Contents

Dedication/Acknowledgements

To the children who are "veterans" of divorce, I deeply regret that you have had to live through the breakup of your family. You know, all too well, that the fallout from it never ends. We as parents have let you down. I and many other parents are deeply sorry.

To our children, Shawn and Mike, and to Jennifer, our daughter-in-law, I'm so sorry for the burdens you have had to bear these many years. There's very little "nice" about divorce in the physical. Its redeeming "grace" is that it has drawn many of us closer to the LORD. I am so grateful for all of your love, support, and outreach and especially your encouragement and help as I continue to fight, not only for our family restoration, but for many others that they might be led to see beyond what often are very destructive and painful circumstances.

And to the TEAM who never gave up on my constant revisions and rewrites of the rewrites that have been a part of this book, I thank you for your tender loving and "long-suffering" care with your many corrections and suggestions concerning this manuscript: Mrs. DeVern (Ruth) Fromke, Mrs. Allen (Marion) Hardin, Mrs. Mark (Lori) Morehead, and Mrs. Roger (Ann) Nixon.

To Judy Shannon, a friend of forty years, who knew us as the loving couple we once were, I appreciate your writing skills which helped to express many difficult passages.

To Fran Austin, thank you for editing and proofing suggestions.

To Mrs. David (Nancy) Sullivan, thank you for writing copy for the back cover of the book.

To Ann Nixon who has been that loving "thorn in the flesh" urging me for the past ten years to share some of my autobiographical sketch, thank you for laboring with me for many years in the ministry of RFI and for the many hours creating the Index, and the many words of encouragement to complete this book.

To those who have been and are continuing to pray for the ministry, Restoration of the Family, Inc., and who support it financially, thank you so much. We cannot DO the *works* without your much-needed help and support, whether it's done here in Florida, or from your home many miles from here.

To those who are Standards, may you never grow weary in well doing, for you shall reap IF you faint not!

To those, named and unnamed in this publication, who have reached out to me in so many ways, may the LORD reward you abundantly.

For those attorneys who reviewed the manuscript and gave me so much encouragement: Kelly Dodd, Claire Ford, Dr. Charles E. Rice, and Shelby Sharpe, thank you.

To Dr. Rice whose critique helped me to see the necessity of rethinking the focus of this book, thank you.

To Dave Hall who resurrected our computers when they crashed during the writing of this manuscript, thank you.

To those at Old Paths Printing, thank you for your guidance and direction for the printing of this manuscript.

And most of all, I'm grateful to Jesus Christ my LORD and Saviour without whom I could not have endured the breakup of our family nor met the challenge of recording it in this manuscript. Above all, I treasure the awesome peace and joy that wells up within me. May I walk worthy of the calling that You have placed upon my life. I thank you with all my heart.

And last, but never least, to Doug, my husband of 43 years, I continue to hold within my heart God's kind of love (charity) that never gives up ... until death us do part.

Introduction

To what lengths would you go to get help for a close friend or relative? What about your spouse? What if he were so ill that he would die if you didn't get medical attention for him immediately? You might rush him to the hospital. You might arrange to airlift him to the nearest emergency center. If he refused to go for help, you might even be willing to borrow a large sum of money to try some unconventional ways to help him understand what was happening to his body, which he either was unwilling or unable to grasp. Do these efforts seem extreme? As this book unfolds, you may recognize similar activities that became a part of my life as providential circumstances taught me the meaning of marriage from God's perspective.

There is a contrast between the evils of what I have presented as the Trojan Horse of No-fault Divorce and the unique kind of love that God addresses as *charity* in I Corinthians 13. The latter is a characteristic you give away with no strings attached, often getting nothing in return except perhaps hatred, divisiveness, and maliciousness. Yet, that something that comes from God's love within empowers the beholder to continue to not grow weary in the task that is put before him.

True love is severely tested when the wall God prepared to surround a marriage is breached. That love is longsuffering, it "beareth all things, believeth all things, endureth all things." It will go to extremes with both personal sacrifices and financial investments to protect loved ones from destructive behaviors. They will resist, they may hate, they may retaliate.

The focus of this book is autobiographical in nature—an overview of a 25-year outreach of the love of a wife for her husband and family in ways that may seem extreme to many and will probably be misunderstood by most. It narrows in focus to six years of what I call *"court-ship."* It was a period of my life which, unfortunately, still continues, but it also taught me a new meaning of love. My "providential" experiences during this time forced me into a different way of living—really depending on the LORD in ways I could never have imagined, nor would have volunteered to experience.

On one side of the coin were periods of depression and brokenheartedness more intense than I had ever previously experienced. On the other side, even though I am still dealing with some of the fallout, I have hope, joy, and peace that I can share with others. My wish is that you will follow along with me as I open some of the recesses of my heart to encourage others who are forced into fighting for their families, and as I urge them to not grow weary or give up.

How immensely blessed I have been to have had the wide range of people come into and, in some cases, go from my life as my circumstances moved me from one crisis to another; and, during one period of my journey, from house to house. I have learned that every person and experience in our lives can be used for good or bad. Therefore I cannot begin to thank everyone who reached out with a helping hand—and even those who did not for they, too, have helped create the person I have become.

There are many legal terms used in this book as my six years in the court system demanded that such become a part of my life. That doesn't mean that I comprehended then, or now, all of their nuances; but they became a part of my journey. May you not miss the intent of my heart—to call loved ones back home to their covenant husband or wife. May those be awakened in the church and government who have lost sight of one of their basic functions—to foster and protect families.

Prominent in this book are several phrases that include the word *color*. This word's application in my life took on new meaning many years ago when I studied a book by J. M. O'Neill, *Religion and Education Under The Constitution*. *Black's Law Dictionary* helped me to see the vital truths this little word encompasses. It is "... concealing a lack of reality, a disguise, or pretext." Doesn't that remind you of what you can do with a crayon? We, with a box of crayons, *color* the surface in front of us with our biases, with our favorite colors, with our skills or lack thereof. We mask what is really underneath with *our* strokes.

That's what this author experienced in our judicial system—the courts. I saw and endured many injustices and inconsistencies. Most citizens would assume we are protected against such through the inalienable rights guaranteed under our Constitution. What was "right" legally seemed to be set aside (usurped/colored) through manipulation of the judicial process. I learned firsthand that our courts are not "equal justice for all," as a number of judicial procedures and activities were/are "colored." Almost a quarter of a century of the clock's ticking has erased numerous hurts and memories, but they have also driven deeper into my heart a special love for my husband that some will find difficult to understand.

As I reviewed my records for much of the information contained in this book, names were renewed in my mind along with some devastating experiences that, thankfully, I had totally wiped from my conscious memory. The letters, several of which are a part of this text, gave me a renewed sense of many of the activities that filled my life and provided "some" semblance of a timeline for what happened when and where and with whom. However, if the reader seems confused by the narrative of legal events, that's because it was confusing to me and still is. What is presented here is the way I lived through it. It was not an organized systematic path, but one with many curves, detours, and events that tossed me back and forth between what I often viewed as legal machinations and the personal tragedies that were forced upon our family.

Most of the names from personal letters and the main "players" in this text have been changed, especially if a negative light would have been cast upon them had I included such. Those of most government employees, however, have been retained. The exception is the fictitious name, *Judge Fuller*. The purpose of this narrative has not been to target any one group or person. It is to alert others to see the dangerous patterns that are re-forming who we are as a nation because of whom we have become as families. Historically, the downfall of any nation can be traced to the breakup of the family.

My sincere desire is that this book will awaken some sleeping giants and alert some busy ants to take up the torch and join the fight for families by supporting financially and prayerfully those standing in the gap for lost loved ones. We must realize that *doing* the work to restore families is a command that not one of us can afford to ignore any longer.

Judith

Chapter 1

TO STAY COMMITTED ...
IT'S THE ONLY ANSWER

HEADLINES: "Home invaded, husband disappears, wife beaten, left with permanent injuries"; "Wife's identity stolen after being forced to sign properties over to thieves, dragged from home, and left in the street to perish." "Children abducted, family treasures stolen." Upon investigation, these domestic crimes were found to be different from most because the thieves were not some derelicts off the street but "representatives" hired by the United States government. No charges could be brought upon these "home breakers" because they were allowed to act with impunity—under *color of law* they had created for such crimes.

These hypothetical, perhaps surrealistic, scenarios may sound extreme, even bizarre—but they metaphorically describe some of the realities of what happens when the judicial system brings the gavel down on a marriage. You may not recognize the specifics, but as you read this book you will see many similar injustices played out in the life of a wife once dearly loved by her covenant husband. His love, however, turned to acts of hatred never thought possible by his wife. This was twenty years after their lifetime commitment had been signed and sealed—"until death they do part."

One of the basic functions of our government is to protect the family. The states, however, have abdicated their duty to fulfill this obligation. Instead, they have actually ratified anti-family statutes which are systematically destroying the very institution they are charged to defend, violating, in the process, the Constitution of the United States of America.

No-fault Divorce is inhumane and unconstitutional.

This Trojan Horse, No-fault, invades more than one million homes every year. A retired Circuit Court judge wrote the following to an individual who was fighting to preserve his family:

To your characterization of No-fault Divorce laws as both "ungodly" and "inhumane," I would add "unconstitutional" as well. The Fifth and Fourteenth Amendments of the U.S. Constitution guarantee citizens the right to *due process* in respect to safeguards against violation of life, liberty, and property.

> **To your characterization of No-fault Divorce laws as both ungodly and inhumane, I would add unconstitutional as well.**

A plausible argument can be made that No-fault Divorce laws violate a nonconsenting spouse's *due process* as well as Article I, Section 10's prohibition that "**no state** shall ... pass any ... law impairing the obligation of contracts ..." **The intent of this latter clause is to prevent state governments from passing laws that would release a party from an obligation to which his contract bound him.**

America is paying a heavy price for its acquiescence in such errors, as the data show that divorce increases the national incidence of crime, abuse, addiction; decreases the capacity to learn, decreases graduation rates, lowers income and raises incidences of poverty, adult and juvenile suicide, and harmful mental and physical health effects. Furthermore, within family life, divorce has the effect of increasing the incidence of: weaker parent-child relationships, destructive ways of handling conflict within the family, troubled courtships, premarital teenage sexual activity and cohabitation of these children. It also keeps the cycle expanding through higher divorce rates of the children of divorced parents. *Let's pray that right-thinking Americans will become energized to bring about needed reform.* (Emphasis author)

This is just the tip of the iceberg of the unconstitutional issues that are promulgated, with or without jurisdiction being established by the court over civil lawsuits in matters of family law. What is it that gives rise to more than a million families **a year** coming before an officer of the court asking him to lower the dissolution axe because of irreconcilable differences? People from all walks of life who once stood at an altar to take vows of marriage to someone with whom they were deeply in love, not only changed their minds, but now are encouraged to do so using an easy legal exit—No-fault. There is strong empirical evidence that **laws of the land have a huge role to play in family stability.** For example, when Ireland had a legal ban on divorce, recorded family break-ups were the exception rather than the rule, and in the U.S., No-fault has been accompanied by a tripling of family dissolutions.

> **Laws of the land greatly affect family stability.**

Those who abandon a marriage let the cares of this world such as changing priorities, financial pursuits, or—as in most instances—changing affections, deceive them. The winds of such form into an eye of the storm called lust.

This "eye" distorts their vision causing them to think that their spouse is their problem and thus file a lawsuit asking the government to dissolve the marriage. The government, which considers marriage to be a legal contract, readily does so. Consequently, in a clean sweep, the Plaintiff is given "jurisprudential sanction" to walk away from the obligations encompassed in the "for-better, for-worse, until-death-us-do-part" commitment. The government has turned this powerful marital commitment into a lifeless, irresponsible contract by providing an easily accessible legal dissolution for spouses.

Perhaps you've been the recipient of such heartbreaking behavior. Perhaps you've wanted to, or in fact did, make an appeal to stop such an unconstitutional strike against your covenant of marriage. I did 22 years ago when I entered my plea: "Judge, please don't strike that gavel on my marriage." As with millions of others, the judge, a representative of our judicial system, struck his gavel firmly on the bench: Marriage dissolved! Dead! He, under color of law, declared void the marriage between Douglas and Judith Brumbaugh created on June 30, 1962.

Color of law is a term mentioned above with which you may not be familiar. Its meaning, however, points to a very important principle about marriage that runs throughout this book—how man destroys and "paints" or "colors" a false picture of marriage. In the Christian culture, marriage was always meant to be a relationship of mutual love and respect between a husband and wife—"to love and cherish, to forsake all others, until death they do part." It, however, has become almost unrecognizable because marriage has been corrupted (colored) by selfishness, sensuality, a lack of commitment, and a government promoting dissolution.

Here's how *Black's Law Dictionary* describes *color of law*: "An appearance or semblance as distinguished from that which is real; the absence of legal right; misuse of power possessed by virtue of state law and made possible

4

only because *wrongdoer is clothed* with authority of state." (*1:241) This would include unlawful acts or abuse of power which are wielded by an official only because he is an official. Such abuses were a major part of the civil suit upon which this book is based. (*See bibliography.)

The home is the incubating place
to teach children godly principles.

The home created out of the love between Doug and me was not one characterized by domestic violence. Instead, it was a partnership of trust, love, and admiration one for each other; of community projects; of 15 years of service and leadership with youth church groups. Throughout the years of this 20-year marriage, the Plaintiff, who filed a lawsuit to **legally** dissolve this permanent marital bond, confirmed his love not only physically, but in many of his poems written to me:

Fifteen years have come and gone
First you and me, then Mike and Shawn
Seventeen and a half years is more a reality
The span of the love between you and me.

As we look back across time's pages
We must conclude that we've had good ages
Work, health, friends, fun and, of course, our rings
Titan, boat, cars, and many other material things.

Then we've been blessed with two kids of our own
*Not to mention the spare ones** through which we've*
* grown*
There must be something they can see here
I guess it's just our class A house, my dear.
[**As youth leaders for 15 years, we had many youths who visited our home and refrigerator (!) and called us "Pa" and "Ma."]

5

It's getting tuff to make things rhyme
Besides, I am running out of time
Class, kids, bills and other things to do
It's time to say, "I love you."

That's really what this whole thing is
Other words don't come, well, gee whiz
I've known and loved only you for all these years
Any more sentimentality might bring tears.

My husband often traveled out of town doing consulting work. On one of the many such occasions, he wrote the following poem:

Words can't describe the way that I feel
Wow, Super, Fantastic aren't even ideal
There are some things I'd like to say
But we'll have to communicate in our own way.

I guess you'll never know the depth of my feeling
Suffice it to say that you sure have me reeling
Your smile, your laugh, your smell, your touch
They all make me want you so very much.

Forever I'll cherish our moments together
Sure is funny, we seldom discuss the weather
When we are there, no matter what we may do
Time passes too quickly for me and you.

I wish you were with me right now
But then I would probably only say, "wow"
It's funny how lonely these trips can be
Oh, how I wish you had come with me.

But then I'll get busy and forget all about it
At least until the next chance I get to sit.

Then as my head clears and my thoughts unwind
Once again you will flit through my mind.

I'll stop trying to make dumb words rhyme
And hope that you've gotten the point by this time
You are the greatest satisfaction of my life
And I am so very proud that you are my wife.

Since judges' gavels come down on more than a million marriages every year, "Why," one might ask, "is there concern about one marriage out of the millions severed by the hand of man?" It's because *Brumbaugh v. Brumbaugh* (and many other marriages) involved legal acts beyond the rightful and judicial authority of man. Some acts, however, are unique to this case and were exacerbated because of my unchanging love for my husband, my love for my family, and my belief that God means what He says as recorded in the Bible—that marriage is only dissolved by the death of one of the spouses. My husband affirmed this latter fact when during one of our court sessions he made the comment, "She's doing this because of what the Bible says" [about marriage].

Why wouldn't I sign?

Unlike most court appearances whose purpose it is to destroy and divide, Judith's purpose was to bring about reconciliation. Here are some statements from a newspaper article that will give a little preview of some of my challenges in the fight to preserve our marriage and family: "Always and Forever: Woman founds ministry on belief that marriage is an unbreakable bond."

REPORTER: "Why wouldn't Judith sign?" [the divorce papers].
JUDITH: "According to the Bible, we are married till death do us part. We made a vow and a

7

covenant with God that's an unconditional promise."

REPORTER: "Doug didn't agree. He, like many Americans, spoke the vow, *Till death us do part*, only to regret making it and breaking it later in life. While an ex-husband or wife might hold it against a person, surely God wouldn't? Nobody really believes that anymore, do they? Judith believes it, with every fiber of her being. That's why she continued to file briefs through the 1980s. The litigation went on for six years. Standing among the ruins of her family, Judith didn't like what she saw."

JUDITH: "I have seen the statistics of what is happening to children because of the breakdown of the family. It's all about the breakdown of the family and what it's doing to this country," she said, "but nobody wants to pay the price to fix it. By doing what I am doing. I am willing to wait. I am not going to 'fix it' by finding someone else."

REPORTER: "Judith believes this passionately."

JUDITH: "[Many] people don't know what it's like to have a mother and a father at home. They're in. They're out. Life is dinner at McDonald's. They don't know how to build permanent relationships or sit down to dinner together."

REPORTER: "According to Judith, there is no such thing as divorce or annulment in the eyes of God. Only death can separate a man and woman made one flesh by God. For this reason, she says, she can never remarry."

JUDITH: "This does not say you have to stay in a situation and get beaten and your children abused. If you do depart, you have two choices. The first is to remain in an unmarried state. The second is to return to your spouse. **We are not called to be beaten and have our children abused.**"

REPORTER: "Many would say that neither are we called to stay in an unsatisfactory relationship."

JUDITH: "It sounds like I'm trying to put people in a box—I'm not—it's all about the breakdown of the family and what it's doing to this country. You cannot hold anybody. Physically Doug has left. He knows that I love him and that I am standing ... Waiting ... Standing on what the Scriptures say. To stay committed—it's the only answer." (2:A10)

The pilgrims acted. The colonists acted. It's time for us to act.

My purpose is not to offend you, the reader, if you hold a view on marriage different from "until death us do part" and especially if you have different religious beliefs. My purpose is to share from my heart a fight I would never have entered if it had not been for what God has made clear to me—His perspective on marriage. If you follow along through the fight for my family, you will see there were some major Biblical **and** especially legal issues that must be addressed—laws and procedures which were and are violated in divorce lawsuits. As part of a *class* of wronged/usurped people, like the colonists (who were subjected to a "jurisdiction foreign to their constitution"); like civil rights' leader Rosa Parks (who was sick and tired of giving up her seat, tired of giving in to inequalities); it's time collectively to DO something. The legislative and judicial restructuring of the family, the attendant destruction of children, and the unconstitutional financial redistribution of family assets must be halted. There is a plethora of empirical evidence that the family unit—a husband and wife and their children—is being erased from the landscape. A person would have to be totally disassociated from reality to dispute such a fact. The purpose of this book is not to present a research paper on such, but to share with readers how our government and many of those who once voluntarily became a part of a life-time commitment to a marriage are now working, often tyrannically, to dissolve marriage and thus destroy the family.

Consider this from the perspective of a wife who was unaware of what can happen to her personal, spiritual, and financial life when her husband rejects her. As you journey through this book, observe how the government became hostile to a layperson who was at the mercy of the legal system—how it harassed, manipulated, and took advantage of her inability to defend herself.

> **I was convicted of a "crime" for which I was not guilty— irreconcilable differences.**

Yes, it was I who was forced into a legal situation against people who had years of legal training and experience while I was a homemaker and mother with a master's degree in Clothing and Textiles. Because of this David-Goliath encounter, I became indigent, was court-ordered from my home, forced to become an itinerant evacuee, and finally convicted of a "crime" of which I was not guilty and could not define—irreconcilable differences.

Prior to this encounter with the judicial system, our family had enjoyed an above average standard of living, having acquired a 4-bedroom marital home, a commercial building, a motor home, ski boat, etc. Our family traveled extensively and pursued recreational activities on a regular basis. Using the motor home in this way also provided us with many hours of fun and strengthened our family bond.

I, like many wives in agreement with our husbands, chose homemaking as my primary career while simultaneously assisting my husband in activities to build his career, and spearheading other home-based business endeavors to supplement our income. This support helped him to acquire both master's and doctorate degrees. I also participated in many other ways supporting Doug's climb to national recognition in his field. Together, we edited his professional writings, put on seminars, and spent numerous hours on mailings when he was elected an officer for a national mathematics organization.

TOGETHERNESS was the word to best describe our marriage. From tennis to community volunteerism, to church youth and adult leaders (while building home businesses), we were always together, each helping and supporting the other.

We had a quiet, unspoken way of communicating. Doug was never a bully or tyrant. When differences of opinion arose, I accepted his point of view, not because he forced such, but because I loved him, and he was head of our home. Most issues were not important enough to disagree over.

Then, the unthinkable happened. A divorce! Now there was an issue important enough to compel disagreement! Because of a decision on my part to disagree, within a matter of months, I became a person without a family, a court-defined indigent (poverty-stricken), and an incompetent (person not legally educated or qualified for the task— the task of defending our marriage against judicial annihilation).

Detailed in this book, my "court-ship" experiences can perhaps open the eyes of those who are unaware of the rampant injustices perpetrated by the **government whose stated function it is to safeguard families and their proprietary rights.** Perhaps my sharing these issues will awaken you, the reader, to the need to fight for families for they are fast becoming an endangered species.

This is presented as an intertwined blending of my husband's and the judicial system's hostility toward me when I refused to accept its efforts to end our marriage

11

legally by a court decree. Both were accustomed to getting their ways. For the courts, the solution was simple. Got a problem? Rubber-stamp it: Marriage dissolved.

My customary pattern of going along with my husband's ideas and suggestions suddenly took an extreme 180 degree turn. I became unmoveable when it came to destroying our 22-year marriage with its family cohesiveness, numerous good times with friends and family members, along with our difficult graduate school years and interim years with financial struggles.

Yet, when I decided to fight against this altered version of the man I married, he lashed out in ways I never believed possible—a fury I had never before witnessed. The hatred! The venom! How could this person I knew so intimately be so changed? The only explanation that makes sense to me is that his request for a divorce represented a complete denial of his basic character. He had gone against every value he had held dear.

I was the person who represented what he walked away from—family, commitment, trust. I became a symbol of what he used to be. My continued presence and struggle to preserve our marriage and family were constant reminders that he was no longer the person he had been for forty-two years. Someone was wrong. He felt it was I, and he needed to destroy—to get rid of the "evidence." But I didn't go away; I didn't disappear! If I had agreed with him, some very ugly things probably would never have happened.

> He needed to destroy, to get rid of the "evidence." But I didn't go away; I didn't disappear!

What a challenge awaited me as I unknowingly walked into a lion's den in my effort to defend myself legally against a legislative and judicial system which gives criminals more rights and protections than an honest, God-fearing wife, mother, and law-abiding citizen. At the same time, my husband was able to use the same system to aid and empower him in walking away, with impunity, from our 22-year marriage.

I tried to defend myself against a legislative and judicial system that gives criminals more rights and protections than an honest, God-fearing wife, mother, and law-abiding citizen.

Who can be usurped?

In the civil suit, *Brumbaugh v. Brumbaugh*, there were many issues which I perceived as violations of the law and my rights. Most of these arose from two **fraudulent** statements written in the box below taken from the *Final Judgment* which recorded the dissolution on April 18, 1984:

This court has jurisdiction.
This marriage is dissolved.

This court has jurisdiction of the subject matter and of the parties.

The marriage between DOUGLAS K. BRUMBAUGH AND JUDITH A. BRUMBAUGH is dissolved because it is irretrievably broken. (3:1)

These will be discussed later, but first, consider a little review of the background of our country's struggle to protect some of the rights violated in this divorce suit. Please don't take this lightly. It is a very serious issue to know that we have come almost full circle to the same abuses the Colonists faced and which many citizens are now facing in the area of family law.

The Colonists not only recognized the evils of tyranny and having an unjust government usurp their rights, but they also understood the importance of fighting for those inalienable rights.

Black's Law Dictionary defines an act of usurpation as "The unlawful encroachment or assumption of the use of property, power or authority which belongs to another. An interruption or the disturbing a man in his right and possession. *The unlawful assumption of sovereign power ... in derogation of the Constitution.*" (1:1385)

Notice how this closely parallels the definition of *color of law* given on page four. We can read of specific tyrannical acts against the Colonists as recorded in the Declaration of Independence. They experienced first-hand many injustices. Excerpts from the Declaration of Independence are given below. Notice especially the clauses and phrases I have italicized:

> ... [The] King of Great Britain [has] a history of repeated injuries and usurpations, all having in direct object the establishment of an absolute Tyranny. To prove this, **let Facts be submitted** ...

> *He has made Judges dependent on his Will alone ...* He has refused his Assent to Laws, the most wholesome and necessary for the public good ... *He has combined with others to subject us to a **jurisdiction foreign** to our Constitution, and **unacknowledged by our Laws**; giving his Assent to their Acts of pretended Legislation ... **For depriving us in many cases, of the benefits of Trial by Jury** ... In* every stage of these oppressions, ***we have petitioned for redress ... our repeated petitions have been answered only by repeated injury ...***

Those who haven't experienced such injustices may not understand the seriousness of this abbreviated list. I certainly didn't until I was forced into a civil suit and, on a personal level, lived through many of the same type of abuses that are summarized in the Declaration of Independence. Perhaps we have become complacent or have been too ignorant to connect the dots. Families are being restructured by judicial acts similar to those listed by the Colonists as "repeated injuries and usurpations ... the establishment of an absolute Tyranny." Such would be in *"derogation of the [our] Constitution."*

In *Brumbaugh v. Brumbaugh*, the judge, likewise, under several acts of what I perceived as legal tyranny, usurped his office (in "derogation of the Constitution" and many of my civil rights*)* by illegally bringing down the gavel against our marriage. This dissolution on the judge's part was followed by other acts that became tyrannical and discriminatory—from a layman's point of view.

> **The way families are being restructured by divorce reflects the same type of acts listed by the Colonists as tyranny.**

Who is to be the watchdog?

The government was designed to punish evil and promote good. It has, however, in the arena of family law, instead, turned the tables and created laws in opposition to this purpose. In so doing, the legal and judicial systems have punished good and rewarded evil, and thereby have embroiled millions in their webs of destruction.

As Thomas Jefferson wrote "To prove this, let Facts be submitted ..." Using the civil suit, *Brumbaugh v. Brumbaugh*, **let Facts be submitted** regarding the "life" and **"legal** death" of the marriage-covenant of Douglas and Judith Brumbaugh. This "legal death" will focus on our judicial and legislative systems working tyrannically by usurping rights guaranteed to citizens by the United States Constitution. I'm not broad-brushing ALL judges and legislators but sounding an alarm where there is egregious abuse. Within *Brumbaugh v. Brumbaugh*, there were a series of events which took place that hopefully will awaken readers to the importance of the protections that our foundational legal and political documents were created to provide. The wake-up call is not only to make people aware of these protections for us as individuals and families, but also to awaken us to the need for us to DO something to restore and protect these freedoms and rights. The institution of marriage is basic to our cultural and social structure. With marriage comes many other related issues—those pertaining to our children, our properties, and many basic freedoms which we often take for granted. These are *legally* protected through sanctions embedded in our Constitution and rights declared in the Declaration of Independence. Inalienable rights and related laws and statutes, however, are being eroded, often through judicial powers being applied in an unconstitutional manner resulting in the mass destruction of our families and properties.

Have too many years passed since our Founding Fathers personally suffered these acts of injustice? This passage of time may be the reason we now take for granted the many rights we freely enjoy every day—**rights that are quietly being eroded.** Thus, we don't understand the urgency to restore many of our God-given inalienable rights embedded in our country's foundational documents.

Inalienable rights are "**those which are not capable of being surrendered or transferred without the consent of the one possessing such rights.**" (1:683) Yet, as will be shown in this book, by legislative sanction and judicial enforcement, many of these rights are being surrendered or transferred with—and more often without—the consent of the person possessing such rights.

Chapter 2

JUDICAL TYRANNY HAS MANY FACES

"If your God were with you, He would have done something by now." This was the cutting remark Judge Fuller made to me as I begged him not to drop the gavel on our marriage. This chapter gives an overview of many injustices I experienced from our judicial system. The information shared was learned by me, a layperson, through the judicial experiences I was forced into because of my husband's divorce lawsuit **and** the unbridled liberties under No-fault. These proceedings permeated every area of my life as I changed from a happy, cheerful, upbeat wife and mom to a frantic, depressed, frightened person who begged God to take her life as the pain became so intense. It seemed at times as if I were in a living hell. Each new judicial encounter produced increased torment and agony.

To guide you through my six years of "court-ship," I will provide two aids to help you follow along as I switch back and forth between my legal and personal experiences. The first aid is a summary of just eighteen of the issues which to me, **as a layman**, constitute acts of injustice. This may seem like a boring list until you read the rest of the book to see some of their realities as they applied to my life while I fought to preserve our family. **The inescapable *perceptions* that I was left with were the following**:

1. It is a matter of fact and law that our judicial system flagrantly discriminates against parties contesting divorce actions.

2. It is a matter of fact that the state will act and issue decrees and orders when it does not have jurisdiction of the subject matter and of the parties.

3. It is a matter of fact and law that the government treats the marriage-covenant as a contract, but does not afford the *minority sect* (those opposing) any recognizable defense to protect this "contract."

4. It is a matter of fact and law that our judicial system violates the principles of *ex post facto* guaranteed by Article I, Section 10 (retrospective laws) in dissolving "marriage-contracts" under the No-fault Divorce Law that were properly executed before this law was in effect.

5. It is a matter of fact and law that in the absence of any criminal charges, pleadings, etc., that our **judicial system**, with its use of tyrannical power, **can divest a person of marital status and family, monies, and properties** violating inalienable rights of life, liberty, and property.

6. It is a matter of fact that the court can unconstitutionally remove a Defendant from her home without any legal precedent or proven legal cause of action to do so, specifically violating the Fourth Amendment—the protection of the people against unreasonable seizures.

7. It is a matter of fact and law that the government is treating the marriage-covenant as a contract, but does not afford Defendants equal protection (under the law) of that contract. We have the constitutional guarantee that laws may not be passed which impair the obligations for performance of contracts. This is part of Article I, Section 10, wherein **states may not pass any law impairing the obligations of contracts**.

8. It is a matter of fact that indigents are deprived equal access to courts and equal legal representation because of expenses required to retain legal representation and, thus, become unprotected and legally unskilled persons without a guardian or means to "redress" the government for "grievances."

9. It is a matter of fact and law that the judicial system has unconstitutionally established the framework for a monopolistically discriminatory sect to emerge—those filing a suit to dissolve a marriage—and awards to it rights and privileges not afforded Defendants (*minority sect*)—those objecting to a dissolution of marriage, and/or being financially disadvantaged.

10. It is a matter of fact that the judicial system can unconstitutionally deny access to the court (by refusal to provide legal counsel and deny hearing of issues filed) to an indigent and leave such Petitioner legally unprotected without *due process* of law; can refuse right of appeal to same; can refuse to forward appeals properly filed by an indigent forced to act for self; and can manipulate away basic civil rights to an unprotected, legally unskilled person.

11. It is a matter of fact and law that the legislative system provides forms, formats, and aid by state employees for parties who agree to a divorce but discriminates against legally unskilled, indigent Defendants. Most are instead forced to follow the Rules of Civil Procedure, Rules of the Supreme Court of the United States, etc., an impossibility for most laypersons.

12. It is a matter of fact that the judicial system is abandoning procedural *due process* and "promulgating" substantive *due process* by using

19

personal bias to interpret what it considers within its present value system as "reasonable."

13. It is a matter of fact and law that the court in dissolution proceedings has no authority to award a "former" husband his "former" wife's joint interest in a business and the property upon which it is located unless the parties agree to this division or the "former" husband properly pleads for partition. In the case, *Brumbaugh v. Brumbaugh* commercial property was awarded to the Plaintiff despite absence of the wife's approval and any recognized partition. From a layman's point of view, it would appear that, under color of law, contractual rights were invalidated, inalienable rights violated, and properties wrongfully transferred by authority of an official of the state acting unjustly.

14. It is a matter of fact and law that our judicial system is under color of law serving as a catalyst to obtrusively and tyrannically destroy the family unit in America.

15. It is a matter of fact that the judicial system does not provide a trial by jury for a matter which "kills" a marriage, divides families, strips parties of their marital status, and divides properties and other family assets. It invokes the Marital Communications Privilege against the Defendant as the Plaintiff's weapon.

16. It's a matter of fact and law that courts show "judicial prejudice" in favor of the Plaintiffs in an action for dissolution.

17. It is a matter of fact that the court strips Defendant (Wife) of the spouse's career assets, retirement, insurance, and other intangible and tangible assets acquired and appreciated during the marriage.

18. It is a matter of fact and law that our government discriminates by giving legal rights to criminals but denies these same rights to Defendants/Respondents summoned to defend themselves in a divorce lawsuit.

While in the finishing stages of this book, I was blessed to have a Circuit Court judge review this manuscript and give me feedback for reorganization and "tweaking." He pointed out that I needed to clarify that not ALL judges are guilty of tyranny. I know this to be true for he does wonderful proactive work for families. Unfortunately, I did not have such a person preside over our case. My "court-ship," like thousands of others, was a nightmare of what I perceived to be judicial abuses working against the preservation of the family and in violation of our Constitution.

Have we come full circle?

Have we come full circle? Is it not today as it was with the colonists? The King of Britain became a despot and usurped the people's liberties—violations listed in the Declaration of Independence. Likewise, the above eighteen issues summarize some of the liberties and rights that were usurped and/or voided in the lawsuit *Brumbaugh v. Brumbaugh*. Most of these will be discussed later in this book. **Listing these abuses is NOT meant to imply legal expertise. They were injustices experienced from the viewpoint of a Defendant whose purpose it was to fight against the legal destruction of her family.**

These issues—empirical evidence—show **what happens when a Defendant (Wife) lacks the financial resources to retain qualified legal defense** and when government becomes hostile to religion/God. Abuses happen.

The second organizational aid to guide you is a six-page chronology to reference if you get lost as to where we are going or where we have been.

21

CHRONOLOGY*

*Names other than Douglas and Judith are fictitious.

Dec. 28, 1982	Petition for Dissolution of Marriage filed by Douglas K. Brumbaugh States: This is an action for dissolution of the bonds of marriage between DOUGLAS K. BRUMBAUGH, the Husband herein, and JUDITH A. BRUMBAUGH, the Wife herein ... The Parties were married to each other on June 30, 1962 ... The marriage between the parties is irretrievably broken. Husband requested: **dissolution, children live with him, wife to pay child support; permanent and exclusive use and possession of marital residence, et al.**
Jan. 31, 1983	Sheriff's office served Summons on Judith Brumbaugh regarding Dissolution.
Feb. 23, 1983	Notice of Appearance - Judith's Attorney (Grier)
March 4, 1983	Wife's Answer to Petition for Dissolution of Marriage: **Marriage not irretrievably broken; objected to other requests in Dec. 28 petition.**
April 18, 1984	**Trial for Dissolution of Marriage**: Court-ordered dissolution without jurisdiction being established. Jurisdiction is based on whether residency is established per corroborating witness (not a party to the lawsuit): 61.052(2), Fla. Stat. (1971). This error alone **requires reversal**: *Gillman v. Gillman*. Wife objected to dissolution; offered "verbal contract" by Judge Fuller for right to contest: dismiss attorney and move from home.
April 23, 1984	Entry of Open Court Sheet and Court Minutes for nonjury *Dissolution* of April 18, 1984: "Court granted Dissolution."
June 11, 1984	*Final Judgment of Dissolution* with Reservation as to Primary Residence of the Minor Child, Alimony, Attorney Fees, and Property Distribution. (Note: jurisdiction cannot be reserved from a void decree.)
June 21, 1984	**Motion for Rehearing filed by layperson, Wife.**
July 25, 1984	Trial to hear Motion for Rehearing, distribution of assets, and child custody. Instead; April 18 "verbal contract" enforced, **under color of law:**

	wife ordered to move out of house within six days and release Attorney Grier in exchange for having Motion for Rehearing heard.
Aug. 3, 1984	Order related to Wife's Motion for Continuance.
Aug. 9, 1984	Order signed by Judge Fuller for withdrawal of counsel of Attorney Grier.
Nov. 29, 1984	Hearing: **Husband's attorney acknowledges husband failed to have corroborating residency witness at trial for dissolution.**
April 9, 1985 (Information not made part of *Final Hearing* 5/29/85)	Husband's contract to purchase newly built house from realtor/builder friend Toby Finacher using jointly owned, adjoining home property lot as down payment.
April 11, 1985 (Information not made part of *Final Hearing* 5/29/85)	Loan application for purchase of house, listing as **personally owned property, jointly owned commercial building and lot adjoining home.** Also listed home "to be transferred to 'ex-wife' when divorce settlement completed." Income sources included professorship at UCF, Consultant for School Districts, Publication of book, carpenter, et al.
May 17, 1985	Court recorded Lis Pendens against all properties owned by parties.
May 29, 1985	Motion to Stay filed by Defendant's attorney to keep properties from being transferred: No properties may be transferred, sold, mortgaged or encumbered of any jointly held properties.
May 29, 1985	*Supplemental Final Judgment* signed and entered; marital assets divided; Notice of refusal to hear Motion for Rehearing filed June 21, 1984. Quit-claim deed to be given on properties within 10 days of this judgment. If not, this judgment shall act as a conveyance. Husband awarded commercial property and lot attached to home property; wife awarded home.
May 29, 1985	**Notice of Appeal** of *Supplemental Final Judgment* filed in Fifth District Court of Appeal by Judith's attorney objecting to above decisions.
June 4, 1985	Judge Fuller discharged Motion to Stay and Lis Pendens.
June 11, 1985	Warranty Deed: Plaintiff (Husband) transferred ownership of lot adjoining home to Toby Finacher (Builder, Realtor, Friend). It was part

	of contract signed April 9, 1985 to purchase lot and house built for Plaintiff (Husband).
June 14, 1985	Mortgage signed by Plaintiff (Husband) for funding house contracted on April 9, 1985: took possession prior to May 29 *Supplemental Final Hearing.*
June 24, 1985	Judge Fuller signed Order to Stay: Parties not to transfer properties (stamped received in court June 26, 1985). **Included bond of $17,000; to be paid on or before June 24 by Defendant** (Wife). Notice was signed by Judge June 24. Defendant didn't receive until after bond was due.
July 1985	Petition for Disqualification of Judge Fuller from the case *Brumbaugh v. Brumbaugh.*
July 11, 1985	Motion to Vacate Reassignment: Husband's objection to having Judge Fuller removed from case. Granted Sept. 10, 1985.
July 26, 1985	**Appeal filed to Fifth District Court of Appeal.**
August 22, 1985	Motion to Appoint Special Master to Sign Deeds to Real Property prepared by Attorney Simon, Attorney for Plaintiff/Husband.
Sept. 10, 1985	Order Related to Motion to Vacate Reassignment GRANTED, signed by Judge Fuller.
Sept. 10, 1985	Notice of Hearing before Judge Fuller on 9/10/85 to appoint Special Master to Sign Deeds regarding Motion of August 30, 1985. (Judith has no record of this hearing/action. Information taken from Court Docket Sheet.)
Nov. 26, 1985	5th DCA Appeal 85-983 Appellant's Reply and Answer Brief to Cross Appeal: Final Judgment void (lack of corroborating witness) cannot be cured subsequently, **Is void *abinitio*** [from beginning]; defense of marriage not irretrievably broken; objection of denial of Motion for Rehearing, property division, alimony, child support.
May 8, 1986	Meeting with Attorney **Durant**. He notified Judith he was **no longer representing Judith**. Gaye her files and instruction how to act for self.
May 9, 1986	**Letter from Judith's Attorney, Durant, confirming end of legal representation.**
May, 1986	**Pleading for court-appointed attorney by layperson, Judith Brumbaugh. (Denied hearing.)**

May 14, 1986	Letter from Attorney Durant with letter and Quit-claim deeds from Attorney Simon (Plaintiff/Husband's Attorney) requesting that Judith sign Quit-claim deeds on lot (part of home property) and commercial property.
May 29, 1986	Received order (forwarded by Attorney Durant) which dismissed Layperson/Defendant's pre-trial conference and trial of Set Aside Issues from *Final Judgment of Dissolution of Marriage.*
June 9, 1986	Judith, acting for self as Layperson, pleaded Motion for Rehearing of May 29 order and filed subsequent motions for court-appointed attorney, Fla.R.App.P. 9.430, Indigent Person and for Stay of Proceedings. Court refused to recognize any of these motions. DENIED ACCESS TO COURT AND LEFT LEGALLY UNPROTECTED.
June 30, 1986	Trial court entered order stating Petitioner, Defendant, Judith, could not act for self as she had "counsel of record." (Attorney Durant had notified Judith that he had withdrawn by personal meeting May 8, 1986 and confirmed by letter.)
July 7, 1986	Judith filed a second Motion for Rehearing of above denial of constitutional rights, etc.
July 7, 1986	Filed request for Notice of Hearing for Motion for Rehearing of Order of June 30, 1986 which denied Motion for Rehearing of Order of May 29, 1986 regarding set-aside issues, etc. (Judith was instructed by Fuller that no hearing date would be given for the above motion because Durant had not withdrawn.)
July 8, 1986	Judith (Petitioner-Defendant) entered a Notice of Appeal to Clerk of Court and Motion for Indigency. Judge held Judith's records hindering constitutional right of appeal. Because of time limits on appealing, Judith was forced to file an Amended Appeal and pay fees to meet deadlines even though "filing of fees is not jurisdictional" (Fla.R.App.P. 9.430). **Court, in effect, made filing of fees jurisdictional and was denying right of appeal.**
July 21, 1986	Letter received from court denying right to represent self (DONE WITHOUT *DUE PROCESS,* WITHOUT ANY RULE TO SHOW CAUSE, WITH

	NO OPPORTUNITY TO ACCESS THE COURT, AND DENIAL OF FOURTEENTH AMENDMENT, CIVIL AND HUMAN RIGHTS ABRIDGED).
July 24, 1986	*Designation of Record* ordered by Judith to transmit record-on-appeal to Fifth District Court of Appeal.
July 28, 1986	Writ docketed, U.S. Sup. Ct., Judith, Layperson.
Aug. 11, 1986	Court ordered that Attorney Durant be dismissed as Attorney of Record for Judith. Judge struck all motions Defendant had filed after Durant had quit. Judicial tyranny against an unskilled indigent giving no access to court, no representation or protection of life, liberty, and property when Attorney Durant quit May 9 (because of the state of poverty the Defendant had been placed by actions of Plaintiff, his legal counsel, and the State of Florida) until August 11, 1986. During this time Defendant was blocked from court, from right to appeal by Judge Fuller, **denying right to represent self and to have court-appointed attorney.**
August 27, 1986	Argument of Judith A. Brumbaugh, Wife, Defendant for Hearing of September 5, 1986 to support her Motion for Rehearing of Order of August 11, 1986 (Attorney Durant's withdrawal).

#3 PROCESS, 41 Fla. Jur.2d page 325:
"Until notice is given to the Defendant of the actions or proceedings against him, and **he is given thereby opportunity to appear and be heard, the court has no jurisdiction to proceed** to judgment against him even though the court may have jurisdiction of the subject matter."

October 7, 1986	**Civil action filed against Judith Brumbaugh by Attorney Durant for Attorney fees owed.**
Nov. 3, 1986	Motion for Rehearing filed with U.S. Sup. Ct.
Nov. 4, 1986	Petition rejected because of time frame.
Nov. 6, 1986	Motion resubmitted showing petition was timely.
Nov. 12, 1986	Motion returned saying must have member of Bar of Court sign Appeal.
Nov. 15, 1986	Motion resubmitted showing person filing *in forma pauperis* is exempted from above requirement.
Nov. 20, 1986	Motion returned for Nov. 12 reason.
Continued filing until petition was docketed May 16, 1987.	
Nov. 21, 1986	**Order from Fifth District Court of Appeal to**

	show cause why case should not be dismissed for failure to file a record-on-appeal.
December 3, 1986	Fifth District Court of Appeal: Reply to Show Cause Order of November 21, 1986: Appellant replies to the Show Cause Order of This Court of November 21, 1986 and shows cause why her appeal should not be dismissed for failure to file a Record of Appeal to the court.
February 16, 1987	Notice of Appeal Filing fee Receipt $100
February 17, 1987	Supreme Court of Florida Petition for Review dismissed and no Motion for Rehearing will be entertained by the Court.
United States Supreme Court Brief, 1987	**"This court, the section asserts, should not rely on 'do-it-yourself procedures' but should instead _provide legal consultation so that the rights of the poor are protected ..._"** Amend. to FRCP 1.611 Sup. Ct of Fla. Case No. 62,147, Dec. 8, 1983 effective Mar. 1, 1984, Section 454.18, Fla. Statutes 1981 pg. 4.
May 13, 1987	Brief filed with United States Supreme Court.
May 16, 1987	Case #86-6907 docketed before Supreme Court of the United States (Second Writ docketed.)
May 26, 1987	Lis Pendens on commercial property filed by Defendant, Layperson, Judith A. Brumbaugh.
June 10, 1987*	Letter to Clerk of Circuit Court asking why it had closed my case and refused to give me a hearing since there were still unresolved issues.
June 12, 1987	Letter from Supreme Court of United States that petition for Writ of Certiorari on May 16, 1987 had been docketed. (Second Writ docketed.)
June 17, 1987	Letter to Doug's Attorney notifying case docketed before US Supreme Court May 16, 1987 attaching appearance forms supplied by Supreme Court.
***June 19, 1987**	Letter from Clerk of Circuit Court saying they cannot advise me in any legal matters or offer any remedies at this time.
Nov. 16, 1987	**Petition for rehearing is denied, United States Supreme Court. No reason given.**
THE ABOVE IS AN ABBREVIATED LIST OF THE ACTIVITIES. LOWER COURT DOCKET SHEET HAS 256 ENTRIES, NOT INCLUDING APPELLATE COURT FILINGS.	

Divorce: The ONLY "contract" where judges are prohibited from "hearing" defense for BOTH sides of the case.

The abuses summarized in pages 17-21 were what I experienced from a legal system that is charged to hear, in an *unbiased* manner, *both* sides of a case brought before it. The judicial officer in charge is to have no prejudice regarding race, religion, gender, etc. What I found was that this holds true EXCEPT for lawsuits dealing with family law—divorce in particular. It's only in divorce litigation where conclusions drawn by the Plaintiff become evidence to convict the Defendant, and the Defendant's testimony has no bearing on his guilt or innocence. The Defendant is guilty as charged by the Plaintiff.

> **It's only in divorce litigation where *conclusions* drawn by the Plaintiff become evidence to convict the Defendant.**

Steal a car, murder someone—get a free attorney; defend your family—hire an attorney and go deeply into debt and/or become a potential pawn of judicial discrimination and oppression.

As I was doing additional research for this book, I visited the courtroom of a judge who was setting hearings for cases involving citizens charged with felonies and/or misdemeanors. Here are the statements made by the judge to EACH and EVERY person coming before him for these alleged criminal charges:

1. Do you understand that you have the **right** to have a lawyer appointed on your behalf?
2. Do you have enough money to hire a lawyer?
3. Would you like the court to hire an attorney for you?

It is a legal **right** for those who might be incarcerated because of a subsequent ruling to have the government provide FREE legal counsel to represent them. Those so charged are also given important information concerning their specific **rights** to appeal forthcoming court decisions:

1. You have a **right** to appeal.
2. You have 21 days to appeal any court decision.
3. If you plead guilty, you give up your right to appeal.

What I discovered is that as a nation, we pay for the legal defense of many criminals, yet, subject Defendants in a divorce suit to cruel and unjust punishments. I was incensed to learn that as a Defendant in a divorce suit— I was an innocent victim, not an accused and possibly guilty felon—I was offered neither a free attorney nor free legal advice: "You have a right to appeal ..." This VITAL information is misunderstood by many Defendants. There is not only a **right** to appeal but also **a time limit to appeal**.

> **As a nation, we pay for the legal defense of many criminals, yet, subject Defendants in a divorce suit to cruel and unjust punishments.**

I, like other divorce Defendants, had to protect myself in a situation that I did not create and do so in a no-win environment. If we are to defend (what we cannot defend), or to even minimally respond, attempting to do so can put Defendants into debt for years to come. In a divorce lawsuit, the government legally dissolves (impairs) the "marriage-contract" between the Plaintiff and Defendant, an act that violates the Constitution. **Impairing the obligations of a contract is an unconstitutional act according to Article I, Section 10.** Furthermore, the state exonerates the Plaintiff—this person who wants to walk away from the obligations of his "contract."

A Defendant sometimes doesn't "answer" the summons to appear thinking the divorce will not go through if she does nothing. Not responding might be for a variety of reasons. **One such is that she often doesn't know that by doing nothing, the divorce will be granted and she, by default, can be subject to whatever the Plaintiff files.** Another major reason for not replying to a summons (especially if it is a woman, and even more so if she is a full-time homemaker) is her lack of financial resources. Her spouse often controls the family assets. Such a Defendant lacks the legal knowledge to protect herself and because of inadequate finances cannot hire an attorney to provide her with vital **accurate** information necessary to survive. Contrast this with the criminal defendant who will not only be offered free legal advice from the judge ("You have the right to appeal," etc.), but may be GIVEN a **highly skilled attorney.** (See page 115.) Not only might the Defendant not even be told that she has a right to appeal, but she can be "evicted" from her home by trying to do so and can actually be denied a right to appeal—and equally as important to be **heard**—as was the case with this author.

A Defendant might also not respond because she lacks emotional resources. To begin with, she may be so traumatized that she cannot function properly or think clearly. Then again she sometimes feels that her responding could jeopardize the possible return of her spouse: "If I give him the divorce and whatever properties we have, he will love me again and return home." Love, however, cannot be bought or "sought" in this manner.

Or she may feel there is a question of religious submission involved and believes she should do what the other spouse wants her to do. The Bible, however, teaches that you do not obey man over God, and God says to not divorce or partake in "putting apart" a covenant-marriage and actually, in many places, gives direction to fight for families and properties. Unfortunately, Defendants who do respond often seek the cheapest—not the best—attorney because of their lack of money (as was the case with me). **They try to find someone who will file the necessary paperwork with as few dollars as possible for something that will negatively affect the rest of their life.**

In a divorce action, the Defendant is charged with irreconcilable differences for which she is summoned to appear in court. **It is for such an undefined "crime" that the court allows no recognizable testimony that could clear the Defendant of the charge of which she is usually innocent.** To appear in court, the Defendant will be forced to incur thousands of dollars of debt to defend the charges. If "convicted," the Defendant's marriage will be struck dead, children will be fractured and strewn among multiple new "parents," "grandparents," "brothers," "sisters," "cousins" ... and forced into a lifestyle that would send many adults to a mental hospital. **AND OUR LEGISLATIVE AND JUDICIAL SYSTEMS DO NOT SEE THESE ACTS AS CRIMINAL?**

> The government exonerates the person who files a suit to have it break his legal "contract."

Even though the law provides otherwise and the Defendant has not committed a criminal act, she can have properties taken from her—including her home—and if a homemaker, she can be stripped of her husband's career assets, retirement, insurance, etc.—these items she partnered to build with and for the Plaintiff—future earning power which he takes with him—often to a "new spouse." The Defendant is not given the option of a trial by jury **because the government has placed divorce lawsuits in a classification (in equity)**

> Children will be ... forced into a lifestyle that would send many adults to a mental hospital.

31

which exempts governmental dissolution acts (except in some set-aside issues) from potential protections afforded by a trial by jury. This very important historical *due process* protection (from the days of the *Magna Carta* [See Legal Terms.]) has been considered a fundamental of justice **to curtail judicial autonomy.** George Mason fought for our Bill of Rights including extending trial by jury to civil cases: "In controversies respecting property, and in suits between man and man, the ancient trial by jury is one of the greatest securities to the rights of the people, and to remain sacred and inviolable." (See page 271.) Thus, a provision for trial by jury in civil cases at common law was added to the Seventh Amendment: "In suits at common law, where the **value in controversy shall exceed twenty dollars, the right of trial by jury shall be preserved.**"

There's nothing more important to the furtherance of civilization than the family. This truth was reflected in our legislative and judicial systems for many years as evidenced in numerous court opinions. For example, the Supreme Court of the United States characterized marriage as "the most important relation in life, and the foundation of the family and of society, without which there would be neither civilization nor progress." (*Maynard v. Hill*, 125 U.S. 205, 211, 1881.)

Judicial tyranny has many faces: "Impeach Henry Fuller," they wrote.

For the last several decades, we have had quite the opposite set in place by our legislative environment and its no-responsibility, family-law legislation. We have judges who, themselves, may be involved in a divorce lawsuit with their wives and yet preside over the guillotine on another's marriage. Would such a thing as this be allowed if this were "truly" a criminal suit? That is, if a judge were being tried for first-degree murder, would he be permitted to sit in judgment on a murder trial? However, this was the "draw" of the lot assigned to *Brumbaugh v. Brumbaugh*. J udge Fuller was himself embroiled in an alleged heated divo1 ~e with his wife. Even so, he was appointed to **LITIGA1 E** (See page 34.) over the Brumbaugh lawsuit while also being a party to his personal divorce "litigation." It would seem that Judge Fuller should have excused himself from presiding over like cases, especially because decisions as to the "contractual" rights of the Plaintiff and Defendant under the current vague No-fault Law are subjective. A motion to remove Judge Fuller from *Brumbaugh v. Brumbaugh* was filed by the Defendant after having experienced what the Defendant perceived were cruel and unjust acts for almost three years, but the motion was denied after the Plaintiff filed a brief to reinstate Judge Fuller.

There were numerous complaints filed by citizen's groups, governmental agencies, and even the courts themselves against Judge Fuller's alleged, unjust judicial acts as he sat on the bench. A billboard was erected in the county seat where he presided with a bold message: "IMPEACH Judge Fuller."

Shown below are several examples from newspaper articles reporting on Fuller's conduct that others perceived as being cruel, unjust, and unusual punishments. These included those who came before his bench and even from those of a higher court. Statements from newspaper reports regarding many of the allegations against Judge Fuller are given below. (None of these are from the author of this book.)

> "Accusations made by Fuller's wife during divorce proceedings could be damaging to the couple's children."
> "He ... handed out unreasonable punishment and caused them and their families extreme emotional and mental stress."

"I didn't get a fair deal in Fuller's court. What happened to me shouldn't have happened to a dog."

"Calling Fuller's actions an 'abuse of judicial power,' HRS in June filed an emergency petition asking the Fifth District Court of Appeal to remove him."

"The 5th District Court of Appeal overturned a juvenile custody order issued by Seminole Circuit Court judge, Henry Fuller, and removed him from the case. In the ruling, handed down by a three-judge panel, the appeal court found that Fuller's order 'departs from the essential requirements of law,' ... a polite way of saying the order was incorrect."

Judge Fuller resigned his judgeship as of September 30, 1986. (Judge Fuller is a fictitious name, but the newspaper clippings about him are not fictitious.)

Carry with you throughout the reading of this text the definition of **LITIGATE** from *Black's Law Dictionary*: to carry on a suit; any controversy that must be decided **upon evidence**.

Governments are instituted among men to secure our God-Given unalienable Rights.

Chapter 3

NO-FAULT INFLICTS CRUEL AND UNJUST HARDSHIPS

"It's insanity. It's really the worst form of child abuse." This is one of the oppressive results of the breakdown of the family that will be discussed in this chapter (page 38) as I continue to share some of the realities of the fallout of judicial tyranny—especially as it affects our children.

Black's Law Dictionary tells us that oppression is "a misdemeanor committed by a public officer, who under color of his office, wrongfully inflicts upon any person any bodily harm, imprisonment, or other injury ... an excessive use of authority; an act of subjecting to cruel and unjust hardship." (1:986)

The affects of oppression are far-reaching.

As a result of the passage and implementation of a no-responsibility law—No-fault—the judicial and legislative branches have brought upon millions of victims, especially women and children, cruel and unjust emotional and economic hardships. They do this each time, when under color of law, a marriage is legally dissolved. No-fault breaches civil rights as well as Amendments to the Constitution, including impairing the obligations of contracts, *due process*, and in many instances *ex post facto* (passing a law which invalidates the rights in a contract that have already been legally executed). Millions may seem like an exaggerated number of victims, but there have been more than a million divorces **every year** since the institution of the No-

35

fault Divorce Law nationwide. Think of all those affected: the children, the relatives and friends—all of society. In her research study, *The Economics of Divorce*, Dr. Lenore J. Weitzman states that divorce is a financial catastrophe for most women. "In just one year they experience a dramatic decline in income and a calamitous drop in their standard of living. Women and children almost immediately become impoverished. **Men experienced a 42% improvement in the post-divorce standard of living, while women experienced a 73% loss.** (4:1251, 1252)

Men experienced a 42% improvement ... women, a 73% loss.

The longer the marriage, the greater the disparity between the incomes of the husband and wife. "The pattern of support and property awards tends to impoverish the long-married woman while providing the long-married man with a continuously comfortable standard of living." "Economic changes alone have drastic psychosocial effects on the child." (4:1248, 1266)

The plight of children was specifically addressed in an appeal a friend and I wrote to President Reagan as we pled with him for help to preserve families. (See also page 154.)

Cruel and unjust hardships cannot be measured socially or emotionally in adults and children. Children are caught in the middle of an emotional crisis that deeply affects their lives because of the situations into which they are forced—trying to please two differing sets of beliefs between parents who are not unified in their morals, religious convictions, and/or standards for raising and disciplining them. In causing our children's loyalties to be divided through divorce, we divide them in two in their spirit, tearing them apart. **We cannot separate "one-flesh" [marriage] and any assets** *thereof, tangible or intangible, in even an economic way that is just; how much more difficult to separate the psychological, social, emotional, and spiritual aspects of "one-flesh" living.* (5:4)

Let the lifestyles of the children testify!

Consider some of the realities of the normal lifestyle of children caught in the throws of a divorce between their parents. In many shared parenting agreements, the children pack up their clothes and favorite toys or possessions every other weekend and move to the "other" household. (You could be pretty sure that things would be different if the parents had to practice this fiasco by being the ones who packed up every other weekend!) Like a piece of luggage, children are transported back and forth and are expected to adjust to a totally different environment with a second set of adults who are, for this period of time, supposed to be their parental authority.

> **You could be pretty sure that things would be different if the parents had to practice this fiasco by being the ones who packed up every other weekend!**

Instead of two parents, children many times have four people acting as the parent and who knows how many newly acquired relatives and other household children with whom they are to "blend." In some situations, the "other parent" may be cut out of his/her children's lives because the "custodial parent" does not honor visiting rights and responsibilities.

Each household tries harder to please the child. There are double birthday and Christmas gifts. Often times the noncustodial (What a repulsive term!) parent wines and dines the children or one household tries to outdo the other in winning the affections of the child. What a deal! No, it's a tragedy! The child learns that he has to keep secrets, that he can't "tell everything" to the "other" parent, and he may be forced to learn to lie to protect his sanity or to keep peace. Some children realize that they hold a control card in the deck. "If this parent doesn't do what I want, I will tell the other parent ..." He learns that he cannot say or do certain things in one household but has free reign with these behaviors in the other.

And then we wonder ... Why do they rebel? Why are they filled with anger? Why do some become aggressive while others are quiet and behave perfectly as both types internalize what they do not know how to express or are not allowed to. They sometimes look for affection or release among their peers by over-performing, by entering the drug scene or promiscuity arenas.

> **It's insanity. It is really the worst form of child abuse.**

The court's "plan" is called *shared parental custody*. It's insanity. It is really the worst form of child abuse. Read the testimony of Midge Decter, one of the many witnesses who testified before the U.S. Subcommittee on Family and Human Services for their study, *Broken Families* in 1983:

For a generation now, millions upon millions of Americans—I will not say all—have been engaging in **child sacrifice.** Less bloodly, perhaps, but no less obediently than certain ancient groups of idol worshipers, we have been offering up our children on the altar of a pitiless god. Nor do I mean this as a flowery metaphor. In our case, the idol to whom we have sacrificed our young is not made of wood or gold, but of an idea. This idea, very crudely put, is

> **We have sacrificed our children to an idol, an idea that everyone has a right to make up his own preferred mode of living.**

that we are living in an altogether new world with not yet fully understood new moral rules. As inhabitants of this supposedly newly ordered world, we tell ourselves we have no right to cling to or impose on others outmoded standards of behavior.

On the contrary, everyone has a right, even an obligation, to make up his own rules—and with these rules, to make up his own preferred mode of living ... And **we have, as I said, literally sacrificed our children to it.** One thing about which we seem to have achieved near-universal agreement is that something is going wrong with the constitution of our private lives. (6:5)

Miss Decter continues by questioning the rationale parents give for divorce:

And, of course, there are all those divorces; all those lonely and self-seeking men and women, hopping from marriage to marriage in search of they know not what ... all those children abandoned by their fathers, and even, nowadays, abandoned by their mothers.

How is it that people blessed by God with better health, longer lives, greater comfort, and personal freedom and economic well-being than any previous people in human history should give so much evidence of deep trouble?

Are there *any words that can be strong enough or graphic enough to bring selfish, unforgiving, bitter, self-seeking adults to their senses?*

How severe does the storm and its destructive aftermath have to get before each of us wakes up and follows what is best for us and our children?

Miss Decter discusses moral irresponsibility and the fact that none of the authorities in the lives of children will tell them what they need to know:

> Life is real and weighty and consequential: that it requires discipline and courage and the assumption of responsibility for oneself and others ... We are permitting ourselves to become a society that punishes the virtuous. That **punishment is every day being incorporated into the laws of the land, written and unwritten** ...
>
> In attempting to erase its uniqueness as an institution, we remove from the family the community affirmation that is the absolutely essential ingredient to its strength as an institution ... Indeed, by **turning the family into a merely voluntary, optional relationship**, we have ironically increased its capacity to make its members unhappy. Thus our divorce rate.
>
> To be a parent is to discover, sometimes with considerable surprise, at first, that **there are lives more valuable to one than one's own.** To be a child of parents is to incorporate into one's being the knowledge that human life, as opposed to animal existence, is a system of mutual obligations and dependencies. To get beyond self is the only possibility for happiness; **to understand obligation is the only possibility for genuine individual freedom.**
>
> That may, as little children are wont to say, be "no fair," but it is the truth. **Thus, the family to me ... is a mother and a father <u>and</u> <u>their</u> <u>children</u>.** (6:5-7)

When we make one or both parents inaccessible to their children through the deliberate, devastating, tragedy-perpetrating act of divorce, we ravage our homes. **We force "cruel and unusual" punishment on our children** through an act of rapacious violation of their inalienable right to two genetic, committed, and loving parents. They need parents who will nurture and protect them, provide vital character training, set an example of responsible, committed "love-by-doing" rather than feeling, and by their life's example to bring problems to peaceful solutions, using discipline and developing good character qualities. **[Even though a divorce does not initiate parental irresponsibility, it usually exacerbates it.]** This most perfect system of joint custody was invented by God and called marriage. When we allow "No-fault" construction to deal a deathblow to our marriages, we remove vital protections from our children. They lose a real (opposing Disneyland or Zoo-daddy), strong, bonded relationship with their father [and sometimes the mother] and his absence also causes loss of and inaccessibility to the maternal relationship due to economic (forced labor outside the home) and emotional hardship. (5:4, 5)

> **This most perfect system of joint custody was invented by God and called marriage.**

On the following page is a drawing done by our daughter when she was young, entitled, "Love is Having a mommy and Daddy like you." At the left of the drawing is a poem laboriously typed by our son which he titled, "You." You can observe that children discern more than some adults what real love is about. They also *know* that discipline is important, and many *know* that "… **the family … is a mother and a father <u>and</u> <u>their</u> <u>children</u>**"!

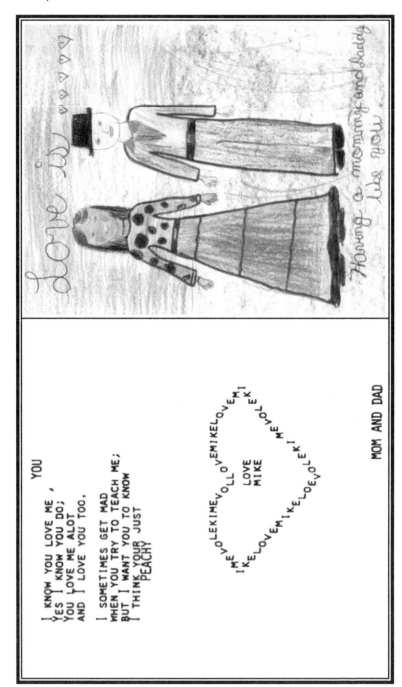

Another person with a heart for families is Dr. Amitai Etzioni, director, Center for Policy Research; professor, George Washington University. He, like Miss Decter, testified before the 1983 U.S. Senate hearings on *Broken Families*: (7:20-22, 27)

> If we continue to dismantle the American family at the accelerating pace we have been doing since 1965, there will not be a single American family left by the year 2008. We dare not allow the family to collapse. There never was a society throughout all of history—and many variations society exhibited—without a family as the central unit for launching the education of children, for character formation, and as the moral agent of society.
>
> Now, I would like to go specifically to the question of the effect on children. Let me say first of all that in all my professional and personal experience, **I have never seen a single child, not one, who did not suffer, in one way or another, psychically or psychosomatically, to one degree or another, from divorce.** Sometimes, the effects are deeper; sometimes they are shorter lived, but the notion that you can have a divorce without an effect on the children, I think, simply has no support in any evidence.

> **"The notion that you can have a divorce without an effect on the children ... simply has no support in any evidence."**

Many reading this text may be part of a family in which one of the spouses has left the family. That does not preclude your home being considered a family.

43

Chapter 4

WE EACH WENT TO COURT FOR DIFFERENT REASONS

It was on one weekday afternoon that a six-year nightmare in the courts began for a homemaker, mother, and devoted wife of twenty years. That was following the devastating, demoralizing experience of having a representative from the Circuit Court serve me with notice of my husband's lawsuit.

I had taken our daughter for her college physical. The doctor had at one time also been a personal family friend. He asked me to come into his private office and asked if Doug had remarried yet. My heart dropped to the floor. One of the men he ate with at our local restaurant had told him that Doug was getting married. I think I kept my composure quite well responding that I knew nothing about it.

With shaky knees, I went to the exam room where our daughter was and told her I would wait for her in the car. She asked what was wrong. I told her I would explain later. Shawn drove me home as I was quite unable to drive. I told her what the doctor had shared with me. She tried to comfort me by telling me, "Dad wouldn't do that," or something along those lines.

Doug had ceased living at home several months earlier, preferring the company of another female companion.

When we rounded the corner to our house there was a strange car in the driveway with an officer leaning against the fender. I said, "Oh no, I hope that isn't court papers." Shawn said, "Let's just drive on by." "No, we can't do that. Drive in. You go into the house with Michael." I went up to the officer and was served with papers.

He read some legal jargon and asked for a signature on a document prepared by my husband's attorney. The husband, the Plaintiff, named me, the wife, as the Defendant in his civil suit—a *Petition for Dissolution of Marriage.*

> This is an action for dissolution of the bonds of marriage between DOUGLAS K. BRUMBAUGH, the Husband herein, and JUDITH A. BRUM-BAUGH, the Wife herein ... The marriage between the parties is irretrievably broken ...

I went into the house and to our bedroom and cried uncontrollably. That whole evening I had the shakes with intermittent crying—not knowing when the tears would again start flowing, but they continued to come. My whole body was ice cold. I wrapped myself up in a wool blanket.

The next few days were not very productive. The following weekend Doug talked with me about his getting Mike and the house. I said, "What will I do if you do this?" He responded, "The same thing I've had to do—go find a place to live. Right now there's a boarding house with rooms listed on the board at UCF (where Doug was working as a university professor). It has about 15 rooms for rent, and you only have to cook a few times a month. You could live there." That was only the beginning.

As a consequence of Doug's new desires, I was forced into the legal arena (and eventually out of our home for almost a year); learned how to write and file legal briefs; introduced a bill to amend the No-fault Divorce Law; and started a ministry, Committee for the Restoration of the Family—now called Restoration of the Family.

Little did I know the changes in my life that those papers would create. Every decision made relating to them would greatly affect the rest of my life in some ways of which I would never have volunteered to partake! How does a person so distraught with emotional pain think clearly? How does one, almost overnight, understand all those legal terms and what they have in store for a homemaker who is nonconversant with legalese? Yet this same homemaker must prepare to respond and to defend herself in her best interest. How does she know how to find the right kind of help? How does she gather strength to continue when her weight drops from 135 pounds to 110 ... and the many times when she pulls the shades on the windows and the blankets over her head as she cries herself to sleep? The exhaustion—it's overwhelming!

> **How does a person, distraught with emotional pain, almost overnight respond to terms she doesn't understand, but that will affect the rest of her life?**

Another disappointment. My husband was putting, in writing, evidence of his changed priorities for our family **and me**. After twenty years of marriage with one set of priorities, he was now telling me through a lawsuit that **my** priorities were to be changed as a result of **his** changed priorities. It devastated me to read this new information in his *Petition for Dissolution*:

> Wife is currently unemployed, however, is capable and able to be **gainfully employed** but has refused to engage in **productive employment**. The Wife has a degree in economics, home economics, and English.

As an undergraduate, I majored in economics and had two minors, home economics and English. Additionally, I also earned a master's degree in Clothing and Textiles while my husband was working on his master's and doctorate degrees. My advanced degree increased my sewing skills. It enabled me to design and sew for my husband who had difficulty finding clothes to fit his 6'3" 250-pound frame.

How could he after all these years say that I was "unemployed"? We had mutually decided that family was more important than a second full-time income. I was a full-time homemaker. He never criticized this arrangement because we had decided together on our parental priorities. In addition to my being a homemaker, I also supplemented our earnings with several income-producing, home-based businesses and some out-of-home undertakings. Now after encouraging me for years in these endeavors, he states that I refuse to engage in "productive employment."

Was it not "productive" to help our daughter learn to develop her sewing skills to the point that she could construct a dress, to take our children to their weekly music lessons and encourage them to practice daily, to teach them the importance of giving to the community by involving them in projects for the less fortunate, to teach them business skills by giving them jobs to do in our home businesses, to become a 4-H leader thereby encouraging our daughter to develop additional social and business skills through projects I designed for this organization, to teach responsibility and instill industriousness? What better employment is there than to be at home full time teaching our children values, being there when they come home from school; being a homeroom mother at their schools; involving them in do-it-yourself, gift-making projects; baking Christmas cookies in our flour-decorated kitchen (!) providing full-time, at-home supervision for them and their friends; being excited as our son brought home fish that he caught in a

> **Was it not productive employment to teach responsibility and instill industriousness?**

47

nearby lake, or proudly presented berries he had picked for Mom to make a pie?

Let's cut a deal!

Several months after filing his lawsuit, my husband came by the house ... to talk. He, at one point, put his arms around me in a quick embrace but then said, "I love you but not as a wife. I felt nothing when I hugged you. Just let me go and maybe I will be back in five years. If you sign the papers (divorce), I will give you everything and just walk out. You can have the house, the vacant lot, the boat, the commercial building, the motor home, and I will give you a thousand dollars a month. All you have to do is to sign so we can move on with our lives." What a "great offer," it would seem.

> A seemingly great offer, but my marriage was not for sale!

It took me no time to give my reply, as I looked Doug directly in his eyes: "My marriage is not for sale. I will never sign." "Your choice; then I will take everything." My precious husband of some twenty years turned and walked out the door. I fell to the floor numbed emotionally with grief, pain, and disbelief.

My prayers and fasting (and those of many friends), my begging him to return, my baking him his favorite pecan pie (!) did not intercede in any way to stop my husband from fulfilling his promise to take, for a period of time, everything. Everything included not only the material possessions that were difficult to part with, but also the more valuable and meaningful core of my being—our children and home.

To save my "everything" I even begged him to allow me to speak to his "woman friend." They were driving in our motor home and stopped so that she and I could talk. I asked her to please at least let Doug go until the children graduated from high school. She said that she wasn't interested in that. She said that Doug had done things for me and the kids all these years and now he wanted to do something for him and for her. Regarding the children she said, "Your kids are tough; they will get over it." With that I exited the motor home and walked toward Doug who had been waiting outside. "What did she say?" "She said that she didn't want to give you up." "Well, you're both fighting for the same thing." "No, Doug, we're not both fighting for the same thing" and I turned and walked to my car.

> "No, Doug, we're not both fighting for the same thing."

After receiving the court papers and learning that I had to respond within twenty days, my next step was to hire an attorney. I didn't understand what was written in the document. I didn't know what to do. With a few phone calls, however, I learned that I MUST DO something or everything that was written in those papers, whether I understood them or not, would become a permanent reality.

How do you find an attorney? Go to the yellow pages. There were more than one hundred pages listing attorneys. Where do you begin? Ask God. Ask friends. Lots of suggestions. Phone calls. With the ensuing phone calls came reality: "What do you charge? You have to be kidding! Where do I get that kind of money for a retainer?"

Our bank accounts had been cleared out without my knowledge (and it wasn't identity theft!), so I didn't have that resource on which to draw. I found this out when a notice came in the mail that I was overdrawn. How could this be? I had just recently deposited a check. This was the first time in my life I had ever bounced a check. Oh, I was sooo embarrassed—not only that the check had bounced, but because I would have to go to someone I knew and respected to explain and

> It wasn't identity theft!

49

to get help for restoration of the money. That someone was the bank president. I personally knew him because we attended the same church and one of his daughters attended the youth group my husband and I led for many years. He was compassionate and helped me to restore my "financial accountability" and to establish another account in just my name. The latter was something I didn't want to establish—an account just in my name; but, for my financial protection, I was now forced to do so.

Hire an attorney. I finally made arrangements for borrowed funds to retain an attorney. With every phone call, every appointment, my meager funds were decreasing as the attorney fees were proportion-

> **How do you find an attorney? Where do you begin?**

ately increasing. I was teaching part time, but the legal bills were fast consuming money needed to buy gas, food, and to sustain myself. That was just the tip of the iceberg. Over the next several years, professional legal defense became not only limited, but eventually totally absent in what grew into a very lengthy, wicked, expensive judicial experience.

Hiring legal counsel was necessary to respond to this civil lawsuit that sought to force me to agree to and sign a sworn statement that said the judicial system could dissolve forever the marital bond between my husband and me, splinter our family, and divide our marital assets. The lack of legal defense was forced upon me because I didn't have the finances necessary to continue to retain legal counsel.

> **I would not only find myself deeply in debt and evicted from our home but forced to learn how to write and file legal briefs.**

During the next six years, I, the Defendant, would not only find myself deeply in debt and temporarily "evicted" from our home, but forced to learn how to write and file legal briefs. The latter happened because my first attorney, Mr. Grier, was dismissed as part of an unconstitutional "plea bargain" that PURCHASED my constitutional **right** to file a *Motion for Rehearing* and to have it heard. Several months later another attorney was hired, but he subsequently quit because I had accrued thousands of dollars of debt with no foreseeable capability to pay.

We aren't prepared ahead of time for an unfaithful spouse.

I didn't understand what was going on in my life. After talking with many others who were or had been forced into court against their will by deserting spouses, I began to see a pattern. Everyone's situation is specifically different, but generally the same. The issue is the destruction of families. Husbands and wives will be attacked where they don't even know they are vulnerable. Their weakest link will be exploited and used to destroy what once seemed an impermeable, loving relationship.

> **Everyone's situation is specifically different, but generally the same.**

Mary Smith who lives at 323 I'm Asleep Street, My City, USA doesn't know that she may one day be required to defend her family by writing a legal brief that requires using terms of which she is totally unfamiliar. Or, Trusting Harry doesn't know that his wife will have an affair with someone at work, and he will be unprepared to deal with her infidelity when it is exposed. But they are all put on the same track—the one that leads them to a court which tells their spouses they are not at fault for initiating bringing the gavel down on their marriages.

> **They are on the same track—the one that leads them to initiate the gavel ...**

Your Honor, please don't strike that gavel.
As mentioned earlier, my husband moved out of our home. Several months later, he commissioned an officer of the court to serve me with notice of his lawsuit. Through many miracles of God, what normally is a quick "execution" (a few months), our *Hearing for Dissolution* and subsequent hearings were extended many times—a total of almost three years.

We had countless formal and informal hearings, motions, and many opportunities for the attorneys to take ownership of our lifetime family assets by their hourly fees which both Doug and I were racking up. There were also many opportunities for my husband to change his mind and return home. That did not happen. Finally, there were no more ways to stop this runaway legal train. No way of staying the court's guillotine.

The court date for this grievous, destructive event was scheduled. Testimony was taken from my husband and me. Doug swore that our twenty-two-year marriage was irretrievably broken. As I recall, he gave no supporting evidence. Sadly, the only required "evidence" to "legally sever" a family is for the Plaintiff to speak the words: "This marriage is irretrievably broken."

> **My husband swore our marriage was irretrievably broken with no supporting evidence.**

Doug's legal interpretation of our "marriage-contract" was in direct violation of the holy vows he made on June 30, 1962—"until death us do part." Additionally, we had what Article I, Section 10 of the United States Constitution deems is a valid "contract,"—not to be "impaired" **by the government**: "No state shall ... pass any ... law impairing the obligation of contracts."

My testimony was quite the opposite. Part of my testimony is reproduced on pages 53 and 54.

Marriage Not Irretrievably Broken

Your Honor, I do not believe that our marriage is irretrievably broken because as a Christian I don't believe that any marriage relationship is irretrievable or unredeemable as long as there is at least one party willing to "stand" for that relationship.

Doug and I began our marriage almost 22 years ago. A marriage-covenant was entered into by Doug and me on June 30, 1962, each party giving of his own free will – a vow sworn and witnessed before God – until death us do part – to remain otherwise betrothed to one another. Doug and I have, on several occasions, in church restated these vows since that time.

This marriage-covenant, as directed by God, is not to be broken by man. God states: A man will leave his father and mother and be united to his wife and the two will be one flesh so that they are no longer two but one. Therefore what God has joined together LET NOT MAN separate. God states that He hates divorce and marital separation. He commands a wife not to separate from her husband and says to the husband you must not divorce and specifically states that we are bound to each other as long as we live.

The court has asked Doug and me to "swear" on the Bible. Why do we do that? Is it not that we believe in the AUTHORITY of God's Word? This Book is used not only in the courtroom but has also been the focal point of our marriage, our family activities, and our basic beliefs.

This Book on which we have sworn today gives a direct command: it says man don't do anything to put a marriage apart. It says when a man makes a vow to the LORD or takes an oath to obligate himself by a pledge he must not break his word but must do everything he said. This "Authority" also says that we should not take our Christian brother to court and that we should "train up" our children in the way they should go and when they are old they will not depart from it. This latter Scripture is one encompassed in a hanging we have had in our bedroom since the birth of our second child, Mike. The banner is entitled, "Children Learn What They Live."

To train up a child in the way he should go says that children learn from example:

I have been forced into court which God says a Christian must not do.

I am being asked to consider the dissolution of something which God
    overwhelmingly says not to do.

The petition presented is asking for vows to be broken which God says not to do.

But even more significant is that I am being asked to "train up our children" that God's Word is not Truth: that breaking up families by divorce is all right ... and thus, by inference, through example set by adults—that children can do anything they want to in life and that God and man will not hold them accountable to their given word.

In our married life we have been a one-flesh team. We have supported each other in educational achievements, family activities, and work-related projects. We have cooperated in and out of the home as each stage of life required.

Doug has spent a great deal of time developing and fostering his career, and I have supported him by being directly involved by doing backup things. I admire my husband for his industriousness. He was building for the future of our family in God's name, and I was doing my job by taking primary responsibility for the children while he provided financial security. As an outgrowth of our activities, we were involved with the church, the community, and several families.

Doug's behavior and beliefs that he is presently expressing are so inconsistent with our past 20-year history. He has stood for family unity. He has taught and lived God's principles. He has had a concern for the welfare of his wife and family. His own words can best describe his love for me.

In 1976, he wrote to my parents inside the cover of a book he had just published: "Perhaps this will reflect the pride I feel in having the honor to be married to your daughter. She is so very special to me, and so are you."

In the copy he gave to me he wrote: "I mean what I said to your folks about the pride I feel in you. Maybe I should have saved that poem and put it in here. Anyhow, the things I do, the efforts etc. are all for you and in my dumb way are attempts to show you my love for you. People tell me how fortunate I am to have you, and I certainly agree. These past years have been great, and I'm sure the next 100 will be too."

At another time, he wrote: "The three qualities I appreciate about you are – your energy, your leadership and how you care for the kids."

In a poem he wrote, Doug stated:
"To list all of your special talents is no small chore.
You do so well in all the regular things and many more.
You patiently love the kids and me through ups and downs.
Often your tolerance for us and our actions clearly abounds.
You're behind so much of the acclaim that comes to you and me.
You organize, motivate, lead, generate, work.
They seem to be a part of perceived duty you won't shirk."

About a year before Doug left the home, he wrote the following poem to me:
"Friends are important of that I'm quite sure
Because it's through the rough spots friends endure.
You've shown me that you are in fact a friend
For that I'll love you till my life does end.
The way I feel right now dictates a thrill and joy.
I think of us and what we are going to do – Oh, boy.
Just remember that what I say now is true.
Keep on loving me – I need it – and I do love you."

The breaking of this pattern by Doug is not a permanent thing. I understand that many people, especially men, go through a period of dissatisfaction in their life, especially between the ages of 40-55 where they want to break ties with their spouses and enjoy freedom that they feel they have missed in life.

I am willing to wait out this period in my husband's life as his wife—and for us as a complete family. I do not want the children to continue their lives with the stigma of divorced parents—with holidays broken between parents and relatives—with a home that is half empty—with the loss of the stability of a family unit.

I ask you, Doug, as my husband—and as a Christian—to forgive me for anything or any way that I have hurt you. I ask you, Doug, to stop these proceedings, which so dishonour God and your family, and to return home as my husband and as the father of our children so that we may be a complete family.

I give you my unconditional love,

Judy

As stated on page 52, the government is not to change the terms set forth in a contract (of marriage). For example, if you sign a contract to purchase a $200,000 house on a 30-year mortgage, you are responsible to pay for it. If later the floor plan no longer suits you and you move out, you are still obligated to pay the mortgage. It would be unconstitutional for the government to pass a law saying that because you no longer liked the floor plan, you no longer had to pay the remaining mortgage.

Likewise, if a spouse wishes to opt out of a "marriage-contract"; i.e., to refuse to fulfill the "until-death-us-do-part" terms of his "legal contract," he shouldn't be aided, empowered, and rewarded by the government to do so. What he perhaps should do if he deserts the other contracting party is to forfeit those things that have accrued as an inherent part of the contract such as the children, property, and other assets. BUT as with other legal agreements, he is still responsible for the financial obligations that are a part of the contract. If this were enforced, there might be a slowing down of people exiting what the government calls a legally binding contract but does not treat as such. Most "exiters" who are **unfaithful** to the spouse of their agreed-upon lifetime "contract" are unbelievably **faithful** to the assets accrued during the marriage!

> **What I didn't realize was that, unlike all other lawsuits, there was no legal defense one could bring, in this type of lawsuit, to stop a divorce.**

Sadly, however, our government has passed a law that releases Plaintiffs from the contractual obligations inherent in the contract and rewards them with what is subjectively determined to be an "equitable distribution" of the assets. The state causes faithful spouses to become Defendants who are powerless to stop proceedings for which they have no defense. Without its No-fault contractual loophole,

Plaintiffs would have no "cause" to name the Defendant in what otherwise would be a frivolous lawsuit.

Thus, because of the legislative act which instituted No-fault, I was, for the first time in my life, involved in such a lawsuit. **Not only was this a lawsuit, but one which would have rules,** like the "marriage-contract," **unlike all other lawsuits.** There would be no legal defense to clear me of the "crime" of which I would be charged—a "crime" of which I would be convicted and sent to the death chamber. My family would be splintered and properties would be, under color of law, judicially taken from me. I would be charged thousands of dollars for defending that which I didn't do—and no one would be at fault. That's right, it's no-fault—no one is at fault for destroying a family! Who in the world made up these rules in this "equal justice for all" country in which we live!

> **The government "caused" me to become a Defendant in a lawsuit with rules unlike any other lawsuit.**

What if I don't sign?

My defense of our marriage, my testimony, did not move the hardened hearts in the courtroom. As I entered my testimony, Judge Fuller looked at my husband. No hope. The judge legally and the Plaintiff emotionally were firm in their resolve that the gavel should come down. I begged Judge Fuller to not strike the gavel on our marriage. But, the legal strike of DEATH resounded in my ears and tore at my heart as the gavel firmly struck the bench.

Unknown to me, the devastation had only begun when I told the judge that I would not sign.

A quick response came from my husband when I said that I wouldn't sign. He didn't feel it was fair that the proceedings be prolonged. He felt that I had already "dragged this thing out too long." Furthermore, he said that

I lived in our home and he in a dumpy apartment. So the judge struck a deal. Here's the deal! If I refused the court decision and planned to contest, he would only "hear" my objections to the dissolution if I would immediately dismiss my attorney and argue the remaining issues myself. AND, **I would have to agree to be court-ordered to leave our home** allowing Doug to move back into our home.

Doug had chosen to move out, but knew he was always welcome to return, which he had done from time to time.

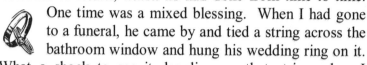 One time was a mixed blessing. When I had gone to a funeral, he came by and tied a string across the bathroom window and hung his wedding ring on it. What a shock to see it dangling on that string when I returned home and walked into the bathroom.

I cut the string and removed the ring. I clutched it in my shaking hands, stunned at my husband's attempts to hurt me. Nonetheless, I learned to be thankful that he brought the ring back home for safekeeping and that I could have this treasured reminder of our "until-death-us-do-part" commitment.

Back to the courtroom. I had just learned that my husband would soon be returning to our home. However, I would never have dreamed that his return would have meant my being forced to leave, followed by a life-threatening keep-out warning from him via a later phone conversation. Judge Fuller made it clear that only if I consented to the above "verbal contract" would he agree to hear my objection to his decision, which I later learned was a *Motion for Rehearing*. I didn't even have a clue as to what a *Motion for Rehearing* was or what the legal process to object to a court decision would involve. What I did know was that I would not agree to sign something—a divorce decree—that in essence said that God's Word was a lie—that Doug was no longer my husband.

I turned to my attorney: "If I don't do this will this be over today? Does it 'end' my marriage?" He said, "Yes, you need to sign." By telling me this, he unknowingly supported the Judge's attempt to mislead me. I found out later that I had a constitutional right to appeal. I didn't need Judge Fuller's "verbal contract" to do so.

I quickly considered the options. The pressure mounted. Then, I spoke: "Your Honor, I do not believe that our marriage is irretrievably broken. I'll never sign a paper that says our marriage is dissolved by man and indicating that I am no longer a married woman."

> **"I'll never sign a paper that says our marriage is dissolved by man and that I'm not a married woman."**

"If your God doesn't recognize divorce, what does it matter whether this is entered or not?" the judge asked. I felt unfairly attacked when he said this. By signing the court decree, it would incorrectly show that I had given my permission for others to continue the destruction of our family, and so I responded, "Because then you also think you have the right to divide our family and our assets." "If your God were with you, He would have helped you by now and if you're worried about the property division you better check your motives," replied Judge Fuller.

> **If your God doesn't recognize a divorce, what does it matter whether this is entered or not?**

Goliath had again attacked David. I felt so intimidated, so frightened. My thumping heart questioned, "How could it be morally wrong for me to be concerned about our children and about my having a right to the assets I helped us acquire during our marriage?" I was afraid to speak what I was feeling.

I responded: "I will not sign." Thus, I agreed to his stipulations, not knowing that this was an unconstitutional order. I did not have to purchase my constitutional **right** to file an appeal and to have a *Motion for Rehearing* heard by the court. So, under much emotional duress to protect our marriage, our family, and our properties—and my ignorance of the law—I agreed to follow these bizarre stipulations.

> Goliath had again attacked David. I felt so intimidated.

Even so, the gavel came down, firmly striking the bench, on April 18, 1984: MARRIAGE DISSOLVED— with the conditional **right** to file a *Motion for Rehearing*. And, as the "icing on the cake," the state had taken away my legal counsel by judicially maneuvering me into dismissing my attorney.

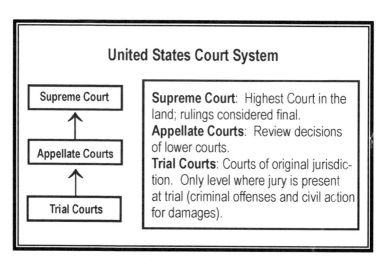

United States Court System

Supreme Court

↑

Appellate Courts

↑

Trial Courts

Supreme Court: Highest Court in the land; rulings considered final.
Appellate Courts: Review decisions of lower courts.
Trial Courts: Courts of original jurisdiction. Only level where jury is present at trial (criminal offenses and civil action for damages).

Chapter 5

THERE IS NO DIVORCE AGAINST THIS FAMILY

As my shaking legs carried me out of the courtroom, a still small voice brought to me a puzzling thought: *"There is no divorce against this family."* That's crazy! I KNEW what had just happened in that courtroom. Over the next twenty-two years, I would learn the true significance of the message within those words: *"There is no divorce against this family."* In the midst of all the confusion and broken-heartedness, I met briefly with my attorney at which time he told me that I would probably be receiving papers from Doug's attorney, Mr. Simon, to which I would need to respond. Most laymen would not realize that with such court-related documents, there are accompanying response deadlines that normally CANNOT be extended. I found there are unforgiving consequences if a deadline is ignored.

My focus turned to the reality of the day. I had just been told that I would be forced to "evacuate" in the near future—to move out of what had been our home all these years and away from the children. Surely, this won't happen. God, please don't let them enter such a cruel order. What an unbelievable injustice!

The one thing that I knew was that I somehow had a short time to file this "strange" document, *Motion for Rehearing.* I left the courthouse with a heart shattered beyond what I thought was repairable, rejected by my husband whom I dearly loved and love to this day. I hated how our family was becoming more and more fractured, and I had no means to stop it. Not knowing when the order would come to move, I started to shop for a place to live. It was another heartbreaking experience. A friend took me to look for an apartment. I tried to keep from sobbing and showing my emotions. How could this be happening? I didn't want to leave my home.

Because of all the emotional turmoil and finding a place to live when that order was enforced, I had forgotten that Mr. Grier had told me that I would probably be receiving papers from Attorney Simon within a few days. It happened. The papers came with legal language and directives very foreign to me. And I would have to respond by following judicial rules of procedure, also totally foreign to me. These were buried somewhere within the judicial system's protocol. "Oh God, where are You!!!" I found that He was there, with that occasional "still small voice" leading me and placing people in my pathway to help.

How do I appeal? The clock started ticking!

Lots of disheartening experiences were just around the corner! From the simplicity of hand writing my first legal document (*Motion for Rehearing*) to the sophistication of my typed briefs submitted to the United States Supreme Court three years later, I began a journey to defend further God's Law of Marriage: "What therefore God hath joined together, let not man put asunder." (Mark 10:9) To you the reader this may seem unusual if you are not a Christian, but defending one's marriage is an inherent part of this life-time commitment. Believing marriage is until death includes defending that belief.

> Ignorance is bliss. Well it was—for a short while.

Most have heard the statement: "Ignorance is bliss." Well it was—for a short while. What a nightmare this became as reality set in. I didn't have a clue as to what to do in the legal arena. It seemed that my husband's lawyer took advantage of the

61

fact that I didn't have an attorney and started firing off briefs to which I had to respond personally. Suddenly, I had been forced into becoming my own attorney. I understood very little of what was said or expected so the first thing I did was to copy some of the expressions Attorney Simon used in the papers I received, typed a form like he sent and returned my reply. This was the only way I knew how to respond, but it did seem to irritate Doug's lawyer.

I didn't have a clue as to what to do in the legal arena.

Also, I went to the courthouse and studied some of the papers that had been filed and took notes trying to figure out what all the legal jargon meant. Before I was served the divorce papers, I was even confused on who the Plaintiff/Petitioner was and who the Defendant/Respondent was. Amazing what a little experience of being a Defendant/Respondent will bring to one's knowledge bank!

I did learn, with haste, the fact that a time clock was ticking on my *Motion for Rehearing*. I would soon be required to properly file my first legal document by the upcoming deadline with no reprieve for tardiness! I had approximately 20 days.

Write! My first legal document, *Motion for Rehearing*, was written on a tablet in my lap as a friend sped in her car on back roads to the courthouse. What led up to this scenario? It was a series of events after the *Trial for Dissolution* when Judge Fuller brought his gavel down upon our marriage saying that it was legally dissolved.

One of the first things I did after the trial was to meet with my attorney, Mr. Grier, to ask him to file the *Motion for Rehearing* based on abuse of my constitutional rights. Constitutional rights. This certainly was not previously a part of my vocabulary! A friend from New Jersey gave me a quick course on constitutional rights and protections, and tried to help me to recognize some judicial errors made and rights violated. I definitely didn't know what to do or how to file the *Motion*—or even what it looked like.

In a meeting with Mr. Grier after the April 18 hearing, he stated that he was not a constitutional lawyer and did not have the proper background to enter into a constitutional battle. **He knew of no legal way to file an appeal—the Motion**—under the No-fault Law. Furthermore, the judge had ordered that I dismiss him, barring him from doing so. "God, how could you leave me hanging like this?"

Many phone calls were made to attorneys and others who had some legal background. I could not find anyone to help me file the *Motion*. **Everyone said that I had no grounds under No-fault to contest and thus no constitutional right of appeal—and these were practicing attorneys!** Yet, I still had hope that there was a way.

Writing letters, making phone calls, and attending meetings to try to find an attorney to represent me became my focus. I was also contacting Christian ministries begging them to join the fight to preserve families. Portions of one of my many letters is below:

June 15, 1984

Dear Mr. Whitemore:

... I am asking you to help me to protect the covenant and my marriage vows which God directs "let not man separate." I'm going to file an appeal.

Mr. Whitemore, I feel that not only has my freedom of religion been violated because it was God who put my husband and me together, but also that there is no real "due process" in the court procedure since there seems

> **There is no real *due process* ... there seems to be no way to "win" if a spouse brings an action against the marriage.**

to be no way to win if a spouse brings an action against the marriage. The person bringing the action is granted "his rights," completely violating those of the party filed against and the vows made to God. A judge is permitted, on a purely subjective basis, to determine that a marriage is irretrievably broken.

My twenty-two year marriage was evaluated by someone who used as evidence a marriage partner who, two years ago, decided he wanted other priorities.

Mrs. Judith Brumbaugh

The above organization as well as most major and minor ministries across our nation that I contacted did not feel they had time to help and/or did not share the "until-death-us-do-part" perspective on marriage.

A Christian constitutional attorney will help??

My thread of hope was partially renewed when I met a nationally well-known Christian attorney at one of the many meetings I attended in my search for legal help. The Jorgensens, one of the families I later lived with, were active in Christian issues and took me to a meeting where Attorney Andy Jones (fictitious name) spoke.

I talked with Mr. Jones after the meeting, told him of my fight against the destruction of the family, and gave him a brief overview of my case. He promised that if I could keep my case alive for several months, he would defend it. Legally, that looked like an impossibility. At the time, I didn't have a lawyer to file papers to defend me. Additionally, of the many attorneys I called, **not one of them** felt there were grounds under No-fault to make an appeal. It would not be easy to keep my case alive, but I held onto that thread of encouragement—his promise of help. I wrote Mr. Jones the follow-up letter on the next page:

June 16, 1984

Dear Andy:
I certainly do thank God for leading me to your office. I will be in prayer each day that your heart will be touched to defend my rights as an individual, a mother, and a Christian. There are many items involved here in addition to the constitutional and "due process" issues that are being violated. I compliment you that you are willing to take an active stand to defend our marriage ...
Mrs. Judith Brumbaugh

I called Mr. Grier, the attorney who had represented me through the April 18 *Trial for Dissolution* to share the good news about the offer for free council from a constitutional attorney. My follow-up letter is below:

Dear Mr. Grier:
I am writing this letter in hopes that you will please give Andy positive encouragement to take on litigation for my situation ... You know I have a limited income at this point. If Mr. Jones takes this on, he will do it free. You know how strongly I feel about the permanency of marriage ... You know that I feel Doug will return.

> **I see children being filled with anger, hostility ... as they are forced to choose sides, dividing their loyalties between parents.**

I have been praying and fasting for God not only to provide the resources to fight this ridiculous No-fault Divorce, but also the finances for it. What a miraculous answer to prayer to find someone who is showing an interest in this case who is a Christian, and who will provide the finances for it. I am sick of seeing, not only my home, family, and rights being violated but that of the many others I have met through this horrible experience.

I see children become filled with anger, hostility, resentfulness as their physical, social, emotional, psychological, and spiritual protections are removed as they are forced to "choose sides" dividing their loyalties between parents (man cannot serve two masters). Their hearts are broken; the quality of their lives damaged forever. The loss of a parent through death is a devastating tragedy. The loss of a parent through divorce carries with it the added component of willful abandonment. Children, instead of coming home to a parent after school, are placed in a situation where they come home to a television set, or a babysitter, or they bum around somewhere.

No-fault provides an incentive for people to leave their families.

Some of the issues to which I object regarding the proceedings on Monday include: violation of the Fourteenth and First Amendments; violation of my right to be a homemaker as my chosen profession; violation of our children's rights (divorce is not in the best interest of our children); being put in an adversarial position of strife against my husband; a humanistic presumption against my marriage calling it dead; the presumption that it takes two to make a marriage

The loss of a parent through divorce carries with it the added component of willful abandonment.

66

reconcilable (as opposed to just one praying, loving partner and God as witness to the covenant); a breaking of my marriage-covenant of "until-death-us-do-part" vows and of my "marriage-contract"; use of the term "separation" or "divorce" instead of desertion.

> **The court forces children's loyalties to be divided.**

No-fault provides an incentive for people to leave their families rather than to stay and honor commitments and work on problems and by holding marriage in honor, having a united, healed family rather than tearing it apart, **forcing children's loyalties to be divided***.*

The common "excuse" that many spouses are expressing is based upon Hollywood love: "I don't feel *any love for her; my life is empty; I'm not happy." Most spouses have at one time had these types of feelings. Love, however, is rooted in something stronger than emotion and feelings.* **That love has to be a willing commitment to action ... If you love someone you will be loyal to him no matter what the cost.** *You will always believe in him, always expect the best of him, and stand your ground in defending him. Too many people are talking about mid-life crises today not to take note of this "temporary something" creating the desire for desertion rather than the "fault" being placed on the spouse who wants to leave ...*

> **Love is rooted in something stronger than emotion and feelings.**

So how did the case move forward without an attorney, without funds, without legal representation, with no personal legal background? Let's turn the calendar back a bit to fill in some other details.

A phone call brings another ray of hope.

My New Jersey friend whom I mentioned earlier had called me for the first time when she heard of my efforts to defend marriage. Her attorney husband was in the process of divorcing her. Through their years of marriage, she had learned some legal terms and judicial procedures that were foreign to me but needed for my upcoming battles.

She knew I had a right to appeal exclusive of Judge Fuller's "conditions." She offered to make long distance calls for me in an effort to locate someone to help with an appeal. These were the days before unlimited long distance calls so she incurred the expense for these calls as I did not have the money to make them.

Day after day, we would talk by phone and make lists of people to call. Day after day, the rejections came. The **time** bomb was ticking. The *Motion for Rehearing* had to be filed by 5:00 p.m. June 21. **No one** felt I had a constitutional right to appeal. Four o'clock, June 21, two phone numbers left to try. The first, another strikeout. Oh, there's no way.

> **No one felt I had a constitutional right to appeal.**

Can you get me to the courthouse on time?

Dial quickly! The final phone number! A break-through—a father/son Christian attorney's office was reached. "Which attorney do you want, Senior or Junior?" the receptionist asked me. Crying and frantic, I replied, "I don't know, I just need help to file an appeal by 5:00 p.m. today." An elderly gentleman picked up the phone. He seemed to understand, to already *know* why I was calling. "You have a right to appeal, but you have to file this by 5:00 p.m." "I know, but I don't know how to do it nor

what to write." "Do you have a piece of paper?" "Yes."
"Just write you would like a rehearing and for what reason
and get down there and file it," replied this stranger whom
I've never met. "Thank you, and God bless you," I
hurriedly responded.

I quickly hung up the phone and turned to my friend
Donna from whose home we were making these last-
minute long-distance calls. "We've got it. Can you get me
to the courthouse on time?" I asked her. "Let's go!" she
responded.

We were off. Yes, we did exceed the speed limit! I
wrote the *Motion* on my lap as we raced on back roads. We
arrived about fifteen minutes
before the deadline to legally file
the appeal. Having never been in
the courthouse, I ran in and
frantically asked the lady at the
reception desk, "Where do I file
this paper?" "Which court are you in?" she asked, along
with other questions I could not answer, but she "caught"
the urgency in my voice. Directed to go upstairs, I ran
quickly, stopping at an open window on the next floor.

> **"Where do I file this paper?"**
> **"Which court are you in?"**

"I need to file this paper." "But you don't have a case
number. You will have to go down stairs and get it." "But
where do I go? What is my case? I don't have time." She
looked at the name and said, "Oh, I recognize this case, let
me write it in for you."

Stamped in at 4:45 p.m., this handwritten *Motion*,
recorded on a piece of notebook paper and properly filed
started me on a horrific journey. It was a journey filled
with fears, various states of poverty, many disappoint-
ments, and endless hours of pouring over legal books, case
precedents, typing, making phone calls, driving miles to
file briefs, meeting with people, much praying and fasting
and ... bucketfuls of tears. (See a copy of this *Motion* on
page 70.)

Motion for Rehearing
June 21, 1984
Circuit Court for
Seminole County
Case # 82-3055-CA
Division # 04-E

Re Marriage of Douglas K and
Judith A Brumbaugh

This is a motion for a rehearing
to judge

I would like to move for a
rehearing. I have decided to
file this motion on my behalf
I would like a rehearing
for the following reasons.
I feel that "no-fault"
divorce is a violation of my
first and fourteenth amendment
rights and is not in the
best interest of our children

Judith A. Brumbaugh

Clerk Jim Bruint x 360
received 6/21/84-4 45 P.M

First Legal Paper filed: Motion for Rehearing

70

The Cover-Up

No one thought that it would be possible for me to file a *Motion for Rehearing*. I didn't have an attorney, I didn't have money. But most of all, I was told by numerous attorneys that there were no constitutional grounds on which to file it. Once I had accomplished the seemingly impossible—I filed a *Motion for Rehearing*—and breathed a sigh of relief, I was summoned to court again. I had written my first legal brief. Now I would have to go into court without an attorney. I would be my attorney! This would be a frightening experience. One of my many fears was that they would likely mow me down.

> No attorney. How do I file?

While doing research for this book, I came across a letter that I had written to President Reagan which is part of Chapter 7, pages 154-156. It reminded me that I didn't understand **their purpose** for the hearing on July 25. I thought that I would be acting as my attorney to defend the division of our properties, but more importantly my *Motion for Rehearing* would be heard. I thought I would be presenting case evidence and proofs as to why the dissolution should not have been given on April 18, 1984.

July 4, 1984

... Mr. President, I am pleading with you to offer some assistance to help me to protect my marriage vows and my family unit. I would like to **have the decree overturned.** *I, however, have no money to hire a lawyer to help me to resist this action and* **have been asked to return to court on July 25 for a division of property** *... I have, on my own behalf, filed a "Motion for Rehearing" as I could find no lawyer to do it for me ...*

Respectfully submitted,
Mrs. Douglas (Judith) Brumbaugh

71

During the July 25 Hearing I found that the property division and the hearing of my *Motion* were not what those in control seemed to have had on their agenda. It appeared that my surprise filing of the *Motion for Rehearing* created a judicial stopgap they couldn't gloss over. The true purpose of this hearing *became* to camouflage the fact that I would be required to pay a great personal, egregious cost to buy my **right** to have my *Motion* heard. **This "edict" was given during the trial for dissolution on April 18, 1984: "eviction" from our home and dismissal of my attorney.**

The Court was called to order—July 25, 1984.

MR. GRIER: "Judge, my client is adamant that she needs to have her *Motion for Rehearing* resolved. I therefore must give this as my motion to withdraw as counsel, and I will follow that up with a written motion to that extent ... I indicated to her, to Mrs. Brumbaugh, that I did not believe I had knowledge ... I was not a constitutional attorney, **I did not have that knowledge** to argue the point on the constitutional law issue."

[Recall the *Trial for Dissolution*. **During the trial, Judge Fuller directed me to dismiss Attorney Grier**— that he could no longer represent me if I planned to appeal his decision regarding the dissolution of our marriage.]

THE COURT: **"We do have this document filed, raising the questions with regard to the divorce itself."**

[That was my *Motion for Rehearing* which I filed because I had been ordered to release Attorney Grier during **the April 18 trial**. If I would not have filed the *Motion* the deadline to do so would have passed, and the *Motion* could **not** have been filed—not even by a constitutional attorney.]

THE COURT: **"All issues that are incidental to the divorce do need to be advised in conjunction with a divorce, or in conjunction to a divorce** ... With that being the situation, The Court has gone ahead and will allow the attorney to withdraw from the case. I do so reluctantly because **I have serious concern about trying this case without an attorney** and wondering how we're going to go through, get through the complete case with a **layperson who's not trained legally**.

Now, the next posture I find myself, we're ready to proceed with the trial at this time. Are you ready to proceed with the trial Mrs. Brumbaugh?"

MRS. BRUMBAUGH: "I don't really understand where we are because it was my understanding that the motion for retrial could be presented only if Mr. Grier withdrew. Is that correct?" [As per April 18 trial]

THE COURT: "There are two ways that it could be presented. One is if Mr. Grier was willing to argue it as his motion and file it in your behalf; and second, in the event he withdrew and you argue it yourself or another attorney who you feel comfortable in arguing the motion."

MRS. BRUMBAUGH: "**It was my understanding that it would be heard today** then if that's done."

THE COURT: "The matters that are set for trial today are the matters of property and support issues ... Are you prepared to go forward?"

MRS. BRUMBAUGH: "I don't feel that I'm capable, by myself, of presenting a case for the rest of this trial."

THE COURT: "Okay. So your choice is what then?"

MRS. BRUMBAUGH: "**I would like to have the opportunity to have my *Motion for Rehearing* presented to the Court**. And whatever is done, I need counsel to help me to do it."

[Notice that Judge Fuller's response was what I now perceive to be a "baited question."]

THE COURT: "Oh, you're asking this Court to delay this matter?" [He had already, on April 18, set the terms for my "right to appeal." Frightened, intimated, emotional, and confused about what was happening, I responded to Judge Fuller's question.]

MRS. BRUMBAUGH: "Yes, sir."

THE COURT: "… I need to make sure you understand when **you ask for the continuance** there would be some conditions connected with it." [I didn't know what a continuance was. I, in the only way I knew how, **was pleading for my constitutional right to an appeal.**]

MRS. BRUMBAUGH: **"Are you saying that the condition would be that you would ask me to move out of the house?" [A condition given on April 18.** My attorney had already been dismissed, <u>one</u> of the <u>two</u> conditions that I was ORDERED to do **during** the April 18, 1984 emotional trial for dissolution as "payment" for my RIGHT to appeal.]

THE COURT: "That's one possibility."

MRS. BRUMBAUGH: "Is that what you suggest?"

THE COURT: "It's pretty strong right now. I'm thinking about – **I can't continue to allow you to cause a delay** and inconvenience and keep everything the same. … You just simply stay where you are while I prevent their [Doug's and our son's] constitutional rights. He has constitutional rights too …"

MRS. BRUMBAUGH: "Your Honor, **I would like to have an opportunity to present my** *Motion for Rehearing.*"

THE COURT: "I'm going to find the continuance is, from what I have heard, prejudicial to the Petitioner [Doug] and that in order to try to balance some of the equity, I'm going to go ahead and require a change of the living arrangement of the parties.

I believe that the husband and the minor child, the father and the minor child, should be returned to the residence until this Court can make an ultimate decision as to the Petitioner's interest in the residence at the next final hearing. [**This was nothing new that Judge Fuller JUST came up with. It was one of the two conditions he gave me on April 18 at our trial for dissolution. <u>The court had made no child custody decisions prior to this</u>.**]

THE COURT: "I'm going to require that the transfer take place by August the 1st. ... **The *Motion for Rehearing* can be argued in fifteen minutes, provided Simon [Plaintiff's attorney] doesn't drag it on ...**"

My judicial purpose was that I wanted to exercise my constitutional right to appeal. To do so meant my paying a great, grievous price which was forced upon me. **What happened in the courtroom this day created the perception in me that the court was attempting to camouflage an abuse of justice perpetrated on April 18. Under color of law, the court was "executing" what had already been "ruled" at our *Trial for Dissolution* when Judge Fuller made the "verbal contract" with me requiring me to buy my right to appeal with two stipulations:** "eviction" from our home; dismissal of my attorney. Now the court was **converting ITS April 18 *order* into a continuance requested by me.** See the order written by Doug's attorney on page 76 recording the July 25 trial scheduled to be the *Supplemental Final Hearing* at which my *Motion for Rehearing* should have been heard. This is also when the court would have divided our properties and our children. Instead, it camouflaged, **under color of law**, the unconstitutional acts that transpired on April 18 during the *Trial for Dissolution* and, in the Order, misrepresented the intent of the July 25, 1984 hearing.

In Chapter 2 of this book, I shared what I learned when I visited a judge's courtroom in 2005. I discovered that criminals would not have been subjected to the horrific persecutions to which I was being subjected. They, unlike a homemaker forced to become a Defendant in a family lawsuit, are protected.

They are not only clearly told that they have a right to appeal but that an attorney can be appointed for them at no cost. If I would have embezzled money, stolen a car, or committed a capital crime, these rights would have been offered to me. Because, however, I was not a conventional criminal, but merely made one by being named as a Defendant/Respondent in a divorce suit, I was left to defend myself in an arena where I had no skills. Because the above protections were not available to me, I was made an easy prey for judicial manipulation.

ORDER RELATED TO WIFE'S
MOTION FOR CONTINUANCE

This cause having come on to be heard and scheduled for trial on the **25th day of July**, 1984, and the Court finding that the Wife has dismissed her attorney, and the Court further finding that the Wife is in need of an attorney, and the Wife advising the Court that she is going to seek additional counsel, and the Court considering the equities of this cause, and *in order to balance the equities*, the Court finding that *the minor child of the parties, Michael, is residing with the Husband* [Michael had been with me **until a few months prior to the dissolution hearing** when suddenly Doug said to me that he was taking Mike to live with him] pursuant to this Court Order, it is therefore

ORDERED AND ADJUDGED

The Husband is hereby awarded exclusive use and possession of the marital residence and the Wife is to remove herself from the marital residence **no later than August 1, 1984.**

"Evacuation"

So the gavel came down once again, but this time on the execution of the dreaded **order** that was **given during our initial trial for the legal dissolution** (procedurally unconstitutional) of our marriage **on April 18, 1984.**

Several weeks prior to what I thought was to be another *Final Hearing*—July 25, I had begun to lose the fear of being evicted from our home: "Perhaps they will be kind and not order me out of our home." More than a month had passed since the devastating and frightening April 18 experience and I had not received an "eviction" notice.

I was nervous about going to court when I was summoned for what was to be the *Supplemental Final Trial* on July 25 because I thought that would be when my *Motion for Rehearing* would be heard. Now, not only was I to be evicted (court-ordered to leave), but I also had to be out of our home no later than August 1, 1984—six days!

Where do I move? No funds to pay first and last month's rent, security deposit, etc. The reader may wonder why the people who had been in my life when my husband and I were such strong church and community leaders did not step forward with housing. I had shared very little of specific court happenings with most of them. My sharing was more with several new friends I met who also were going through unwanted divorces. Most of my other friends thought as did the government that the marriage was over because of the court decree on April 18. Many felt it was time for me to look for another husband. They didn't share my "until-death-us-do-part" understanding of marriage. I didn't tell most that I was to be "evicted" and about the financial situation that had been forced upon me.

Along with being emotionally distraught, I was embarrassed at what was happening to our family. Especially on my thoughts were the many young people that had looked up to us—the untold numbers that called us "Pa" and "Ma"; those who visited our home for Bible studies and the many lives we had touched through community projects we had headed as a strongly connected husband-and-wife team.

However, there was a couple who sensed that the smile on my face was concealing some deep needs. They came to my rescue. Their parents were going north to stay for several weeks, and they had agreed to let me move into their home. What would I have done if Dave and Sherrill had not found a place for me to live? What a blessing for me that Elton and Florence would be vacationing in Michigan at "such a time as this" when I needed free housing. Can you imagine the faith they had in letting a total stranger, a friend of their son and daughter-in-law, move into their home!

And what about our children? What would be best for them? Our daughter was 18 and was still with me in our home. Our son who was 14 had been with me, but *Doug took him to live with him a few months before what was to be our final hearing on April 18, 1984.* It was puzzling when he suddenly told Mike, but apparently not Shawn, that he wanted him to move in with him. Perhaps the offer was also made to her and she decided to stay in our home.

Even though I was emotionally traumatized, I wanted the children's lives to be as uninterrupted as much as possible. The only secure element in their lives was our home. It was the only thing that was not changing. It seemed best that they remain in our home. It was obvious they couldn't stay with me. My living arrangements were certainly not stable, knowing I couldn't rent an apartment and that I had housing for three weeks. And then what? Nonetheless, the July 25 order tore my heart further into shreds, leading me at times to beg God to take my life.

Our children loved both of us. Imagine the confusion that must have taken place in their minds when they were put in the position of having to choose one parent over the other. **That's like asking someone which arm they'd rather have amputated. Or which eye they'd rather have gouged out.** Obviously, the answer would be, "Neither one!" The anguish that an adult would experience when having to face such a choice—and these are children! For a child, their worst nightmare is coming true—nothing is permanent, not even love, and life is not safe. **To a child, his parents are like**

A person cannot serve two masters— not even children!

two sides of the same coin. If something were to happen that caused the people of our nation to lose faith in our currency, society would crumble. In this same way, **the lives of our children are crumbling. This is a tragedy!**

I needed to deal with the court-ordered "eviction" by disturbing the children as little as possible. Those who have had to leave their homes, either forcefully or voluntarily, know all too well the uncertainty, the fears, the anxiety that accompany such an occurrence. Will I be able to return? What will be there when I return? How do I decide what to take, what to leave? Where will I live?

I remember so vividly the day. Leaving our daughter added deeply to my emotional turmoil. (Recall that my husband had taken our son to live with him a few months before our divorce hearing on April 18, 1984.) Piece-by-piece, he was doing as he had threatened when I refused his offer to buy a dissolution from me. "Then I will take it all!" he said.

> **Piece-by-piece, he was doing as he threatened when I refused his offer to buy from me a dissolution: "Then I will take it all!"**

But my marriage was still not for sale! Oh, the pain of packing up my stuff. I had to choose only what would fit in my car and a friend's car. What should I take? To leave so many things I had treasured. It seemed that everything was being stripped from me. Why? Because I loved someone who no longer wished to be a part of my life, and I chose to abide by the perspective on marriage—"until death us do part"—to which both Doug and I committed, and to which I was still committed.

Donna came by to help me with the move. I wanted everything to look so perfect. I cleaned, scoured, and polished. Oh, I loved our home! I had made all the draperies and curtains, done the decorating, sewn the children's clothing, my husband's suits, and my garments.

Doug had had a big sewing table custom-made for my sewing room. It was such a dream.

I looked into his closet at the years of labor on his suits that I had designed and sewn for him. I laid my hand on them, wishing that he were in one of them. Doug didn't take the suits I had made when he left our home. He bought a new wardrobe. How that hurt!

There were many sweet memories I carry with me to this day. I can still chuckle that he used to tell people that if a button came off his suit he would have a better chance of my making him a whole new one than getting the button sewn back on. I didn't like to do repairs! And I had a special trademark. I would somehow always manage to leave a pin in somewhere that would find him the first time he wore the suit!

Doug was so proud of my sewing labors that he arranged for a reporter friend to interview me and write an article. She called it "Everybody Meet Judy Brumbaugh! "FTU Wife Tailors Doctor – Husband's Threads":

Dr. Douglas Brumbaugh of Florida Technological University proudly wears duds, including formal wear, designed and created by his wife, Judy.

Energetic! Exuberant! Dependable! Vital! Helpful! Friend! Versatile! And last, but not least, a most gracious person …! Why all of these adjectives you ask? Well, how else could one describe Mrs. Douglas Brumbaugh.

What this very enterprising young lady can do to a piece of cloth is not known. Whenever Judy's scissors "see" her coming to pick them up, I would be willing to wager that they usually sing for sheer joy of it.

Judy not only makes and designs most of her fashions (sometimes dear hubby, Dr. Douglas Brumbaugh, takes his pencil in hand and goes to

work on a special design for lovely Judy), but she also makes all of Doug's suits.
Doug is over six feet tall. His size offers no challenge to dear Judy by any means. She cuts her patterns to meet hubby's specifications, decides upon the type of materials she desires and takes it from there. To say that Douglas is one of the smartest dressed professors on the campus would not be an exaggeration!
Is Judy satisfied with this accomplishment? Not on your tin-type! She makes all of the clothes for the Brumbaugh youngsters, daughter, Shawn, five, and small son, Michael, two. The talented seamstress also makes all of the draperies and a good many of the tablecloths she uses. The Brumbaughs are truly an asset to their community. (8:4B)

Despite my history of making a home for my husband and our children as acknowledged in the previous article, my labors were now being dismissed as unimportant by my husband and the court. However, the Maryland Court of Appeals, in 1978, recognized the role of the "opportunity cost" of the duties performed by a housewife. They felt there was economic value for the housewife who had chosen to perform the "parental services" in her home herself rather than purchasing care for her children. The court determined that the economic position of the family was enhanced by the value of those services. A labor economist calculated their economic value.

There are many women who, likewise, have focused on the home and family; yet, the courts do not recognize the intangibles of years of such devotion. Some wives surely could have established a career and climbed the economic ladder but instead chose to be "keepers at home"—to care for the children and support the husband's career. These wives build up no retirement from which they can draw and may be totally cut off from the husband's when he decides he no longer wants to commit to his responsibilities to provide for his household. Thus, in so many instances, the wife's income drops drastically while his increases. She's without insurance and retirement and is often removed from the home as the court divides not only their marital relationship but also the attendant children and assets.

These sad realities have been statistically proven by many studies, some of which were mentioned in Chapter 4 of this text. But, let's return to my "evacuation."

Our last family portrait taken at our church was hanging on the wall. It was hard not to bring it with me, but my hope was that its image of our family as a unit would be a visual reminder to Doug, Shawn, and Mike. It was one of the things I requested during the *Supplemental Final Hearing* two years later. When I asked about it, my husband said that it had fallen off the wall and had torn. I wondered how falling off the wall could have torn it. But ... it was gone. I was heartbroken—our last family picture taken at our church. More on this later.

As my friend and I drove out of the driveway, I was saddened to see my husband sitting at the cross street watching me load the things into the car. He had told me earlier in the week that if I neglected to meet the deadline to vacate, he would have an officer come to arrest me. The pressure! I had no intention of not following this demeaning, threatening court order. Tears flooded my eyes and my heart was thumping in my throat as I drove out of the driveway. Men probably don't understand the attachment that women have for their families and the

> ... but to homemakers, our home is a part of us. Why in the world did you take the typewriter instead of so many other things?

homes that surround their loved ones. It's often just a place for some men to hang their hat, but to many homemakers, our home is an integral, emotional part of us.

So what did I choose to take with me? Clothing, my sewing machine, and the big heavy IBM Selectric typewriter that I could hardly lift. You may be thinking, "Why in the world did you take the typewriter instead of so many other things?"

The typewriter was not what I would consider a treasured possession. Because the space to transport things was limited (my friend's car and mine), I could not carry much. I chose to take the typewriter because I *knew* the work that I was about ... "fighting for my family." I knew the hours and hours that I had already spent in front of it typing and retyping briefs, legal documents, and letters. It was one of my weapons of this warfare, essential in the fight for my family.

When the court ordered me out of our home, I was not given money to rent an apartment or sufficient funds to maintain myself outside the home. I surely could not go out and purchase another typewriter. I only knew that at the time I had housing for about three weeks from precious people who, before my "evacuation notice," had not even met me. For me, there was no time to process the pain of moving out of our home and away from both children. I had serious legal work to do.

How do I find the books?

I learned that I needed to find additional legal justification for filing the *Motion for Rehearing* and to prepare my defense to support the *Motion*. Where do they get all those quotes and citings they use in these papers I keep getting?

Do lawyers have all this information in their offices? Yes, they have personal libraries, but how do I get hold of these books? Call some attorneys. "No, Mrs. Homemaker, these are not available for your use! Call the local library."

Our local library had a law dictionary that I checked out, but they had no legal books with court opinions, etc. "Check with the main library downtown," I was told, "and the county courthouse also houses a law library." "Can someone like me use these resources?" "Yes."

The downtown central library had a law library on the third floor used mostly by attorneys, but it was also open to the public.

I began to drive there each day to research case law and case precedents in preparation to write the defense for my *Motion for Rehearing* for what I thought would be a quickly scheduled hearing. It actually wasn't scheduled for almost another year. But I didn't know when it would be. So the pressure was still on.

The library became my next unexpected challenge. There were still some details I had to work out before I could begin my research. I discovered that the law library cataloguing system was different from that used in other libraries. I didn't have a clue as to what all this meant: *Dwyer v. Dwyer*, 305 So.2d 10 (Fla. 1st Dist. 1974). Reader, do **you** know what this means? The next logical step. Ask the librarian to help me locate the books.

It, however, wasn't the logical thing from her perspective! She told me that she could not assist in doing legal research. "But I'm not asking you to do research. I just need to know how to find the books where these cases are discussed."

She still felt that she could not help. Another roadblock. I could see this was not going to be a "user-friendly" experience!

When I saw that pleading with her for help was a dead-end road, I gave my oft-repeated plea to God: "Okay God, it's your turn. Please help." As I turned helplessly from the librarian's "HELP DESK," my tear-filled eyes panned the room filled with strangers. These were days when I wondered how there could still be water in my tear ducts as

I cried at the drop of a hat—and there were lots of hats dropping around me!

Attorneys were sitting at the many tables in the law library doing research. They were going back and forth from the shelves bringing to their workspace law books from which they were studying and taking notes. So I cleared from my eyes the tears that clouded my vision and approached them one by one.

> **But I'm not asking you to do research. I just need to know how to find the books where these cases are discussed.**

"Excuse me, I'm doing some research and can't seem to find this book. Would you be so kind as to see if perhaps I'm just overlooking it?" Some said they were too busy; others left no doubt in my mind that they were irritated at my questions. However, each day I could usually find favor with one or two attorneys who would take me to where a book of case law I needed would be located. I continued with this pattern until I learned to proceed on my own.

With my rolls of coins, I fed the copy machines making duplicates of the cases that I thought I needed. Back home at night, I would study the many pages of these court decisions and accompanying judges' opinions with *Webster's* and *Black's Law Dictionaries* at my side as well as books and pamphlets outlining the confusing judicial rules of procedure, filing procedures, and time deadlines which had to be followed.

> **"Excuse me, I'm doing some research."**

I studied the terminology of the cases and legalese from the continuing entourage of papers received from my husband's attorney. Night after night, I incorporated related case law from my library research and typed my responses on my typewriter. Those were the days without a computer. Imagine that! One wrongly worded sentence or a revision meant a retype of the entire page and so, over and over and over, I typed every page!

I waded through the maze of legal books. Each brief had to be filed within the required number of days, in the proper format, and with a certified "certificate of service" to the parties involved. I continued to wade through the maze of legal books, documents, and other resources containing court rules of procedure.

With hundreds of hours of writing and typing briefs, our case went from the Circuit Court to the District and State Courts of Appeal until finally one brief and a supplemental companion petition for Writ of Certiorari were docketed before the United States Supreme Court. This was over a period of several years. More on this later.

When the unlikely number of stays was granted by the court, I excitedly called Mr. Jones, the constitutional attorney: "Our case is still alive!" He, however, had changed his mind saying he didn't have time to take on my case. In a letter he wrote to me he said he didn't think "... the proper foundation was laid at trial to allow us to attack the No-fault Divorce Law on appeal."

Why did this man not keep his promise? His concluding remarks in a letter to me were: "Take comfort in the fact that your request will begin the process that will ultimately result in our challenge to the No-fault Divorce Law." That was 1984. To my knowledge, the organization with which he was affiliated has not yet challenged the No-fault Divorce Law. Why did this man not keep his promise?

I didn't give up on Mr. Jones. I knew it was so important to have a constitutional attorney to not only argue my case, but to do something about pulling down the No-fault Divorce Law. I wrote another letter hoping he would honor his original promise.

Dear Mr. Jones:

I am asking that you reconsider your decision to not help me to uphold God's laws regarding my marriage-covenant. I have filed a motion for a rehearing which I have enclosed. I have also included correspondence to Mr. Grier which states other reasons for my objection to this action.

> **Daniel Shuman posed the question of the legality of having a husband testify against a wife.**

*In an article in <u>Judicature</u>, Volume 67, Number 7, February, 1984, Daniel W. Shuman posed the question of the legality of having a husband testify against a wife and the **subjective nature** of the judge in making his decision **to dissolve a covenant**.*

The "Motion for Rehearing" was filed without a lawyer as I could find no one to do it for me. Please, as a brother in Christ, help me.

My plea was to no avail.

The beauty of the Trojan Horse is deceitful, but few recognize its vicious nature—until it's too late.

Many of my letters were written on paper which had a homemade letterhead of a Trojan Horse. Mindi French, a young woman that I met at church, drew this symbol. I felt the need to be a little more official, so I asked her to draft this symbol to represent my ministry to families as my outreach increased nationwide, and as I became involved in the legislative process. More

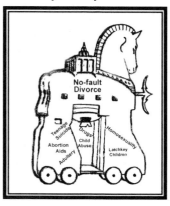

on my legislative "education" in Chapter 7.

The Trojan Horse she drew was to picture how the destruction from varying sins from within an individual precedes the breakdown of the family and affects many lives. Collectively, these can be called lust. It is an innate weakness of man—the desire to possess those things which he does not presently have, does not need, and/or should not possess or desire. Some of the societal "ills" resulting from these inappropriate desires are written on the horse.

Lust was the underlying cause of the destruction of an ancient city, Troy. It was destroyed because the citizens removed their protective gates and part of their walls to pull this huge, beautifully crafted wooden horse into their city. The enemy built it as a gift but purposely made its dimensions taller and wider than the protective city gates. What the citizens of Troy didn't know was that the horse was hollow. Inside this gift were fiercely armed war soldiers, waiting to descend through a secret door in the underside of the horse.

> **How could anything so beautiful be destructive?**

Late at night, when the people in the city were partying, the enemy escaped through the trap door and beckoned their comrades waiting outside the walls. A vicious siege took place.

This is what happens to families. Husbands and wives neglect to follow principles that will keep in tact their protective walls. These principles are summarized in the vows that many speak during a wedding ceremony:

> To have and to hold, from this day forward, for better, for worse, for richer, for poorer, in sickness and in health, to love and to cherish, *until death us do part*. Will you love her, comfort her, honor and keep her ... forsaking all others, and **keep yourself only unto her**, so long as ye both shall live?

When one of the spouses replaces these standards with unfaithfulness, the protective wall is torn down, loosing an army of destruction to overtake the family.

I hired another attorney.

In October 1984, I hired another attorney, Mr. Durant, with funds from a small loan. I also continued my pleas for help. I knew that it was important to find a constitutional attorney who could take this to the United States Supreme Court, regardless of what happened in the lower courts. I was aware that my small loan for a down payment on the retainer would not fund that type of battle.

I met with yet another attorney, Jan Miracle, at one of the meetings I attended. She too wanted to challenge the No-fault Law and was willing to work *pro bono* (free) to help me to go to the United States Supreme Court. With this renewed encouragement, I wrote another letter to Mr. Jones after meeting with her. The follow-up letter to Jan and a final plea to Andy are below:

January 19, 1985

Dear Jan:

Thank you so much for meeting with me on Friday and for being a willing vessel to work to reestablish marriage. I have had so many people respond: "Judy, this is too much of a hot potato for me to touch." "Judy, this is too big of a mountain to move." So, Jan, I do not take at all lightly your decision to step out and help.

> **They told me, "This is too much of a hot potato for me to touch."**

I have enclosed a copy of the letter you asked me to write to Andy.

January 15, 1985

Dear Andy:

When you were in Orlando in December you met with Jan Miracle. Through contacts at this meeting, I also met Jan. She has shown an interest in protecting the bonds of marriage. Jan asked that I write to you to inform you that should you decide to litigate my case, she, as part of her ministry, would act as a liaison for you. She requests that you contact her so that she will know how she can assist. I do have a Florida Senator and a Representative who are willing to work on getting the No-fault Law amended. I have given the Senator your name and address. He has asked me to speak before the Senate Judiciary Committee in either February or March ... I am anxiously awaiting to hear from you...

Once again, there was no positive response from Mr. Jones.

I continued to write letters, call, and meet with religious and political leaders and attorneys. An excerpt from an attorney someone hired to look over my case is below. It refreshed my mind about my multifaceted efforts to find help and the continued hindrance of pursuing my defense because of funds needed for legal help.

"She [Judith] is hampered by a lack of funds to support her fight, but money is not the only issue. The arguments raised to support her allegations that the state has no right to dissolve her marriage are creative but, in my estimation, unlikely to succeed ..."

Chapter 6

MY DAY IN COURT:
A LONG TIME IN COMING

Many trips to the library. STOP! WAIT! What do
these unfamiliar terms mean? What is a corroborating
witness? What has been decreed? What does it mean to
have jurisdiction? I'm totally confused. Below are several
examples of divorces that had been reversed because the
jurisdictional requirement (F.S. 61.021) was lacking:

> Evidence of the residence requirement of Section
> 61.021 Florida Statutes must be corroborated.
> **Reversed**. *Wise v. Wise,* Fla. App. 1st 1975, 310
> So.2d 431. This court has held that the uncorro-
> borated testimony of complainant is insufficient to
> support a decree of divorce. **Reversed.** *Chisholm
> v. Chisholm,* Fla. 125 So. 694. (See also: *Gillman
> v. Gillman; Kutner v. Kutner; Wade v. Wade.*)

Another divorce case's record on appeal contained
the transcript of a hearing held June 26, 1974. At
that hearing petitioner Patricia Jane Lemon testified
that she had resided in Florida for about sixteen
years, but her testimony was not corroborated by
any other witness ... the courts of Florida have held
that the residency requirement of 61.021 F.S. and its
predecessor is jurisdictional ... The Florida residency requirement may not be established by the
uncorroborated testimony of the petitioner. Since

petitioner failed to establish the statutory prerequisite of residence, the lower court lacked jurisdiction to enter a *Final Judgment*. **Reversed**. *Lemon v. Lemon,* Fla. App. 324. So.2d 623. (See also: *Caizza v. Caizza,* Fla.1974, 291 So.2d 569.)

Back to my "friend," *Black's Law Dictionary,* to see what it says about jurisdiction:

> The word [jurisdiction] is a term of large and comprehensive import, and embraces **every kind of judicial action** ... It is the authority by which courts and judicial officers take cognizance of and decide cases ... It exists when court parties are present, and point to be decided is within powers of court ... Power and authority of a court to hear and determine a judicial proceeding ... **The right and power of a court to adjudicate concerning the subject matter in a given case.** (1:766)

In Florida, the residency requirement (1984) is what **legally** gives a court jurisdiction over a divorce lawsuit. Without an outside witness to verify the fact that the Plaintiff has met the required residency of six months within the state in which the case is being heard, the court has no jurisdiction over the parties to the lawsuit. Only if this requirement has been met can the Plaintiff then affirm that he wishes for the court to agree with him that the lifetime "marriage-contract" no longer exists. The Plaintiff is required to swear that the marriage is irretrievably broken. With these two requirements met, the judge can then rap his gavel: "Judgment for the Plaintiff!" **The Plaintiff's testimony becomes evidence to support the dissolution. The Defendant's testimony has no bearing on whether the marriage is irretrievably broken. To reiterate: The Plaintiff (1) must merely satisfy the jurisdictional** requirement by having someone not a party to the case verify his residency of six months, (2) must then state, "the marriage is irretrievably broken." The marriage is regarded as irretrievably broken and, magically, the State of Florida's No-fault dissolves the marriage. As shown on pages 91 and 92, even these simple jurisdictional procedural requirements are sometimes not satisfied.

It's important to note that when there had been no corroborating witness, the attendant divorces were **all** reversed. **They were void** for lack of

Everything was unconstitutional for lack of jurisdiction.

jurisdiction. Why were these particular cases so important from this author's point of view? It was because Judge Fuller decreed in favor of the Plaintiff when he had no legal right to do so. QUESTION: Why didn't he have the legal right to do so? ANSWER: There had been no corroborating witness to testify and give him jurisdiction over our case **prior** to the dropping of the gavel on April 18, 1984. Thus, his decree was **void for lack of jurisdiction**. Consequently, I would perceive that there had been no judicial authority on which to hold any additional hearings. According to FRCP Rule 1.540 below, there is no statute of limitations that restricts the time frame to invalidate such acts of injustice by the court:

… judgment alleged to be void for lack of jurisdiction **may be attacked at any time**. West's F.S.A. FRCP Rule 1.540 (b); US Const. Amend. 14.

The *Open Court Sheet and Court Minutes* on page 94, dated April 18, 1984, verifies that no witness for the Petitioner was present to corroborate residency in the nonjury trial held to legally dissolve our marriage. The ONLY witnesses to testify that day were Douglas Brumbaugh Petitioner and Judy Brumbaugh Respondent.

APPENDIX F

OPEN COURT SHEET AND
COURT MINUTES FOR _Non Jury Dissolution_

CASE NO. _82-3055-FAM_

IN THE CIRCUIT/~~COUNTY~~ COURT
OF SEMINOLE COUNTY, FLORIDA

Civil DIVISION

SANFORD FLORIDA

Douglas Brumbaugh
~~STATE/PLAINTIFF~~/PETITIONER

DATE: _April 18, 1984_

SCHEDULED TIME: _3:00 pm_

-VS-

Judy Brumbaugh

~~DEFENDANT~~/RESPONDENT

COURT OPENED AT: _3:09 pm_   IN COURTROOM _Clark_

HONORABLE _____ / _____   COURT REPORTER —

~~STATE/PLAINTIFF~~/PETITIONER/ATTORNEYS _____

~~PUBLIC DEFENDER/DEFENSE~~/RESPONDENT/ATTORNEYS _____

PROBATION OFFICER _____   DEPUTY SHERIFF _____

BAILIFFS _Gerzea Robbins_   TRIAL CLERK _Clarice Irvin_

Parties present and sworn at 3:09 pm. Court spoke
with parties, testimony a dissolution only.
Petitioner Witness No 1 - Douglas Brumbaugh
testified at 3:10 pm
Respondent witness No 1 - Judy Brumbaugh,
testified at 3:19 pm
Entered in evidence as Respondent Exhibit 1 -
Statement prepared by wife.
Recess at 3:32 pm until 3:50 pm
Continued with testimony of Mrs. Brumbaugh.
Court spoke with parties. The Court finds marriage
irretrievably broken and Granted Dissolution
Recess while Court spoke with child, Michael.
Parties agreed to mediation for parenting issues
and other issues if necessary. Order to be
prepared. Guardian to be appointed.

COURT RECESSED AT: _5:12 pm_

WITNESS the Clerk and seal of said Court this _18_ day of _April_, 19 _84_.

ARTHUR H. BECKWITH, JR., CLERK OF CIRCUIT AND COUNTY COURTS.

BY: _Clarice Irvin_, Deputy Clerk in Attendance.   50⊄

**_Open Court Sheet and Court Minutes_ showing there
was no corroborating witness to give the judge
jurisdiction to legally dissolve this marriage.**

Below is an excerpt from what was entered as the *Final Judgment* on June 11, 1984. The bolded portions fraudulently state that a corroborating witness was present on April 18, 1984 and that the court had jurisdiction.

This cause coming on to be heard on the 18th day of April, 1984, and the Court being advised in the premises, and the **Court having taken testimony of a corroborating witness as to residency**, and the Court further having taken the testimony of the parties, it is hereby

ORDERED AND ADJUDGED
1. **This Court has jurisdiction of the subject matter and of the parties**.
2. The marriage between DOUGLAS K. BRUMBAUGH and JUDITH A. BRUMBAUGH is dissolved because it is irretrievably broken.

The above bolded information became significant to me ONLY after I later had been doing research for supporting evidence for my *Motion for Rehearing*. To my astonishment, it seemed to this layperson that a serious judicial error had been committed and that **I was not really legally divorced**. Neither did I understand the vital necessity of this *due process* requirement, the corroborating witness.

So what do I do with this information, and why hadn't my attorney caught this serious procedural error? And why wouldn't anyone that I shared this with agree that it was significant?

I needed to find answers to these questions. In a brief filed **by my husband's attorney** (August 7, 1985) when our case was before the Fifth District Court of Appeal, he apparently knew something was lacking during the *Trial for Dissolution* because as part of his argument for dismissal of this issue he gave as evidence that this procedural requirement had been met by the **Defendant's testimony**. Surely he must have known that the Defendant cannot serve as the corroborating witness. Here's what Attorney Simon wrote in my husband's brief:

> On June 11, 1984, the lower tribunal received testimony relating to the marriage being irretrievably broken. The [sic] serve as corroborating witness. No transcript of the June 11, 1984 hearing is available because a court reporter was not present. However, **Appellant has never suggested that she did not act as the corroborating witness for residence at the hearing of April 18, 1984 which resulted in the order of June 11, 1984.** It should be noted that the *Final Judgment of Dissolution of Marriage* dated June 11, 1984 states:
>
> > "This cause coming on to be heard on the 18th day of April, 1984, and the Court being advised in the premises, and the Court having taken testimony of a corroborating witness as to residency ..."
>
> Certainly, as the lower tribunal indicated, the Appellant waived any rights she had to argue that she was not the corroborating witness or that the *Final Judgment of Dissolution of Marriage* of June 11, 1984 is void.

By researching this matter after the fact as indicated at the beginning of this chapter, I found that "... admission, in wife's answer that husband had been a resident of state for more than six months before he filed a petition for dissolution could not substitute for proof of such residency and that **where *husband* failed to properly present proof of his residency, Circuit Court lacked jurisdiction to render a *Final Judgment*.** Residence for statutory period is jurisdictional and must be **alleged and proved** <u>in action for dissolution of marriage</u>." **Reversed.** *Wise v. Wise*, Fla. App. 1st 1975, 310 So.2d 431.

In another similar case where reversal of the dissolution was ordered, the Defendant was also awarded court costs, etc: "We, therefore adjudge that the Plaintiff in the court below, appellee here, be required to pay the costs of this suit in the lower court and in the Supreme Court and shall be required to pay a reasonable sum to the Defendant in the court below, appellant here, for her solicitor's fees in the Circuit Court and in this Court, all of which the court below may determine subject to review by this Court." *Phillips v. Phillips,* Fla. 311, 1 So.2d 186.

I also found that judgments that are void or fraudulent or are **based upon a prior judgment or decree which is void *can be vacated at any time*;** i.e., **"Judgment absolutely void can generally be set aside and stricken from record on motion at any time."** *Kroier v. Kroier,* Fla. 116 So. 753 and *Chisholm v. Chisholm,* Fla. 1196, 25 So. 694.

No money. Apply for legal aid?

At this point in my case, July, 1984, I did not know about the corroborating witness requirement and the fact that without that requirement being fulfilled, Judge Fuller had no authority to legally dissolve our marriage, divide our family, and judicially remove my legal rights to some of our jointly owned properties. I, at this point, had no attorney to represent me. This was because I refused to accept Fuller's legal *Dissolution of Marriage* on April 18, 1984 and my following his subsequent order stemming

97

from that decision that I dismiss my attorney, Mr. Grier. I wanted to proceed with my *Motion for Rehearing*. The only way I could do this was to represent myself (*pro se*). So, where do I acquire funds to continue my quest? To pay another retainer? I don't know what my rights are. I live in fear of what Judge Fuller and my husband's attorney can do to me through their motions and orders that I often do not understand.

I wrote several people and made many phone calls, including some to governmental agencies pleading for help. One of the responses is below:

Department of Health & Human Services
Administration for Children, Youth and Families
Washington DC 20201
July 18, 1984

Dear Mrs. Brumbaugh:

I have reviewed the records which you sent to me, relative to your pending No-fault Divorce situation. It is regrettable that this family dissolution is underway and that it has caused such distress.

I regret that ACYF is unable to offer assistance to you in your case. As you know, the states have traditionally had jurisdiction over matters dealing with family separation. Therefore, this is an area in which the federal government does not involve itself directly. **[See page 158 and 168 Article VI.]**

Your best source of help would be from an attorney in Florida who could most astutely argue your case. I would suggest you call the Florida Bar Association or a family assistance service association with your church.

Sincerely,
Elizabeth Ruppert Ph.D.

As suggested by Dr. Ruppert, I contacted the Florida Bar Association as well as churches and several individuals. No financial or free help for this type issue was available. I next made a plea to have the state provide legal counsel for me. Papers were filled out for legal aid and an appointment made to discuss my case. Once again, my candle of hope was extinguished with my meeting:

> **"You do not qualify for a court-appointed attorney because your name is on the mortgage to your home and commercial property."**

LEGAL AID: "You do not qualify for a court-appointed attorney because your name is on the mortgage to your home and commercial property."

JUDITH: "I'm not even living in my home nor do I have the income from the commercial property."

LEGAL AID: "That doesn't matter, your name is on the properties so we cannot help you because you own too many assets to qualify."

JUDITH: "All this just does not make sense, God. It seems so unjust."

"Another day older and deeper in debt"!

At this point there was growing disparity between Doug and my standards of living because of the vast difference in our incomes. Doug's teaching salary, consultant fees, book publishing, and monies from our business property and other miscellaneous income-producing activities provided him with the ability to retain consistent high-quality legal counsel **while I was left to flounder as best I could.**

Seemingly all efforts to enlist free help were exhausted. My *Motion for Rehearing* objecting to the whole issue of Dissolution had not been called up for a hearing. I didn't understand at that point that the party who has made the

Motion is the party who sets the Motion down for a hearing. There were a lot of papers being filed that I didn't understand including child custody and property issues. I knew that I needed legal GUIDANCE and so shopped for an attorney—once again—**with the cheapest retainer fee** and gathered enough money to get started with him.

Sid Durant became my attorney October 12, 1984. Depositions were taken so that the property issues could be argued with more facts. He immediately **discovered** there were **significant** assets that would **not** have been considered by the court as part of our equitable distribution at the April 18, 1984 *Dissolution Trial* **had the trial not been halted** because of my refusal to accept the dissolution. Despite Durant's discovery, these assets still were not considered at the *Supplemental Final Hearing* May 29, 1985. This included thousands of dollars for one of Doug's female friend's household and entertainment. (The reader might be interested in rereading the last sentence in the previous two paragraphs. Can judges not also *read* between the lines?) As with the legal marital dissolution, so it is with the assets that are an inherent part of the "marriage-contract." *It becomes a matter of subjective empowered parity*: "In most states with equitable distribution standards the courts have the discretion to divide property 'as **justice** requires.' Since equitable distribution standards **give judges considerable latitude**, there is typically more variation in awards under these rules." (9:47) "Equitable standard is meant to 'allow judges **to do justice'** according to **the circumstances of the parties** and, where appropriate to award women more than half of the property ..." (9:73)

The Discovery—Mr. Durant's depositions

Deposition: "A discovery device—statements taken under oath outside the courtroom ... to obtain information for evidence to be used by the court in a civil action or criminal prosecution." (1:396) Mr. Durant learned through this discovery device about a written statement Doug had made to a mortgage company when he applied for a loan during the divorce proceedings. The loan was for a new house one of his realtor/builder friends was constructing and which was transferred almost immediately to Doug after a *Supplemental Final Hearing* on May 29, 1985. The financial information he provided the mortgage company that helped him qualify for the loan differed from that used to determine our equitable property settlement May 29, 1985.

The down payment for the above property purchase was in exchange for one of our jointly held assets, a vacant lot adjacent to and part of our home property. The contract pledging our parcel as Doug's personal property was signed on **April 9, 1985**. We had purchased this lot several years earlier to create a barrier from anyone building next to us. Even though it was considered to be a part of the home property, it was divided from our home property during the *Supplemental Final Hearing* on **May 29, 1985** and given to Doug. Following are statements written by my husband on his behalf to qualify for the loan on his new house:

> ***Judy has resisted the divorce on a religious basis. She will accept a separation but not a divorce.*** *She has repeatedly stated that she will sign no property settlement and thus refuses to sign the court mandate. Hopefully the session on 5/14/85 will settle the issue. [This was moved to 5/29/85.]*
>
> *I am currently working on two books as an independent consultant. The first is a student workbook that will accompany a student text on computers. I will be paid $10,000 upon completion. The second is an 8th grade text with Harcourt, Brace and Jovanovich. I am rewriting the text. Contractual arrangements are still being discussed. But I will be paid at least $30 per hour for my work. It is possible I will be paid a flat rate for a chapter.*

The items mentioned in Doug's statement were in addition to his retirement fund and the income of almost $50,000 listed on his 1984 tax return, fees from consulting for school districts, work as a carpenter, and various other employments, many of which were not considered in the equitable distribution of our assets. (Notice this was income in a 1984 economy.) Dr. Weitzman in her book *The Divorce Revolution* says, "Even wives of well-to-do men often did not have immediate access to cash to pay for lawyers' retainers and the expensive discovery necessary to uncover and document their husband's assets." (9:48)

Is the fox guarding the hen house!

One might wonder about the necessity of mentioning the above information. These empirical facts reveal a common major weakness in what the courts define as equitable distribution. Even though a judge is to follow equitable distribution guidelines and case law, application of the law to the facts does allow subjectivity. In the No-fault Law which allows for **subjective** judicial opinions, Defendants can be placed in a compromised position not only regarding the legal dissolution of the marriage, but also for child custody decisions and property distribution. These Defendants, especially if they lack financial resources equal to those of the Plaintiffs, often become pawns of a judicial system which affords them little or no relief. Additionally, because of emotional stress, they don't recognize until too late what has really happened to their economic future—poverty!

> **It's a law which is redistributing major family assets to the legal profession.**

The stage for all this injustice has been set by a law supposedly designed to **protect** families and **their properties** but which, in practice, is actually affecting more than a million family members negatively in some way every year. **It's a law which enables the redistribution of major family assets to the legal profession.** **It is a law which almost makes the Plaintiff a judge in his own cause because of the power of his unilateral position.** It is a law which has as one of its purposes and rationales:

*To prevent disrespect for the law and its processes and **to curtail perjury.***

As if one does not need more evidence regarding what the Florida Bar is NOT doing to protect and strengthen families, it passed the *Marriage Preparation and Preservation Act* in 1998. Sections 2 and 3 of this act give findings from yet more taxpayer-funded studies for what we already know and what the No-fault Law it has promulgated has created:

It is the finding of the Legislature based on reliable research that: (2) The divorce rate has been accelerating; (3) Just as the family is the foundation of society, the marital relationship is the foundation of the family. Consequently, strengthening marriages can only lead to stronger families, children, and communities, as well as a stronger economy.

As part of this *Marriage Preparation and Preservation Act*, the "Family Law Handbook" had been made available at the various courthouses in Florida. State funding had provided these for couples applying for a marriage license. Here's the first paragraph on page one:

"CONGRATULATIONS! You're getting married —hopefully for the rest of your life. It may surprise you to learn that the State of Florida has an interest in your marriage ... in whether the marriage is long lasting and happy."

103

Sounds great, doesn't it? However, turn to page two. Instead of providing materials for building relationships to keep marriages together, the remainder of this publication focuses on DIVORCE! Here are typical headings: "The process for **ending a marriage (Divorce)**, Making decisions for the children **after divorce**, Where the children **live after divorce**, Child-related issues (upon **divorce** or separation), How the court divides assets and liabilities upon **divorce**, Economic issues upon **dissolution**."

On the last page the following statement is made: "This handbook has been prepared **as a public service** by the Family Law Section of the Florida Bar." Printed on the front of the booklet is: "Such handbooks shall be available from clerk of the Circuit Court upon **application for a marriage license**."

I tried for several years to garner governmental support to create a proposed booklet that would strengthen families with topics such as "A love that lasts, Debt management, and Conflict resolution" to replace this booklet that is designed in content for dissolution. No support was found.

There have been and will continue to be many examples in this book showing conflict between what is stated by the government as its purpose to strengthen and preserve the integrity of marriage and safeguard family relationships and the opposite reality of the effect of its legislative acts played out in the lives of its divorce victims.

Many of my court experiences are not uncommon, especially when it comes to the division of assets. This is one place where the Plaintiff, especially if he is the primary breadwinner, can use his financial power to put the Defendant in financial jeopardy not only during the trial but for the rest of her life. This misuse of the Plaintiff's financial power can invite the court to act under color of law to use legal gymnastics to partner in a continuum of what an unskilled Defendant such as I in *Brumbaugh v. Brumbaugh* would perceive as discrimination and infliction of fear.

It's time for the Motion—I thought!

Lots of motions had been going back and forth until the date was set for another *Supplemental Final Hearing*, May 29, 1985. At least now my *Motion for Rehearing* which objected to the dissolution of our marriage would be heard.

May 1985. We were motioned to go back to court. I, with anticipation and fear awaited this opportunity to have my *Motion for Rehearing* regarding the legal dissolution of our marriage heard. I had incurred a huge financial debt, grievous loss of personal time with our children, and additional loss of finances. **All of this just to be granted my constitutional RIGHT to be heard.**

But ... once again, the unexpected. The court was called to order. Doomsday! What did Judge Fuller say? "The court will not hear Mrs. Brumbaugh's *Motion for Rehearing*." How could he make such a statement? I had fulfilled my part of the verbal contract to buy my right to have the motion heard. I had missed the daily contact with our children, untold hours and special moments with them which **could never be replaced**. I had moved out of our home, going from house to house with my boxes of belongings like a vagabond for almost a year.

Even though the homes in which I was privileged to stay were wonderful, so many nights I cried myself to sleep begging to go back to my home—and to our children. And, remember, I had also dismissed my first attorney Mr. Grier as part of my "purchase price" to file and have my appeal **heard**. And now—no reason, just—"Motion denied."

Back to the courtroom

My mind was reeling. What is going on? I went over and over the following in my mind: I released my original attorney as ordered/bargained for and hired another. I fulfilled my part of the verbal contract. How could Judge Fuller renege on his commitment by refusing to hear my *Motion for Rehearing*? From an untrained layman's point of view, to give your word and refuse to keep it; or, even legally justify it, would be considered a misuse of justice.

I could not believe he did this. "Where are you, God? How could the legal system be so unjust, so cruel, and so inhumane?" I could not concentrate on what was being done. I was in the courtroom physically, but not mentally.

My thoughts were focused on the fact that varying segments of my life would no longer be recognizable. They would be shredded and thrown away, my identity changed, my rights mutilated by people who had no regard for the "marriage-contract" to which I had been faithful for more than twenty years.

> **Varying segments of my life would no longer be recognizable.**

Henceforth, for purposes of legal matters and for filing tax returns, I would be considered "single." I would be forced to pay higher taxes because my marital status was torn from me.

One might compare divorce to the ravages of living with the destruction left by a level four catastrophic hurricane! The hurricane-force winds attached to divorce strike the "house" leaving litter strewn throughout the lives of those caught in its devastating path. Those who have a part in bringing down the gavel upon marriage truly know not the effect of what they do!

> **Those who have a part in bringing down the gavel upon marriage truly know not the effect of what they do!**

Appeal to a higher court.

What happened in court that day was a blur. Until I read the judicial summary several weeks after the hearing, I didn't consider what had taken place the day I thought my

Motion for Rehearing was to have been heard. It took several years to only partially understand what took place! Even today through the writing of this book I have become more aware of many unjust acts enabled because of a law that is vague, partial, and unjust—unconstitutional.

Those papers summarizing the *Supplemental Final Hearing* recorded the division of property, assigned our son to live in dual households, and stated "Wife's *Motion for Rehearing* dated June 21, 1984, is denied."

All three of these decisions misrepresented who I was and the rights I felt I should have had. As noted in our court hearings and in his mortgage application, Doug acknowledged: ***"Judy has resisted the divorce on a religious basis. She will accept a separation but not a divorce."*** Both he and I had based our marriage and lives on a "religious basis"—what God says about marriage. Sadly, with Doug's lawsuit, I now realized how he and the government defined our marriage—a legal contract. **Yet,** *neither my husband nor the government were following the rules of either of the **rulers over our marriage and its acquisitions**: The Bible and the United States Constitution.*

Doug's turn against our "until-death-us-do-part" Biblical covenant meant I would alone uphold this commitment to God. The denial for the rehearing meant that I had no constitutional avenue to object to the court's legal dissolution and its further division of our family and our marital assets. What do I do now?

There was a thread of hope, however, because my friend from New Jersey told me I could appeal to a higher court. I had asked Attorney Durant to prepare the papers to file an appeal prior to the May 29 hearing. He agreed, but I would need to come into his office to do some of the work (research and typing) to make it happen by the deadline and to save on some of the hours he could not give to the case. It was believed that my husband would be responsible for my attorney fees. Doug held a financial advantage over me, the Defendant, and had acknowledged some liability for such fees. This was supported by Fla. Stat. 61.16, *Canakaris v. Canakaris,* Fla. 382 So.2d 1197; *Seitz v. Seitz,* 471 So.2d 612 (Fla. 3d DCA 1985). Not only did my husband not help with my legal fees, but he filed a Motion to have me pay some of his! Some of these abuses were discussed as part of one of the briefs I later filed without an attorney before the United States Supreme Court in 1987:

Monies and properties taken from the Defendant by the Court's actions were available to the Plaintiff to use in the hiring and retaining of legal counsel to effect further blockage of the Defendant's protection of her assets. Not only could the Defendant not retain legal counsel but was not permitted to have any representation—even by self ... whereby self-executing rights provided under the Fourteenth Amendment, etc. of the United States Constitution and Statutes of Florida have been made void and her Civil Rights, protected under U.S.C.A. 42-1983-5, et al., have been abated.

The court decision not to award payment of incurred attorney fees affected Attorney Durant's desire and ability to continue to represent me and his eventual withdrawal from my case. He had filed many motions and represented me in court on several occasions, for which I was thankful. Unfortunately, all this greatly increased my financial indebtedness to him, which seemed to him beyond my ability to pay—and at the time—was.

> **He gave me the records and instructions on how to represent myself.**

A year later, on May 8, 1986, Attorney Durant called me to come to his office. The meeting was to tell me that he would no longer represent me on any matters because of the amount of money owed him. He gave me the records for my case and instructions on how to represent myself. But ... this was **right in the middle of my Appeal** to the Fifth District Court of Appeal which he had helped to file!

Attorney Durant followed the May 8 meeting with a letter dated May 9, 1986, confirming our meeting the previous day. However, the reason he gave in the letter was [because I am not] "... admitted to the United States Supreme Court, my representation of you on your case is now at its logical end." It didn't mention the real reason.

A million dollars! My family is worth it!

With indebtedness of thousands of dollars now owed to two attorneys, I approached some friends and business people in our community to try to find funds to take this injustice against our family to the United States Supreme Court.

> No price tag could be put on the value of my family.

One very successful businessman said, "It would take a million dollars to do this." He felt it was a "foolish venture." Many would agree with this decision from a business point of view. In my estimation, however, no price tag could be put on the value of my family. Needless to say, he would not extend the money!

I was totally on my own again. I studied to learn more about the rules for the Fifth District Court of Appeal. The knowledge gained hopefully would allow me to continue my mission to save my marriage and rectify the inequity of treatment many others and I had received. More legal barriers presented themselves as I persistently searched for funds and the help to go forward with the Appeal.

To gather support, I continued to attend and speak at many meetings: church groups, political gatherings, and, citizens' groups. After one of these, a man approached me who said he could help me frame my case with proper legalese for the appeal. Jonathan also gave me some books to guide me. What a blessing. I know now even more so what a miracle it was that this man was placed in my life at that particular time. He was willing to help because he could see that I had been denied several crucial constitutional rights.

He seemed to understand the importance of the absence of the procedural *due process* requirement at our *Dissolution Trial* (the corroborating witness for residency). Not fulfilling it **invalidated everything** on which the judge had ruled, especially the dissolution itself; i.e., the divorce.

Hurry! Hurry! The clock was ticking again for the filing of another appeal. By the time I met Jonathan, there were just a few days left and we would miss the window to file another appeal. With his help, this and additional appeals were written and court documents prepared and filed. Excerpts from one such—a legal-size 25-page brief to plead my defense objecting to the nonjurisdictional dissolution against our family—are reproduced on page 111. In addition to the above, my brief also included several pages listing the constitutional issues violated during the trial including violation of the Fifth, Seventh, and Fourteenth Amendments.

A third attorney? Surely not!

Jonathan had been a great deal of help, but I needed an attorney. A third attorney. I didn't know what to do or how to do what I didn't know what to do! No money for a retainer. What could I do? Jonathan said that I would qualify to have a court-appointed attorney.

I filed a motion for a court-appointed one. The court refused to recognize my *Motion*. The procedure is to file the motion and then call to get a hearing date. The clerk, however, would not give me a date to hear my *Motion* even though I called repeatedly to get one. From a layman's view, this seemed like an illegal action on the court's part.

This cause coming on to be heard on the 18th day of April, 1984, and the Court being advised in the premises, and the Court *having taken testimony of a corroborating witness as to residency* ... ORDERED AND ADJUDGED: 1. This court has jurisdiction of the subject matter and of the parties. **"The above statements from the *Final Judgment* are fraudulent.** There was no corroborating witness at the hearing preceding the entry of this judgment ... Open Court Sheet and Court Minutes for nonjury Dissolution ... are completely void of any mention of a corroborating witness, or even of the proper taking of residency testimony of the husband. At the time of the hearing wife was not aware of this jurisdictional requirement, but through a more recent study of case law, statutes, etc., Judith A. Brumbaugh, Wife, has learned that a judgment or decree rendered where jurisdiction of authority is wanting is utterly void ..."

The Constitution guarantees access to the courts by **any** citizen. You don't have to be a criminal to exercise this right! I didn't understand why I was denied such.

More of the puzzle pieces were taken out of the box and placed before me, but not enough so that I could recognize the picture that was being painted—what was really happening behind the scenes. Almost two months after Attorney Durant withdrew from my case, I received his *Motion to Withdraw* from my case:

The Wife, JUDITH A. BRUMBAUGH, does not have the financial ability to continue to retain the undersigned counsel, and the continued retention of the undersigned counsel by the Wife, JUDITH A. BRUMBAUGH, would impose an unfair imposition and burden upon the undersigned attorney to continue representing her in these proceedings.

Attorney Durant's *Motion to Withdraw* sat somewhere in the court until a month later when I was "noticed" to appear in court regarding his *Motion to Withdraw.* This was on August 11, 1986. I didn't know what to expect or what I was supposed to do, but I prepared my defense.

Durant pleaded his cause to have Judge Fuller allow him to withdraw. I pointed out **with evidence** that he had made false statements in his *Motion to Withdraw* to which he admitted. Even so, Judge Fuller said Attorney Durant could not be expected to continue because I couldn't pay him for his services and thus permitted him to withdraw as my Attorney of Record.

Now I was forced to file another *Motion for Rehearing.* This time the Motion was a request to allow me to present evidence as to why Attorney Durant should not have been allowed to withdraw from my case. Durant knew my case, and I didn't have money for a retainer to hire another attorney to start over again. However, this Motion, like the Motion to request a court-appointed attorney, was also denied a hearing. Judge Fuller refused to let me come before the court to present my objection to his ruling. Once again, he had denied my constitutional right to access the court and "redress my grievances." My Motion stated:

I allege the Order of August 11, 1986, was obtained by fraud, pursuant to FRCP 1.540 and the Fla. Statute of Frauds, and move the court to void and/or to issue one which correctly reflects the pertinent facts.

1. See Exhibit 1, document attached, wherein Attorney Durant requested me to sign this document

"That I agree to allow him to withdraw as my counsel." I did not sign this document and let him know that I did not agree to allow him to withdraw as my counsel.

2. See Exhibit 2, document attached, wherein said document sent to Attorney, Billy Simon, attorney for husband, requesting him to sign this document that states he agrees to allow Attorney Durant to withdraw as my counsel. Attorney Simon did not sign this document.

3. There are no documents filed that show any party has agreed to allow Attorney Durant to withdraw as my counsel or attorney.

*As the present Order of August 11, 1986 **can cause her to be denied a court-appointed attorney which is a motion pleaded by her to this court prior to the motion of allowing counsel to withdraw pleaded by Attorney Durant** ... Judith A. Brumbaugh states she pleaded for court-appointed attorney after her attorney Durant quit her, approximately May 1, 1986.*

In addition to refusing to hear my *Motion for Rehearing* concerning Attorney Durant's withdrawal and dismissal, Judge Fuller also entered an order **to strike all the motions I had personally written and filed prior to August 11, 1986.** As part of a brief docketed before the United States Supreme Court which I had filed acting as my own attorney in 1987, I addressed this issue and pleaded:

The state, by its repugnant actions ... and being an agent for discriminatory actions, left the Defendant an indigent with no possible representation or protection of life, liberty, and property from May 8, 1986, when Attorney Durant quit because of the state of poverty the Defendant had been placed by the actions of the Respondent [Husband], his legal counsel, and the State of Florida, until August 11, 1986, when Judge Fuller states, "Now Appellant can plead for herself."

At the time, I didn't understand nor comprehend the ramifications of Judge Fuller's act of striking all the motions I had laboriously researched, written, and filed. That I would discover several months later. I had filed several very important motions and briefs during the time I was representing myself.

> **I didn't understand what Fuller had done ... until later.**

Unknown to me, Durant was still the Attorney of Record. The motions I filed included the above-mentioned pleading for a court-appointed attorney (See Motion on next page.), property set-aside issues, and Directions to the Clerk of the Court to forward my Record on Appeal to the Fifth District Court of Appeal on July 24, 1986. **Without meeting this time deadline** and giving the order to have my Record forwarded, my Appeal would have been denied.

The government provides free legal forms to help couples obtain an almost cost-free divorce.

In contrast to all I had been doing to preserve my marriage, on one of my many trips to the court house to file papers, I discovered something very interesting: Florida's Simplified Divorce—an almost cost-free divorce—for those agreeing to legally end a marriage (uncontested). While I waited in line to speak with a clerk, the person in front of me was handed a "Simplified Dissolution" divorce packet. He didn't understand how to fill it out. The clerk was ASSISTING him. I listened carefully.

> **I discovered Florida's simplified divorce.**

Motion to postpone hearings and recognize
pleading for Court-Appointed Attorney

---

*JUDITH A. BRUMBAUGH, WIFE, DEFENDANT, PLEADS A MOTION TO THE COURT, TO POSTPONE OTHER HEARINGS ON OTHER MOTIONS UNTIL THE MOTION FOR **COURT-APPOINTED ATTORNEY** IS DISPOSED OF.*

Comes now the Wife, Defendant, Judith A. Brumbaugh, the undersigned, acting for self, layperson, and moves the court with MOTION TO POSTPONE OTHER MOTIONS UNTIL MOTION FOR COURT-APPOINTED ATTORNEY IS DISPOSED OF BOTH PLEADED BY JUDITH A. BRUMBAUGH AND FOR GROUNDS SAY:

1. *As the Motion for Court-Appointed Attorney is pleaded, pursuant to FRCP 1.211, wherein, Judith A. Brumbaugh has no attorney, by order of the court, wherein she is not competent to plead for herself, and after she paying for four years litigation, and the above case of divorce is still active, her legal position, **she is entitled to proper legal representation.***

2. *She states, it is common sense not to allow other hearings to take place until it is decided by the court the adjudication of the **Motion for Court-Appointed Attorney**, for the above actions, this case.*

*Wherefore, Judith A. Brumbaugh, moves the court with this motion for order to postpone other hearings, until the **Motion for Court-appointed attorney** is disposed of and She states, the hearing of this motion will be same time, day, that the Hearing of the Motion for Court-Appointed Attorney takes place.*

Judith A. Brumbaugh, Acting for Self Layperson June 27, 1986.

The above motion was never heard. This is in contrast to Clarence Earl Gideon who was arrested **and convicted** for breaking and entering. He asked for a court-appointed attorney, but was denied. On appeal, he **was *provided* a highly respected lawyer, Abe Fortas, to represent him. The U.S. Supreme Court reversed Gideon's conviction because he had been denied legal counsel.** Justice Black wrote: "… the **right-to-counsel of the Sixth Amendment is 'fundamental and essential to a fair trial'** in both federal and state courts." (10:107) See *Gideon v. Wainwright*, page 261, and civil law rights. (12:49)

When it was my turn to address the clerk, I asked her how to file my paper to get a hearing. Can you guess her response?

She told me that she could not give me legal advice—that I would need to hire an attorney. I cannot believe this. I wonder if she knew the librarian at the public law library who also felt she could not help with legal research!

Yes, here was an additional way the legislature was **NOT** "preserving the integrity of marriage and safe-guarding meaningful family relationships" (along with its No-fault Divorce Law): Florida Statute, Section 61.001 (2)(a).

Yes, the **State of Florida provides an easy and *affordable* exit from a marriage for those who agree to a divorce.** They need no attorney because they have access to a "Simplified Dissolution Packet," prepared for them by the Florida Bar, which at the time of the research done for my briefs had 22 pages of forms and formats to follow for persons **agreeing to divorce** (uncontested). These documents prepared by the Florida Bar are to assist those who would be considered the Plaintiff and Defendant in a non-contested divorce (action for Dissolution of a Marriage):

> The Florida Bar has petitioned this Court to AMEND Florida Rule of Civil Procedure 1.611 (Dissolution of Marriage) to provide a simplified procedure by which dissolution of a marriage ... can be obtained by the parties **without their having to employ private counsel**. [See page 123.] The "Simplified Dissolution" serves several purposes. **It makes the courts more accessible and minimizes costs to the parties, while protecting both the interests of the parties** in the fair resolution of their case ... **a step forward in making Florida's courts available and affordable ...**" (The Florida Bar Re: Amendment to Florida Rules of Civil Procedure No. 62.147)

This is not equal justice for all! What a discriminatory contrast to the millions of Defendants whose purpose it is to preserve their marriages, families, and their assets. In my particular case, not only was I denied equal protection and refused help afforded those NOT contesting, but was further discriminated against by being forced to defend myself **without a lawyer**, and, on several occasions, **without access to courts**. This also included being burdened with thousands of dollars of debt which took 20 years to repay. Yet, there are case precedents that the court should award reasonable attorney fees and costs especially when there is disparity of income between the parties. One such is *McClay v. McClay*, 447 So.2d 1026, (Fla. 4th DCS 1984), etc. (See also page 108.)

Someone called Restoration of the Family as I was writing this manuscript and shared that he was being required to come up with a **$12,000 retainer** as the Defendant in a divorce suit. He, like me, believes in the permanence of marriage and so is hiring an attorney, an attorney who should know that according to the No-fault statutes this Defendant has no way to win. Not only that, but the $12,000 is a retainer, not the complete cost of helping this man legally dissolve a marriage he wants to preserve!

In the county in which Judge Fuller struck his gavel on our marriage, there were that year **985** cases filed for a dissolution of marriage and each and every one was granted. **No** Defendant was able to defend his marriage successfully.

There's so much evidence to show that our government is assisting those who want out of a marriage while opposing those who want to hold a marriage together. It's time to connect the dots and do something to bring about change: DOT, DOT, DOT: $12,000 for a retainer to "defend" an issue for which there is no defense; 985 cases filed—ALL "verdicts"/judgments in favor of the Plaintiff. Dissolution granted. Are the dots connected now?

I tried to petition for another judge.

I filed a *petition for Disqualification of Judge Fuller.* I felt that there was no chance to have equal justice—or at this point any justice—under Judge Fuller so I filed a petition to have him remove himself from my case:

> *Judith A. Brumbaugh, Action for Self, the undersigned, petitions Judge Henry Fuller to disqualify himself from the above-styled cause, pursuant to Code of Judicial Conduct, State of Fla. Supreme Court of Fla. 281 So.2d 21, Cannon 3, (C) Disqualification of Judge (1)A, and F.S. 38 Judges, 38.0l ... Wherefore, pursuant to the above, and in order to have "due process" of laws obeyed, Judith A. Brumbaugh, petitions that Judge Henry Fuller disqualify himself from the cause, case No. 82-3055-CA-04-E.*

My husband's attorney filed a *Motion to Vacate the Reassignment* with some of the following reasoning:

> *Comes now the Former Husband, DOUGLAS K. BRUMBAUGH, by and through his undersigned attorney, and moves this Honorable Court to vacate the reassignment of this cause, and would show:*
> *1. This Dissolution of Marriage proceeding has extended for approximately three (3) years.*
> *2. The only Judge who has been involved in this case and who has knowledge of the circumstances of the parties, as well as matters involving the children, is Judge Henry Fuller.*
> *3. That, as a matter of law, the Court which heard the evidence is required to conclude this matter, and only new matters (post-judgment), such as a Petition for Modification, could be heard by a new Judge ...WHEREFORE, IT IS RESPECTFULLY*

REQUESTED THAT THE Motion to Vacate the Reassignment be granted, and that this cause be transferred to Judge Henry Fuller.

It should be of no surprise that Judge Fuller was reassigned to this case.

A letter that I had written to my parents, at this time, gives some additional details:

Dear Dad and Mom:
I have appeals into both the District Court of Appeal and to the Supreme Court of Florida. This man, who sort of appeared out of nowhere, has made it possible to do the above two things. I really feel that it was a miracle from the LORD as financially there was no way to continue, plus my lawyer would not go forth because of my lack of funds. I have enclosed some of the stuff we have been working on. It seems impossible that Jonathan could have pulled together ... over one weekend ... just before the deadline to have these submitted. I feel like I'm in third year Russian and haven't had the first two years.
There are a lot of issues at stake, statewide as well as nationally, resting on this case, not to mention my personal involvement, so there are, of course, a lot of barriers to overcome.

> **I feel like I'm in third year Russian and haven't had the first two years.**

> **I always tell them that nothing will really ever be right until the husband is back as head of their home.**

I continually speak with women who have had their homes, families, and businesses stripped from them by people in the judicial system who have some time in the past done likewise to their families. It's time to stand up to this.

Most are fighting only for the material part of their marriage, but I feel they also have rights. I always tell them that nothing will really ever be right until the husband is back as head of their home; that is, the children will be out of order, there will be continued conflict; this will be passed on from generation to generation, etc.

Another letter sent to my friend in New Jersey records my continuing efforts to work and earn money for basic essentials and to gather more resources to pay the fees to further this judicial "court-ship" travesty.

Dear Fran:

I am busy day and night, going from one project to another. I need to open the doors for the Lord to send some big finances so this weekend I worked on a correspondence course to renew my real estate license. I turned it in and spent some time with a lady to help me get started in this field. I still have my teaching job, but I only get $485 a month with it, and that will soon decrease.

I was beginning to hear from more people who were going through divorces. Encouragement was something I could offer them as I heard the familiar ring of injustices with their legal dissolutions. They were experiencing many of the same things I had been experiencing. There's truly nothing new under the sun!

Chapter 7

FROM THE JUDICIAL TO THE LEGISLATIVE TO THE EXECUTIVE BRANCHES, I PLEADED

In addition to my judicial "school of learning," I also entered the legislative arena. This was to introduce an amendment to the No-fault Divorce Law which would support those who wished to honor the "until-death-us-do-part" perspective on marriage. **I'm not saying everyone must CHOOSE to fit into an "until-death-us-do-part contractual" commitment, but for those who agree to such they should also be afforded equal legal protection.**

Life's experiences can work for our good.

As we walk through life, many of the things we experience seem as if they are so negative. However, even as I labor over this book with the years of letter writing, briefs, and newspaper clippings surrounding my desk, strewn on the floor and counter tops, I can see from a new perspective. Many experiences which at the time were cruel, were inhumane, were heartbreaking, were things I did not want to accept, have worked out for good. It's just that I could not see the broader view as I was living through many of my "court-ship" experiences.

For example, being court-ordered out of our home was an experience that has had a lasting, fearful effect upon me. However, without that, I would not have moved into the home of two people I hardly knew—the Jorgensens. Jorgy

121

and Grace became my friends, my comforters, my cheer-leaders. They were compassionate with my many tears, shared my fears, and comforted me. They sat outside the courtroom and prayed while I defended our marriage inside. These two people and I bonded together in a treasured friendship. They became so close that I consider them surrogate parents. United, we went forward in our efforts to help others who had been brought into this nightmarish dilemma called divorce. Jorgy and Grace had knowledge about the legislative arena. They personally knew Representative Daniel Webster who became one of the sponsors for the Amendment to the No-fault Law that I drafted.

Even though Jorgy and Grace could not have been more gracious, I would cry myself to sleep, pleading that I might be able to move back into our home, because for me, "There's no place like home." Nonetheless, I learned that leaving our home, although devastating, was important because it forced me to meet others I would never have met who were vital in my "court-ship" journey. As the work to be done took center stage in my life and I became more immersed in the demands of the court proceedings, the tears became more diffused—but the daily time away from our children continued to tear at my heart.

I'm reminded that if I would have been a conventional criminal, the state would have supplied food and housing, and I would not have faced a child-custody issue! Not that I think jail is a desirable place to be, BUT I'm trying to help the reader to draw a perhaps ridiculous BUT REAL contrast between the extremes under No-fault versus laws protecting and providing for Defendants in criminal lawsuits.

How do you get a law amended?

Politics! My biggest involvement in politics had been going to the polling location to cast my vote whenever election time rolled around. One of my friends often "lovingly" remarks, "Judy, we won the war" (WWII') because of my lack of knowledge about what is going on in the world. I had pretty much wiped out all that boring high school civics stuff from my memory bank. You know, the Constitution, the Senators and Representatives, the three branches of government, and other basic foundational documents and historical facts.

Why would I ever need such trivia? Oh my! How vital all that quickly became as I was about to get another crash course. It started with my "court-ship" in the judicial branch through my court "dates" and the writing of my first Motion. Now I would move on to the legislative branch, the lawmakers.

It was time to try to get the No-fault Law changed. As I chronicle these events, does the reader wonder if the Florida Bar passed the same rigors as I when it instituted No-fault and later amended its Rules mentioned on page 116? Through many phone calls, research, meetings, and the added personal realities regarding the ravages of divorce and the injustices in the court system, I moved forward: first by drafting the words for a petition, then gathering signatures needed to support the Amendment so that it could be brought before the lawmakers. With the help of many people, most of whom I have never met, signatures were obtained to help satisfy the first step. See wording below from the petition reproduced on page 125.

We the undersigned believe that any divorce law which allows the dissolution of a marriage when one of the partners resists that legal action on the basis of religious conviction is in violation of the First and Fourteenth Amendments to the United States Constitution and Sections 3, 9, and 10 of the Constitution of the State of Florida and must be amended.

We believe that the "marriage-contract" is enacted between one man, one woman, and Almighty God. The State ... should not interfere simply because one party wants to break the agreement. The State should therefore continue to recognize the validity of the marriage; that is, not issue a divorce in such cases. However, we do feel it appropriate for the State to protect a battered mate by specifying a legal separation when clear evidence is shown of persistent physical abuse.

Next, I needed to find legislators who would become sponsors for the proposed bill. After getting the names and addresses, I started the task of writing and/or speaking to each Florida Representative and Senator. Hundreds of letters were mailed to support these efforts to petition the government to stop its unconstitutional actions against marriage. Many then, as now, did not realize that No-fault is restructuring the family into a picture that totally distorts the beautiful image that it is intended to be. Some of the responses from the legislators to whom I wrote are below:

September 10, 1984
Dear Mrs. Brumbaugh:

Thanks for your letter of recent date regarding the No-fault Divorce legislation.
You and I have discussed this by telephone, and I've expressed my opinion. I do believe some change should be forthcoming but, frankly, do not believe that it will be. The viewpoint that you and I hold is, unfortunately, a minority viewpoint in the Legislature.

Cordially yours,
[Representative] John A. Grant, Jr.

A Petition to amend the No fault Divorce Law of the State of Florida

We the undersigned believe that any divorce law which allows the dissolution of a marriage when one of the partners resists that legal action on the basis of _religious conviction_ is in violation of the First and Fourteenth Amendments to the United States Constitution and Sections 3, 9 and 10 of the Constitution of the State of Florida and _must be amended_.

We believe that the marriage contract is enacted between one man, one woman and Almighty God. The State merely acts as legal witness to this contract and _should not interfere_ simply because one party wants to break the agreement. The State should therefore _continue to recognize the validity of the marriage, that is not issue a divorce, in such cases._ However, we do feel it appropriate for the State _to protect a battered mate_ by specifying a _legal separation_ when clear evidence is shown of _persistent physical abuse_.

Signature	Printed Name	Address	City
1.			
2.			
3.			
4.			
5.			
6.			
7.			
8.			
9.			
10.			
11.			
12.			

Committee for the Restoration of the Family
Orlando, Florida

Petition to Amend the No-fault Divorce Law designed to collect signatures in support of the Amendment of the No-fault Divorce Law

September 11, 1984

Mrs. Brumbaugh:

Thank you for writing me in regards to your concern about Florida's No-fault Divorce Law. While I agree with some of your points, I remember the situation which existed under Florida's law prior to No-fault Divorce Law. Partners consistently lied to get divorced. Do you prefer that situation or would you not allow divorce at all?

Sincerely,

[Representative] Jim Watt

September 12, 1984

Dear Mrs. Brumbaugh:

In response to your letter of September 9, 1984, enclosed please find a copy of the Florida Supreme Court's decision in the case of Ryan v. Ryan, 277 So.2d 266 (Fla. 1973), upholding the constitutionality of Florida's No-fault Dissolution of Marriage Statute. I hope this information is of assistance to you in your litigation.

Sincerely,

Richard Hixson

Staff Director Florida House of Representatives

September 13, 1984

Dear Mrs. Brumbaugh:

Thank you for your letter regarding No-fault Divorce. Many of our laws are not "pro-family." I would welcome any specific suggestions to improve in this area.

Please let me know, and we can work on it together.

Most Sincerely,

[Representative] Elizabeth (Betty) Metcalf

September 17, 1984

Dear Ms. Brumbaugh:

Many thanks for your letter regarding Florida's No-fault Divorce Law. I share many of your concerns.

It is my understanding that the marriage must be shown to be "irretrievably broken" in order for a divorce to be granted. I am not sure how that measure can be reconciled with the "no-fault" concept which you speak of. Consequently, I do not know how I can answer your questions relating to whether I support a No-fault Divorce Law. I can say, though, that I do believe that a marriage should be shown to be "irretrievably broken" before a divorce should be granted.

Again, thank you for your letter. Please apprise if I can be of assistance.

Sincerely,
[Representative] Rick Dantzler

September 20, 1984

Dear Mrs. Brumbaugh:

Thank you very much for your recent letter concerning the No-fault Divorce Law.

You ask about my feelings on this issue, and I say to you, **I am in favor of changing any law where the existing statutes impact adversely on a large number of Florida residents. If such a large scale problem exists in this instance, attorneys should make this known to all legislators, and this is the first time I have been contacted regarding this issue.**

I believe you raise some very interesting points about the existing law. This issue has not arisen during my term in office, therefore, I am not sure what support can be generated in Tallahassee to

*change this statute. I will make some inquiries and
contact you if I feel we can be successful in making
any significant changes in the 1985 Session.*

*Very truly yours,
[Senator] Karen L. Thurman*

September 21, 1984
Dear Mrs. Brumbaugh:
*Thank you for letting me know of your support
for pro-family legislation. I, too, strongly support
laws that are protective of family life.*

*I supported legislative attempts to enact a
community property law in the state which would
divide property equally between spouses. When
that effort failed, I worked successfully to amend the
No-fault Divorce Law to* **require the courts to
consider age, duration of marriage and contributions of homemaking, child care and career
support in assigning alimony.**

*Please be assured that I will continue to work
for the legislation that is protective, not destructive,
of the family unit.*

*Sincerely,
[Representative] Helen Gordon Davis*

September 24, 1984
Dear Mrs. Brumbaugh:
*As of this time I am not in favor of changing our
No-fault Divorce Law. In any divorce proceeding
children are the ones who suffer most. The quarrels
between divorcing partners impact very heavily on
their lives emotionally.*

*I realize this does not answer all your concerns
about the fairness of divorce proceedings for the
partners involved. My primary concern is for the*

children, and this is my reasoning for my support of
our existing laws.

Sincerely,
[Representative] Everett A. Kelly

September 27, 1984
Dear Ms. Brumbaugh:
    Enclosed please find a copy of Chapter 61,
Florida's law regarding dissolution of marriage.
    Your letter requested repeal and replacement
with "Pro-Family" legislation. If you would care
to prepare something more specific, it could be
submitted for consideration.

Faithfully yours,
[Representative] Dorothy Eaton Sample

I not only followed up with Representative Sample but
wrote many other politicians:

October 2, 1984

Honorable Dorothy Eaton Sample:
    Enclosed you will find a brief which a friend
and I have prepared. No-fault seems to be punitive
to those who are standing for morality. **It provides
protection only for the person seeking unilaterally
for a release from a bilateral contract. The person
filed against has no defense that is legally recognizable. No-fault reflects and contributes to
retreat from the traditional view that a person is
responsible for his actions** ... Innocent persons are
injured as all too often a partner wants a divorce
simply because he or she is tired of being married,
or is interested in someone else. The other partner

*may have been a good spouse. The result can be that the spouse who wanted nothing **but a good marriage and family can lose the home, children, estate, and many life goals, simply because of the other's selfish desires.***

Innocent persons are injured as all too often a partner wants a divorce simply because he or she is tired of being married, or is interested in someone else.

For this reason, I strongly believe that if "No-fault" concepts are to be applied at all in civil society, they should apply only if both spouses agree to proceed under No-fault provisions ...

In Summary, three areas on which to concentrate might be:

1. *to allow no divorce when there is one party in opposition;*
2. *to minimally allow for protection provided under previous laws where a party could not be awarded a divorce if that party were involved in adultery;*
3. *to adjust the financial aspect of a dissolution to reflect equality in the living standard of both spouses ...   Judith A. Brumbaugh*

October 2, 1984
Dear Representative Carlton:

Grace Jorgensen suggested that I write to you again and apprise you of my current situation. I have enclosed a letter which I wrote to ACLU in August when I was in desperate need of help in this fight against No-fault Divorce. I submitted to you a brief which was entered into court in my defense and, as additional information for you, regarding support for initiating legislation to repeal this most

This is the third home that I have moved my boxes to since being "forced" out of my home.

ungodly law. I do hope that you will be part of a team to spearhead this legislation.

Grace and Jorgy have graciously permitted me to stay with them awhile. This is the third home that I have moved my boxes to since being [judicially] "forced" out of my home ... Judith A. Brumbaugh

October 12, 1984
Dear Ms. Brumbaugh:
Thank you for your letter and the enclosed information on No-fault Divorce. I really do appreciate your taking the time to send me this additional information.
I have sent a copy of your letter and the enclosed materials to Representative Dan Webster. As the Legislator representing your area I have asked him to review this situation as well.
With every good wish to you,
[Representative] Fran Carlton

October 16, 1984
Dear Ms. Brumbaugh:
Thank you so much for your letter of October 2 and for all the enclosures. You are aware of my feelings on this subject through our telephone conversation and my letter of September 10, 1984.
You can rest assured that whenever this matter reaches the floor, I am prepared to support the pro-family legislation you have referred to.
Cordially yours, [Representative] John A. Grant, Jr.

The following is part of a response from Senator Stuart which gives some of the reasons legislators feel No-fault is a positive option for marital discord.

February 5, 1985

Dear Mrs. Brumbaugh:

Thank you for taking your time to address the Orange County Legislative Delegation last week concerning No-fault Divorce. In response to your earlier correspondence, we contacted the Senate Committee on Judiciary-Civil, and they have provided the following information. It appears that No-fault Divorce was adopted for the reasons enumerated below.

1. *To eliminate the pre-1971 statutory requirement that fault be assigned ...*
2. *To reduce bitterness and hostility between the parties in a divorce proceeding, particularly when minor children were involved ...*
3. *To prevent disrespect for the law and its processes and to curtail perjury occasioned under the pre-1971 statutes ...*

*To conclude, I agree with you that marriage is a fundamental institution. Certain segments of our society err when they assume that divorce is a matter of little consequence. As indicated in the court cases which you referenced in your letter, **it is the family which is the basic unit of all civilized society.** If I may be of further assistance, please feel free to contact me.*

Sincerely,

[Senator] George Stuart, Jr.

Consider the information that the Senate Judiciary Committee gave Senator Stuart as the rationale for the No-fault Divorce Law. What people write often sounds good because of the way it is worded. But we must examine what is really being said. Look carefully at the four rationales below that are used to justify No-fault. Does it seem logical that we would abolish punishment for crimes such as murder, rape, theft, and embezzlement because we want:

1. to eliminate the requirement that fault be assigned
2. to reduce bitterness and hostility between the parties, particularly when minor children were involved ...
3. to prevent disrespect for the law and its processes
4. to curtail perjury occasioned [caused] under the previous law?

Study the first rationale above. It would be hard to believe that any person with clear thinking would vote for a bill that would **eliminate** the requirement **that fault be assigned** when a person murders another or steals another's possessions or embezzles someone's bank account!

> **We would not eliminate punishment for murder, rape, theft because it might offend the person so charged with such crimes; yet, that's one rationale for No-fault Divorce.**

It's equally implausible to imagine the passage of a bill that would exonerate criminals because they might become bitter if they were convicted. Would we change a law because someone threatens to disrespect the law or because he lies?

Yet, when it comes to preserving the basic unit of all civilized society, the family, we have been made to believe that the above set of four rationales justifying the No-fault Law will preserve the family—a set of standards which **actually does away with** responsibility, commitment, and accountability.

133

Putting the focus on children and employing emotional expressions such as *"particularly when minor children were involved"* and *"prevent disrespect for the law"* can take the spotlight off the real issue—the unwillingness of one or both parents to reconcile. Instead of the government protecting families, it is fostering the prevailing no-responsibility attitude by its promotion of a law which says it will **not hold a person accountable** if he wishes to abandon all responsibilities attending a "marriage-contract." Is it conceivable no one is RESPONSIBLE? Is it possible there is NO FAULT?

> **Putting the focus on the children ... can take the spotlight off the real issue.**

Most who have lived through the ravages of divorce can attest to the fact that the rationales for justifying No-fault are false. The death sentence on a marriage is **not** a deterrent to lying and bitterness. The bitterness and hostility are ongoing with an attendant disrespect for and/ or manipulation of the law. Even worse, lying in and out of the court not only is **not** curtailed, but **it is often made a part of the lifestyles of the children.** They learn to lie to cover up for actions of the "other" parent or to hide activities which one parent may approve while the other does not. Children are made pawns of situational ethics as they learn to internalize many thoughts and fears: "Mom, please don't say anything. It will make Dad mad." "I know it's wrong, but I don't want to hurt Dad's feelings."

> **No-fault divorce rationales are false.**

> **Many children learn to lie as their way to keep peace between separated parents.**

Committee for the Restoration of the Family was birthed.

After several months of phone calls, letter writing, and personal interviews, three legislators agreed to sponsor my proposed Amendment. The initial wording, however, had to be modified to gain any support. The media caught wind of all this activity. An attack on the No-fault Law was definitely news. Reporters began to contact me: "What's the name of your organization?" "What does it do?" "Organization? What organization?" I, with panic, thought. "What do I tell them?" *Committee for the Restoration of the Family* was the answer that came into my mind. So now I had my response to media questions: "It's a grassroots organization (God and me—at that time!) designed to foster families called *Committee for the Restoration of the Family.*" "Thanks, God." The reporters seemed satisfied with these replies. The United Press International wrote an article which was published in our local newspaper, *The Orlando Sentinel*:

Langley proposes tougher divorce law
March 15, 1985

Tallahassee: Senate Minority Leader Richard Langley said Thursday he is sponsoring a bill to require the consent of both parties to a divorce ... Langley said he introduced the ban on unilateral divorce at the request of an Orlando woman who has been fighting for 2 1/2 years to prevent her husband from divorcing her.

He said the bill would allow judges to grant property settlements, award alimony and make child-support judgments, without dissolving a marriage, when one party objects. "The state doesn't marry people, it recognizes the 'marriage-contract,'" Langley said. "The state shouldn't go

135

*in and dissolve a contract if one party to the
contract doesn't want it done."* (11:D4).

I had heard from some homeschooling and other pro-
family groups who said that it was important to lobby the
legislators. So my friend Mindi and I went to Tallahassee,
not having any idea what to do. I made Trojan Horse
cookies which we gave to the legislators. I can imagine the
politicians probably were thinking, "From where did these
'Susie Homemaker women' come!"

One of the first questions we were asked once we were
in Tallahassee was, "Are you a registered lobbyist?" Good
grief, what do they mean by that? How do we get registered? "Oh, yes! Where do we register?" That taken care
of, we were on our way up and down the *halls of justice*
pleading our unpopular cause.

How would I prepare to speak before legislators?

"You will need to present your Bill before the House
and Senate committees," Senator Langley told me. What
do I say? Write a presentation. Practice. Practice. The big
day arrived. With knees knocking and voice trembling, I
eventually stood before the Senate Judiciary Committee to
present rationale for the Amendment to the No-fault
Divorce Law. (See the Bill on page 137.) To put it mildly,
my presentation did not appear to be well received. But it
certainly was an educational experience on many fronts,
even before I spoke!

How I met Judy Civil!

Mindi was with me again on this trip. When we arrived
in Tallahassee, we drove around and around to find a
parking spot and finally found a free one in a parking
garage. We thanked God for helping us find such a great
space and made a special note of where we were so that we
could find the car when we came out later that day.

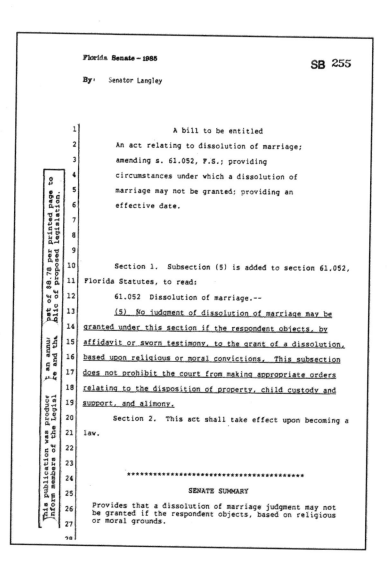

Florida Senate – 1985

SB 255

By: Senator Langley

1   A bill to be entitled
2   An act relating to dissolution of marriage;
3   amending s. 61.052, F.S.; providing
4   circumstances under which a dissolution of
5   marriage may not be granted; providing an
6   effective date.
7
8
9
10   Section 1. Subsection (5) is added to section 61.052,
11   Florida Statutes, to read:
12   61.052 Dissolution of marriage.--
13   (5) No judgment of dissolution of marriage may be
14   granted under this section if the respondent objects, by
15   affidavit or sworn testimony, to the grant of a dissolution,
16   based upon religious or moral convictions. This subsection
17   does not prohibit the court from making appropriate orders
18   relating to the disposition of property, child custody and
19   support, and alimony.
20   Section 2. This act shall take effect upon becoming a
21   law.
22
23
24   ***
25   SENATE SUMMARY
26   Provides that a dissolution of marriage judgment may not
      be granted if the respondent objects, based on religious
27   or moral grounds.
28

Proposed Amendment to the No-fault Law

We met briefly with Senator Langley. Before leaving his office, he told us to go to one of the house phones to call Judy Civil to find the room in which I would be speaking.

We found a phone. I dialed the extension. I don't remember the exact details, only the basic conversation. "Hello, could I please speak with Judy Civil?" "There's no one here by that name," was the answer on the other end. "Are you sure you have the right extension?" "Yes," I replied, "Senator Langley gave me this number to call Judy to find the meeting room where I will be speaking to the committee regarding the Bill we are introducing." There was a silence on the other end and then an outburst of laughter. "Oh, you mean Judiciary Civil!" Judy Civil was their abbreviation on (Florida's) "*Capitol Hill.*" I guess they knew the hometown girls were "on campus"!

We found the meeting room and waited nervously for my turn. As we sat there, I thought that we should have a record of this. "Mindi, I have a tape recorder in the car. Would you mind going to get it so you can record this?" I gave her my keys, and she was off. About a half hour passed. Where in the world is Mindi? Had she gotten lost? Did something happen to her?

Finally, she came just minutes before they called me to speak. "What happened? Where have you been? I was so worried." "Do you want the good news or the almost not-so-good news?" she answered. "What happened, Mindi?" "Well, the good news is that I found the car. But guess what? We were parked in a Senator's parking place. The police were there and had the car on the tow truck ready to take it away." "Oh, no. What did you do? Do I still have a car?" She had explained that we were from out of town—had never been in Tallahassee

> **"Do you want the good news or the almost not-so-good news?"**

138

before. I guess that wasn't hard to believe. They gave her "grace" and agreed to a $2 fine and to permit her to park the car elsewhere. But not in a legislator's spot! Can you imagine us coming out at night, both 100% sure we knew where the car was and not being able to find it? "Oh, God, you're so good to look over us!"

Time for me to speak. With knees knocking, and voice trembling, I went to the podium and gave my presentation. Several did not wait until I finished to let me know that they did not agree with what was being proposed, but I continued until I finished my prepared talk. Someone thanked me, and we left.

We met again with Senator Langley. He said that it didn't go well and that I should get some additional people to testify and gather more support. What a blessing to have his support and help.

But we still had a lot of work to do. We went to the car, ate the food we had packed in a cooler, and headed home. How grateful we were that we had a car to drive! We certainly had enough chuckles to help offset the sadness of the negative response to the Bill.

No time to become depressed or to mope around. Have to keep going. Get support for the bill. Increasing numbers of private and public citizens became a part of my life as I continued trying to gather support for the Amendment through letters, phone calls, and meetings. A brief summary of these activities can be gleaned through some of the letters below. (*Names in letters to and from most private citizens have been changed.*)

March 15, 1985
Dear Mrs. Judith Brumbaugh:
I saw and heard you on Channel 55 today and totally agree with you. Please send me the packet you spoke of. Wishing you success in your effort to correct things. If I can help you in any way feel free

to let me know. Getting a divorce in Florida is entirely too easy. Sincerely, Frank

Dear Representative Dantzler:

I want to take this opportunity to thank you for meeting with me this past week and for your patience with me in speaking before the Judiciary Committee. It is, indeed, a most frightening experience for those of us who are not involved with politics to speak before such a delegation. Your positive reception was certainly appreciated.

I do hope that you will vote for this legislation to provide protection for those of us who must remain committed to vows spoken and to a contract entered into. I do hope that you will vote yes for this Amendment. Thank you again for your time and consideration.

Sincerely,
Judith A. Brumbaugh
Committee for the Restoration of the Family

The above letter was sent to each of the Judiciary Committee members. I received a few responses:

March 20, 1985
Dear Mrs. Brumbaugh:

Many thanks for your recent letter relating to the Judiciary Committee meeting in Tallahassee. I certainly appreciate your taking the time to appear before our committee and offer your opinions.

Please continue to express your concerns to members of the Legislature. Knowing how you feel is helpful in making legislative decisions.

Sincerely,
[Representative] Rick Dantzler

A new friend unexpectedly found me.

As I became aware of various ministries, especially those nationally known, I contacted them to give information about the proposed Amendment to the No-fault Law. One such ministry held a meeting in Sarasota. They gave me permission to speak to the attendees about the pending No-fault Amendment I had drafted. I did so hoping to gain the support Senator Langley said I needed.

After I spoke, a young woman came up to me and said she had a dream that she should attend this meeting, and she would find support for her stand against divorce. She had grown weary and discouraged: "I wondered how in this huge gathering of strangers I would get an answer to such a need," she related. "When you stood up and started to talk, I could not believe it. I knew you were the one I was to meet and could hardly wait to get to you." Not only did I meet Sharon, but she and her parents became precious long-time friends and supporters of the work to restore and strengthen families. Sharon would later testify on behalf of the Bill and her mother Dena would chauffeur us to Tallahassee.

> **"I wondered how in this huge gathering I would get an answer."**

April 1, 1985

Dear Sharon:

I thought that I was going to the meeting on Saturday to get on the agenda, but I really went there to meet you so that we could further this work regarding the reestablishment of the family unit in America.

Sharon, I do look forward to working with you. This is a most difficult position to defend. Many will try to tell you to drop it and "get on with your life" if things continue for an extended length of time ...

Love,
Judith

More people were contacting me as they heard about the Bill. Others joined us in continuing to get support for this important Amendment.

Dear Mrs. Brumbaugh,

Enclosed is one of your petitions that I was able to get filled out over the past few days. I was able to get three signatures when I stopped at a 7-11 store one night.

Please send me a few more of the petitions. I have written and called about six Florida Representatives and Senators supporting the Bill.

Also, did you hear WKIS radio early this week when they discussed this Bill? They spent an afternoon talking about it according to my Dad. God bless you. Keep on pressing on!

George

April 13, 1985

EAGLE FORUM
Dear Mrs. Schlafly:

Kay Yonge from the Orlando Chapter has appointed me Special Projects Chairman to represent Eagle Forum for a Bill which we have before the Florida Legislature. This Bill, Senate Bill #255, is to provide protection for the family from the Trojan Horse, No-fault Divorce. Our Amendment is to stop the state from dissolving a marriage when one of the spouses is trying to hold the family unit together ... Last week when I spoke before the House Judiciary Committee, they vetoed the Bill 7-0. Please help us to fight for our families, our homes, our friends. The Bill will be heard again the last part of this month.

Sincerely, Mrs. Judith A. Brumbaugh

April 13, 1985

Dear Sharon:

I talked with Nancy the other day. She told me that you had received papers [divorce] from Mark. I know the pain you must be experiencing. It is so deep, and you wonder how you can keep going ...

Please call me any time of the day or night. I understand. I know that finances hinder that but know I am praying for you, Sharon ... I have a few more petitions. I was on WAJL this morning but haven't received any responses yet ...We must be diligent in these days ahead and determine to get this Amendment passed.

Love,
Judith

Kaye Yonge, president of the local branch of Eagle Forum, got behind us by also contacting politicians, legislative delegations, and others with potential influence to support the Bill. She helped in Tallahassee with some much-needed contacts and wrote to the Senate Judiciary Committee:

April 15, 1985
Senate Judiciary Committee
Tallahassee, Florida 32301
    I am writing to you in behalf of our organization to ask that Senate Bill #255 be passed out of Committee with a favorable vote. In our opinion, this Bill deserves to be heard and debated on the Senate floor. The present No-fault Divorce Law is unjust and violates the Fourteenth Amendment of the U.S. Constitution which says that "NO STATE SHALL DEPRIVE ANY PERSON OF ... PROPERTY WITHOUT DUE PROCESS OF LAW..." All Americans are supposed to be allowed to have their day in court, a chance to be heard and the issues weighed by the judge ... There is no basis on which a divorce can be denied. As a constitutionalist, I am extremely distressed that there are NO FACTORS to be weighed by the judges and that someone's property can be taken away ... on NO BASIS ...

Kaye Yonge, President

There are no factors to be weighed by the judges, and someone's property can be taken away on no basis.

Below are portions of a letter I wrote to Senator Denton pleading with him to help with the Amendment to the No-fault Divorce Law.

April 20, 1985

Dear Senator Denton:
    I am writing to plead with you to help me in my efforts to salvage the family unit in America. I

know from the works that can be credited to your name, especially the Subcommittee Hearings on Broken Families, that your heart motive is pure in your concern for the children and families of our nation.

In this current legislative session in the State of Florida, we have a Bill which is in great danger of being killed unless we get some help from people like you. The Bill, Senate Bill #255, is written to prevent the state from dissolving a marriage when someone is trying to hold the family unit together. There, of course, is a lot of opposition to the Amendment of the No-fault Divorce Law since many have taken advantage of this "no-responsibility" law.

Almost three years ago, my husband filed against our 20-year marriage. I have struggled for these past years to stop the state from dissolving my marriage through its ungodly, unconstitutional law.

In my efforts to stop the state, I have been evicted from my home, have gone without food, have been forced to go to court without a lawyer,

> **This land of ours is being destroyed from within from the effects of divorce.**

and experienced harassments and embarrassments from the legal system. Friends and family have forsaken me, but I will continue to hold fast to the commitment I made to our marriage. **I have determined to stand not only for my family but for this land of ours that is being destroyed from within from the horrible effects of divorce.**

Senator Langley, the sponsor of the Bill, along with me seems to be standing alone out on the end of a big limb. He asked me to see if I could get

145

some professional experts to testify on behalf of the Bill.

Senator Denton, will you do this? Time, of course, is of essence as our Bill will again come up yet this month. Please help to stop this rampant breakup of the family by assisting us. I am enclosing some additional information to give you more background and pray that you will answer the call.

Sincerely,

Mrs. Judith Brumbaugh

No help was forthcoming. One cannot judge whether the lack of help was because of heavy schedules, misunderstanding of the issue, or opposition to what was being proposed. Many feel they cannot afford to step into waters that might create political, religious, economic, or personal waves and possibly personal enemies.

Midge Decter, who gave testimony before the United States Senate Committee on Broken Families, was asked what the legislature might do to help shore up families. She wrote a reply to Senator Jeremiah Denton:

... Moreover, I have only one answer to the question of what the Senate might do about family stability. It is something important, but something, I am afraid, mainly negative. The Senate, as the representative body of the American people, must refrain from whoring after strange gods, or even from the willingness to discuss the possibility of whoring after them.

Senators, in other words, must take the risk of being square for all the rest of us. It is called leadership, and is just as important in the realm of attitudes as in the realm of lawmaking. Who knows? We must all begin to follow. It is hard to

stand up for old-fashioned virtue; it makes us feel
stuffy and priggish and not at all as we know ourselves to be. But if Capitol Hill could still, as it
once was, be a place shocked by adultery, pederasty
[form of male sodomy], and other sins—if such
things at least still cost one something in the highest
tribunal of the land—it would make an enormous
difference to our entire public tone. Remember
when a divorce cost a politician dearly (e.g., Nelson
Rockefeller)? What does it cost anyone now? Not
even the slightest twinge of disapproval. (6:5)

> **But if Capitol Hill could still, as it once was,
> be a place shocked by adultery, pederasty,
> and other sins—if such things at least still
> cost one something in the highest tribunal of
> the land—it would make an enormous
> difference to our entire public tone.**

Many have found and continue to find it difficult to
address such a political hot potato and an issue of which so
many people have found themselves a part. Representative
Hill's response gives further insight into the difficulty that
elected officials have in coming against such a controver-
sial issue:

April 23, 1985
Dear Ms. Brumbaugh:
*Thank you for your letter concerning the
Florida Divorcement issue before the legislature.
As you might imagine, this is a most complex issue.
I have received input from both proponents and
opponents. I have not, to be quite honest, made up
my mind as to my position on this Bill. Certainly*

147

*your thoughts will be given every consideration as I
continue to gather information to make my decision
on this matter.*

Thank you for your interest and concern.

Sincerely,

[Representative] James C. Hill, Jr.

Many clergy from varying faiths were contacted by
phone and letter:

April 24, 1985

Dear [Member of the Clergy]:

*Again, I thank you for your willingness to
discuss our Bill #255 in providing protection for the
family unit. I do pray that your church will become
actively involved at this "ninth" hour.*

*Please let me know if you have further ques-
tions.*

A local businessman provided two tickets so that a
guest and I could attend the Mayor's prayer breakfast. I
wrote the following letter to the speaker after the breakfast:

April 28, 1985

Dear Mrs. Nelson:

*Your talk at the Mayor's breakfast this morning
was most consuming. Most of us are so far from
suffering that it is difficult to relate, and I do
compliment you for your efforts. My friend Mindi
spoke to you briefly concerning our Bill in the*

Senate #255 (Florida). What we are trying to do is to provide protection for the family unit by stopping the state from dissolving a marriage when there is someone who is trying to hold the family unit together.

I have enclosed a copy of the Bill as well as a letter to Senator Langley with amendments to make the Bill strictly a religious exception. The Bill as written was voted down 7-0 in the House. Senator Langley suggested that I have him "temporary pass" the Bill and to come home, and in a short time, gather more support by additional petitions and by phone calls to senators, as well as letters.

> **I am asking that you will become involved in this last-minute effort to save our bill and thus thousands of families throughout our state.**

He also suggested that I get people to testify on behalf of the Bill. I am asking that you will become involved in this last-minute effort to save our Bill, and thus, thousands of families throughout our state.

Will you testify? Will you call and write and get others to do the same ...

In Christ's Service,
Mrs. Judith Brumbaugh
Committee for the Restoration of the Family

No offer for help came, but my friend from Sarasota continued to help.

Dear Sharon:

Hope this letter finds you on top of things. What is happening with your situation? I do continue to pray for strength for you and for Mark's heart to be softened.

It looks as if they might hear our Bill next Tuesday. I hope that you can gather an army and go along. I still haven't gotten anyone else to testify.

I have a few more completed petitions.

I'm trying to make connections with a lawyer bishop who works in Tallahassee for the Catholic Church. Be in prayer that he will testify. Did you get a copy of the Amendment?

Judith

More radio and TV stations opened their doors to give me the opportunity to discuss the Amendment on the air.

April 30, 1985

ACTS TV

Dear Mr. Hale:

*Thank you for your willingness to help with the No-fault Amendment ... I feel that our nation is in deep trouble and that No-fault Divorce is the internal destructive weapon which will completely destroy this country. **It has tripled the number of family break-ups since 1970!***

I am enclosing a copy of my recent talk before the Senate Judiciary Committee as well as a copy of the Senate Bill #255. The House Bill is #361 and reads the same.

On Friday, I don't want to get bogged down in my personal situation, but I will give you a capsule summary of what happens when someone tries to come against the laws as now written.

Last June, a judge signed a decree. I, on my own behalf, filed a Motion for Rehearing saying that No-fault violated my First and Fourteenth Amendment rights and was not in the best interest of the children. **My lawyer would not file this as he has never defended constitutional issues. That's why I filed it myself ...** I had to go to court without a lawyer—another chapter in and of itself. Anyway, I have been moving from house to house since last August. About three weeks ago, the Motion for Rehearing was scheduled ... The judge denied my Motion without any reason ...

Sincerely, Judith A. Brumbaugh

April 30, 1985

Dear Senator Langley:

I want to thank you so much for your time on Monday and your willingness ... in bringing back protection for the institution of marriage.

Daniel W. Shuman, in the article "Decision-making Under Conditions of Uncertainty," made some unique observations regarding spouses testifying against one another, something not allowed in criminal cases. Another article "An Overview of Domestic Relations Law" is enclosed.

> **In criminal cases, spouses cannot testify against one another.**

Again, regarding the institution of marriage, the couple makes a covenant agreement between themselves and God— <u>not</u> them and the state. It is performed before witnesses. They sign a statement giving evidence that they have done that. Witnesses *sign that agreement. This is presented to the state as evidence that a "contractual agreement" has taken place between these two people. Based upon tradition, the state recognizes the validity of that one-flesh "contract" "legalizing" their living together.*

There were witnesses present so we accept that as a binding "contract."

Important in the "separation of church and state" is that the state did not make the couple one flesh. It only "recognized" this institution. Thus, it has no authority to put apart what God has put together.

As in Section 3 of the Constitution of the State of Florida, **"the state can have no law prohibiting or penalizing the free exercise of religion," and in Section 9 and 10 cannot deny due process nor pass an ex post facto law or law impairing the obligation of contracts.**

Amitai Etzioni who testified before the United States Subcommittee on Family and Human Services regarding the effects of divorce on children said that he would testify for me. This was last summer, but I believe he still will.

Sincerely, Judith A. Brumbaugh

It was time to present the Bill.

The day arrived for our final plea for the Bill. Dave and Sherrill bought fabric for the dress that I made for the occasion. Sharon's mother drove us to Tallahassee. Only two people answered the call to appear for the hearing for the Bill: Sharon and me.

We were both so nervous. Sharon did such an incredible job pouring out her heart before the legislators. I followed. Our presentations were not well received. Parts of mine are given on pages 153 and 154.

I represent a group of citizens called The Committee for the Restoration of the Family. We believe that the family unit is an important part of our nation; that without it, our  *nation will be destroyed from within. We feel that this is happening in America as we see family after family broken with the Trojan Horse, No-fault Divorce. The destruction of the institution of marriage through No-fault is something we do not hear directly addressed by the media; instead, what we experience is the tragic aftermath which is affecting our entire society.*

It was noted in the court case <u>Grigsby v. Reib</u> *that*

> **marriage was not originated by human law and that civil government grew out of marriage. Why? To protect it and to conserve the moral forces of society and free government ... We are not asking to interfere with**

Civil government grew out of marriage.

those who mutually come to an agreement to break their "marriage-contract" but are asking you to enforce our constitutional and inalienable rights.

According to the "marriage-contract" which binds us, it is stated: 1. that "marriage is instituted by God"; 2. that a man and a woman make a covenant agreement between themselves and God; 3. that we swear "until death us do part," to "let not man put asunder," and to be committed "as long as ye both shall live." Friends and relatives duly witness this sacred ceremony.

Important in this constitutional issue is that the state did not make the couple one flesh, nor did it create the institution of marriage; it only "recognizes" the institution once the marriage has been vowed and solemnized. Therefore, the state has no authority to put apart what God has put together. The Constitution reads: "the state can have no law prohibiting or penalizing the free

exercise of religion" and in Sections 9 and 10, cannot deny due process nor pass an ex post facto law impairing the obligation of contracts. No-fault violates these sections.

| No-fault violates the free exercise of religion, *ex post facto* law, and impairs the obligation of contracts. |

As a nation, we have a choice—to rebuild our foundation: to provide protection for those committed to keeping their word and vows in holding the family unit together; or to continue to promote destruction by destroying the family unit.

We cast our vote for protection of the family unit. We thank Senator Langley as well as Representatives Selph and Webster for drafting bills to provide this protection and ask that you, too, support this legislation.

The Bill died.

What's next? The Executive Branch?

No, I didn't forget the executive branch. During the previous year, I had made an appeal to the President of the United States. Fran, my New Jersey friend, and I wrote a nine-page, legal-sized appeal in a petition pleading for help to defend the institution of marriage. We hoped it would be shared among all branches and levels of government as well as spiritual and secular institutions and organizations. Portions of my cover letter and the appeal are on the next several pages.

July 4, 1984

Dear President Reagan:

I write to you on this historical day where we as a nation under God celebrate our country's freedom ... I have been placed in a position, after 22 years of marriage, of trying to protect the rights

154

given to me regarding my marriage-covenant. *I find the same court system that was set up to "insure domestic tranquility, promote the general welfare, and secure the blessings of liberty"* ... trying to **force me to accept a dissolution of a [valid] "contract."**

"The disruption of families not only imposes a vast economic burden on the nation, but it inflicts

> **The court system is trying to force me to accept a dissolution of a [valid] contract.**

upon individual citizens more sorrow and suffering than war and poverty and inflation combined. Once these facts are fully comprehended, I think the entire nation will realize that the problem of divorce can no longer be neglected. **To spend vast sums of money in other areas while neglecting the area of divorce is like placing an expensive roof on a house while neglecting a raging fire in the basement below.**" (Armand M. Nicholi, Harvard Medical School – Hearings before Subcommittee on Family and Human Services: Broken Families) (7:57)

> **"The disruption of families not only imposes a vast economic burden on the nation, but it inflicts upon individual citizens more sorrow and suffering than war and poverty and inflation combined."**

As I mentioned above, I am representing a 22-year marriage; I am 43 years old. Almost my entire adult life has been centered around my husband's and family's needs. With this court

155

action, I can be asked to give up rights to my
family life, rights to remain in my home, and to
now be forced to establish a career outside the
home on a full-time basis.

Mr. President, I am pleading with you to offer
some assistance to help me to protect my marriage
vows and my family unit. I would like to have the
decree overturned. I, however, have no money to
hire a lawyer to help me to resist this action and
have been asked to return to court on July 25 for a
division of property ... I have, on my own behalf,
filed a "Motion for Rehearing" as I could find no
lawyer to do it for me.

I have pleaded with several Christian groups as
well as governmental officials during the past
month to help me. **All have agreed that divorce is**
wrong, but they feel they don't have the power to
fight the court system. Have we reached the
position of having the laws of our land, once set
up to protect the family, to now work to destroy
our institution of marriage so basic to the survival
of any civilization? Has the "Trojan Horse" truly
come to America?

> *Respectfully submitted,*
> *Mrs. Douglas (Judith) Brumbaugh*

AN APPEAL TO THE PRESIDENT
OF THE UNITED STATES
To be shared among all branches and levels of
government and spiritual and secular institutions
and organizations

We entreat and appeal to you to use the authority with which you have been empowered by God
"to establish justice, ensure domestic tranquility ..."

to help prevent family dissolution and to protect and save our families ...

"Our families are the building blocks of our nation, serving to provide its future generations of citizens, and to educate them in all areas of living, most especially in morality and character formation. Families are under attack, and they need protection." (Broken Families Hearings, U.S. Senate, March 1983, pp. 26-29)

> **"Our families are the building blocks of our nation."**

It is not in the best interests of our nation to allow its families to collapse. It is a form of "tearing down our own house."

One weapon used to break families apart is the No-fault Divorce Law ... allowing it to continue unchecked is not just being **the passive witness to the murder of families ... but also providing the weapon—against which there is no defense made possible ... While it may appear that we cannot "force" people to do that which is right, we can _enforce_ that which is right by our laws and by cultivating, rather than relaxing, moral standards.**

In a land whose system of justice calls for "innocent until proven guilty" construction of the law, we allow the unverifiable (except by self-will of the party seeking to divorce) presumption of "death" to be summarily wielded against families, with no defense possible to its life ...

No support for our cause was received from the executive branch. See the letter on page 158 which was written on behalf of President Reagan. You may or may not be aware that President Reagan, when he was Governor of California, signed into effect the first full-fledged No-fault

Divorce Law after which the other states modeled their similar laws. He signed it September 4, 1969. It went into effect January 1970. Mr. Reagan, like probably millions of others, may not have been aware of what the Bill really entailed and the subsequent destruction it would promote. May we each carefully assess all works and activities of which we become a part.

DEPARTMENT OF HEALTH & HUMAN SERVICES

Office of the Secretary
Office of the General Counsel Washington DC 20201
October 5, 1984

Ms. Judith A. Brumbaugh
Box 1342
Oviedo, Florida 32765

Dear Ms. Brumbaugh:

The White House has asked this Department to reply to your recent letters inquiring whether President Reagan will support repeal of the Florida "no fault" divorce law. **See Ruppert, page 98 and Article VI, Page 168.**

> We appreciate your having taken the time to share with us your views regarding broken families, an issue about which the Administration is deeply concerned. We believe that the family is the primary social unit of society, and that prevention of family dissolution is essential. At the same time, we recognize that legal questions relating to divorce have traditionally been within the jurisdiction and control of the states. Because states continue to have an important role to play with regard to such matters, we are not prepared at this this time to recommend Federal legislation governing the grounds for divorce, or to seek revisions in existing state divorce laws.

We are certain, however, that your deep convictions concerning "no fault" divorce would be of value to those responsible for developing state law on this issue. We encourage you to make your views known to Florida state legislators so that they may consider whether a change in the existing law is warranted.

Sincerely,

Terry Coleman
Deputy General Counsel/Regulations

Did the Florida Bar pass the same rigors as I (to preserve marriage) when it recommended the amendment to the already destructive No-fault Law with its "Simplified Dissolution"—an *affordable, quick and easy* **exit** from marriage?

Chapter 8

CONTRACT OR COVENANT, WHICH IS IT?

"Grow old along with me!
The best is yet to be,
The last of life,
For which the first was made;
... Youth shows but half."
Robert Browning

When my husband and I were in undergraduate school, one of the classes we took was English literature. As a part of the requirements for the course, we had to memorize a poem by Robert Browning. It's one that has stuck with me over these many years as it encompasses the love that we had shared for years and the "last of life" to which we looked forward together. One of Doug's poems to me showed that he, too, agreed with Browning:

Friends are important of that I'm quite sure
Because it's through the rough spots friends endure.
You've shown me that you are in fact a friend
For that I'll love you till my life does end.

However, we had never lived through the realities of the second part, "Youth shows but half." Sadly, how true. Sad ... for those who begin the race strong but get off the track in their latter years.

To "grow old along with me" in a marriage requires a decision encompassing the determination to honor the terms of the contract/covenant to which each party had committed himself. The contract/covenant is satisfied or discharged as stated: "until **death** us do part." This leads to the underlying vital truths that will be discussed in this chapter: contract or covenant, which is it?

Whether you are comfortable with the word *contract* or *covenant*, the objective of this chapter is to show that we all need to be concerned with what the legislative and judicial branches of our government are doing that is destroying the protection inherent in these vital instruments as they relate to marriage. This especially includes rights of the Defendant in a family lawsuit should the other party decide not to "grow old" along with him/her. All aspects, legally and spiritually, created out of this agreement that unites two people into one are meant to be both legally and spiritually inseparable.

> We need to be concerned with what the legislative and judicial branches of our government are doing which is destroying the protections inherent within these instruments.

Whether marriage is called a "marriage-covenant" or a marriage-contract, the intent and the laws protecting marriage are the same. Contractual law as taken from the Constitution states that nothing is to **impair** the obligations so stated in the contract/covenant; that is, **nothing is to interfere with the contractual rights that are a part of it**.

This includes a related vital constitutional protection called *ex post facto*. *Ex post facto* means what is done after the fact. As applied to contractual instruments, what is done after it is *duly* executed is not to void or negatively affect the rights and responsibilities of the parties to that agreement. This includes laws passed after it is executed. *Black's Law Dictionary* tells us *duly* is something that is "in proper form or manner; according to legal requirements; based upon a proper foundation." (1:450)

To give a broad overview, a contract/covenant of marriage includes a mutual agreement between competent parties with terms "until death us do part" and conditions which leave no loopholes for voiding the agreement: "... from this day forward; for better, for worse; in sickness and in health, to love and to cherish, until death us do part."

The Constitution—
Yes, it is vital and should be studied.

Until I, against my will, became enmeshed in my husband's lawsuit, I had no interest in reading what I felt were the boring Amendments to the Constitution. A book on such certainly would not have been something I would have curled up in a chair evenings to read! However, after my husband filed asking the government to dissolve our "marriage-contract" (covenant), I soon found I was being forced to study some vital legal issues. These had their principles buried in the laws of our land that are meant to provide equal justice for all. Their source—the United States Constitution.

> **The government has passed a law that invalidates contractual protections.**

Men who had an incredible amount of insight created this document. They had been given wisdom, some of which I would need 200 years after its ratification. Because of their wisdom, we have protected civil rights contained in the Amendments to the Constitution that are **guaranteed** to **every** citizen of the United States. These include: freedom of religion, freedom of speech, the right to petition the government, freedom of one's house and person from unwarranted search and **seizure**, right to have legal assistance in one's defense, freedom from bills of attainder, freedom from *ex post facto* laws, freedom from cruel and unusual punishments.

> **Judges do not use this anomaly when dealing with other contracts.**

Contrary to these safeguards, No-fault Divorce statutes were enacted in most states in the 1970s giving judges and attorneys an open door to violate, in practice, all of the above-mentioned legal protections. Many judges, when dealing with dissolution of "marriage-contracts," use this open door. These same judges, however, do not use this anomaly when dealing with other contracts.

> **Government refuses to honor constitutional rights it affords to other contractual parties.**

Under color of contractual law, the government takes control and invalidates a valid contract and treats Defendants as "nonhumans, as objects to be toyed with and discarded. It is, indeed, cruel and unusual [punishment]." (17:114) In its double jeopardy against marriage, the government not only legally classifies marriage as a *contract*, but then it refuses to honor the constitutional rights which it affords to other *contractual* parties.

"He [King George III] has ... depriv[ed] us, in many Cases of the Benefits of Trial by Jury ... transporting us beyond Seas to be <u>tried for</u> <u>*pretended offences*</u> ..."

Declaration of Independence 1776

"America has always been about rights ..."

So wrote Warren E. Burger, Chief Justice of the United States Supreme Court, 1969-1986. "We are the first people in history to found a nation on the basis of individual rights—a nation governed by 'we the people' ... Americans have made individual rights the foundation of our national identity. As it stands today, our Constitution and the Bill of Rights express the fundamental ideal of liberty, justice, and equality which have shaped the American experience, and have also made us a beacon to other peoples seeking a better life." (12:v)

Merely expressing the ideals of liberty, justice, and equality in this legal document will not effect, in practice, the rights inherent within our Constitution. As our wise Founding Fathers realized, there needed to be a system:

> ✓ to police these rights,
> ✓ to interpret these rights,
> ✓ to contextually and consistently apply these rights.

Thus, put in place was our legislative and judicial systems. Between the lawmakers and the judiciary (those who rule over the laws), the tyranny—the abuses experienced by the founders of our country—were to be avoided. Some of the specifics the Colonists wanted to prevent from happening again were discussed in Chapters 1 and 2 of this book. They are succinctly stated in the Declaration of Independence, part of which is repeated below. It was these abusive acts that gave rise to the protections included in the Amendments to our Constitution but sadly today are often violated in divorce lawsuits.

*The King of Great Britain ... has combined with others to **subject us to a jurisdiction foreign to our Constitution** ... giving his assent to their acts of* *pretended legislation ... for depriving us in many cases, of the benefits of trial by jury ... we have petitioned for redress ... our repeated petitions have been answered only by repeated injury.*

Before proceeding, I **beg** the reader to **STOP** and go to Appendix B, pages 269-274, where there are two tables with vital constitutional information to use as a standard to assess the evils that have crept into our laws and engendered cruel and unjust judicial actions by some of those given charge to administer our constitutional rights.

These tables will also help you to better understand the

> **Because of the vague nature and subjective application of the No-fault Law, these discriminatory practices are running rampant.**

purpose for many of the personal family examples that will be given in Chapters 9 and 10 as well as those already included in earlier chapters. These are necessary, not as an ongoing litany or saga; but without these, the reader would not have specific real examples of how our courts are taking what is brought before them packaged in a family lawsuit and creating horrific nightmares and injustices not likely in other civil suits—assuredly not in criminal ones.

This book is not only about the pain and the agony accompanying the destruction of one "contract," that of Douglas and Judith Brumbaugh, but it's a reflection of a national crisis that has been lost in the statistics of more than a million families legally dissolved every year. **It's the reality of the nationalization of an attitude of irresponsibility which is fueled by a legislature that has passed a subjective, arbitrary law: No-fault.**

This law has empowered Plaintiffs who want out of their "marriage-contract" with the least possible hassle and greatest possible speed and with no questions asked.

Decisions in the courtroom are framed by the subjective but limited powers of a judge who is charged to follow guidelines of the vague, nonspecific "cause," "irretrievably broken"—and bring down the gavel against such "contracts" that are placed before him. Again, if you haven't yet examined Appendix B, please do so. <u>Studying</u> it can give you a new set of eyes to recognize the constitutional abuses introduced in the preceding chapters and those brought to culmination in Chapters 9 and 10.

Within the government's *administration of the laws* lies the greatest potential for tyranny.

Tyranny is used to define the severe autocratic exercise of sovereign power used unjustly and arbitrarily to the oppression of those over whom a judicial officer has rule, either judicially and/or unconstitutionally so invoked. Even though the Constitution and the Amendments were carefully drafted, the application of the intended principles can go awry in the hands of those who wrongfully use their judicial authority. There are many righteous judges; however, there are those who are not and/or others whose hands may be tied regarding the laws handed to them by our lawmakers.

Our nation's Founding Fathers had dealt with rulers who were administrative tyrants. Many of the constitutional Amendments were ratified to avoid such abuses. These Amendments lay down rules the government must follow when it takes action against or decides disputes between citizens. One of their purposes was to spell out fundamentals of *due process* in the government's enforcement and/or administration of our laws. The framers of the Constitution considered *due process* rights the most important because of the abuses they had experienced from the King of Great Britain. "Our Constitution is color-blind, and neither knows nor tolerates classes among citizens ..." [12:69] There is to be equality for all.

165

Due Process is intangible in theory; tangible in its application.

It's impossible to adequately summarize the important protections encompassed under *due process*, but let's go to *Black's Law Dictionary* for some basics. "*Due Process* Clause: Two such clauses are found in the U.S. Constitution: one, in the Fifth Amendment pertaining to the federal government; the other, in the Fourteenth Amendment which protects our citizens from unlawful state actions. There are two aspects: procedural, in which a person is guaranteed fair procedures, and substantive, which protects a person's property from unfair governmental interference or taking." (1:449)

Due process encompasses rules and principles for our legal system for the enforcement and protection of private rights. It gives the **right to be heard** regarding issues of life, liberty, or property. **A defendant's rights are not only to be heard but also <u>enforced</u> and <u>protected</u>.** *Kazubowski v. Kazubowski, 45 Ill.2d 405, 259 N.E.2d 282, 290.*

The phrase *due process* means no person shall be deprived of life, liberty, property or of any right granted him by statute, unless the matter involved first shall have been adjudicated against him upon **trial**. Such a trial is conducted according to established rules regulating judicial proceedings. It **forbids condemnation without a fair and just hearing**. A law may not be unreasonable, arbitrary (without regard to facts), vague, or capricious (unpredictable). *U.S. v. Smith, D.C. Iowa, 249 F. Supp. 515, 516.* Fundamental requisites of *due process* are:

> **Due process forbids condemnation without a fair and just hearing.**

1. the opportunity to be heard,
2. to be aware that a matter is pending,

3. to make an informed choice whether to acquiesce [to agree—uncontested] or to contest,
4. and to assert before the appropriate decision-making body the reasons for such choice.

"Due process requires that every man has benefit of general law ... **It is a law which hears before it condemns, which proceeds on inquiry and** <u>renders judgment only after a fair and equitable trial.</u>" (1:449) Many *due process* protections have been "excised" from No-fault.   In practice, almost all fundamentals of *due process* are violated.   At least, this is what I perceived to be in the case of *Brumbaugh v. Brumbaugh* and many others of which I have learned who have been judged guilty under the vague, undefined cause: *irreconcilable differences.*

Rights of Defendants in a divorce lawsuit are to be protected by constitutional Amendments.

✔ Right to be heard
✔ Right to petition government for redress of grievances
✔ Right to equal protection of laws
✔ Right to reasonable laws
✔ Right to be judged by impartial laws
✔ Right to equal counsel
✔ Right to be apprised of legal rights
✔ Right to and protection of life, liberty, and property
✔ Right to *due process*
✔ Right to be protected from excessive fines
✔ Right to be protected from cruel and unusual punishment
✔ Right to have properties protected from governmental seizure and transfer
✔ Right to laws that do not discriminate or give special rights or impunity to certain sects or classes
✔ Right to have laws that do not infringe on the rights of the Defendant

✓ Right to object to shared parenting: criminals are not subjected to custody procedures as a general rule
✓ Right to appeal
✓ Right to laws which are not vague and give rise to subjective decisions against which a Defendant cannot defend
✓ Right to protection against *ex post facto* actions or laws
✓ Right against laws and acts which impair the obligations of contracts
✓ ET AL.!

The Supreme Court has constitutional responsibility to void laws, whether state or federal, which violate the Constitution.

"There is constitutional and legislative basis of the Supreme Court's general authority to invalidate laws which violate the Constitution..." (13:259) The right to void laws of the states became a part of the Supreme Court's function through Article VI, Section 2:

> *This Constitution, and the Laws of the United States which shall be made in Pursuance thereof; and all Treaties made, or which shall be made, under the authority of the United States, shall be the Supreme Law of the Land, and the Judge of every State shall be bound thereby, any thing in the Constitution or Laws of any State to the Contrary not withstanding.*
> **[See letters on pages 98 and 158.]**

The constitutional right to appeal is an important stopgap against lower court "maladministration" of the laws of our land.

"The first, and probably the most important federal law passed under the authority of Article VI was the Judiciary Act of 1789. Section 25 of this Act provided for appeals to the United States Supreme Court from the highest courts of the states ... In effect, this meant that **appeals would be taken in all instances where the state judiciary assertedly failed to give full recognition to the supremacy of the Constitution ...**" The Judiciary Act of 1914 allowed appeals on a Writ of Certiorari:

WRIT OF CERTIORARI IS A DEVICE FOR REQUESTING REVIEW BY A HIGHER COURT, IN CASES WHERE THE HIGHER COURT HAS A DISCRETIONARY RIGHT TO ACCEPT OR REJECT THE APPEAL." (13:260)

> **"A law repugnant to the Constitution is void."**

Chief Justice John Marshall said that the supreme authority in the national judiciary must of necessity be able to determine whether or not the laws of a state violate the Constitution or laws of the United States. "A law repugnant [in opposition] to the Constitution is void ..." (13:262) This is a key issue of *Judge, Please Don't Strike That Gavel ... On My Marriage.* The law which brought our marriage before Judge Fuller is repugnant. Our marriage is based upon a valid, legal "contract" duly executed on June 30, 1962. I, the Defendant, have not voided the "marriage-contract." I have kept and am keeping the "until-death-us-do-part" vow made.

Our "marriage-contract" was duly executed under a totally different divorce law. The divorce law under which the Plaintiff and Defendant were married in 1962 would have required that the Plaintiff charge and prove the Defendant with "cause," such as the unfaithfulness of adultery. This would not have been a provable defense for the Plaintiff. But, even beyond this legal provision, the point to which we all must get is to forgive the other person. It's not always easy to forgive, but it can and should be done. Those who go on to other relationships take their problems with them rather than to let the sandpaper of marriage force them to look within themselves.

The Defendant was subjectively judged as without any right to contest the legal conclusion that our marriage was irretrievably broken by Judge Fuller who, at the time, was embroiled in a divorce suit with his wife. (It might be enlightening for the reader to review comments concerning Fuller as reported in the newspaper accounts found in Chapter 2, pages 33 and 34.) Under the No-fault Statutes, there is no issue of **whether** the marriage should be dissolved once Doug spoke the magic words, "irretrievably broken." Judge Fuller had the legal authority to grant Doug's *Petition for Dissolution.* I felt the terms under which the dissolution took place became highly subjective.

For example, I felt I had been deemed "guilty" for a vague "cause" without a trial by jury, in violation of *due process*, in the absence of equal rights and equal protection of the law under which our "contract" was duly executed. Time with our children was ripped from me, properties were seized, and life and liberties meant to be an indivisible part of our bilateral "contract" were denied me. These actions were horrific in and of themselves but were made more so because I felt I was judged on charges that were not a recognizable part of the "contract" into which I had, in good faith, entered. The rules had been changed midstream without notifying me! Again, I urge the reader to study Appendix B—the second table—to glean some of the principles of *due process* listed. Below are three examples from that Appendix:

A state that forbids or requires the doing of an act in terms so vague that men of common intelligence must necessarily guess at its meaning and differ as to its application **violates the first essential of *due process*.** (Defendants in No-fault do not know the terms under which they may defend their "marriage-contract.") (See page 272.)

170

Due process requires that the citizenry be specifically informed of their rights and responsibilities and the legal prohibitions with which they must abide. (These rights are violated under No-fault.) (See page 273.)

The 14th Amendment prohibits any state from taking action which would deny to any person within its jurisdiction **equal protection of the law**. (Defendants in a No-fault suit are not afforded equal protection, to defend against the contract being legally dissolved, that is afforded Plaintiffs.) (See page 273.)

It's important to understand what Man considers to be a contract and what God considers to be a covenant because both have been made a part of the marriage laws of our nation.

In the last several pages and the vital information in Appendix B, some groundwork has been laid to help us continue on our journey to learn more about contracts and covenants. A contract/covenant of marriage includes a mutual agreement between competent parties with terms "until death us do part" and conditions which leave no loopholes for voiding or impairing the obligations of that agreement: "from this day forward; for better, for worse; in sickness and in health, to love and to cherish, until death us do part."

Throughout this book, you may have noticed that I have used two terms to refer to marriage: contract and covenant. Covenant is a word with which the reader may not be familiar or seem important enough to investigate— especially to those who are not Christians and even to some Christians. Before you think that, please bear with me because both of these terms, covenant and contract, will take us to the same place—the permanence of marriage— loving/trusting our marriage partner until death parts us.

At one time these two words, *contract* and *covenant*, actually had the same meaning; but today, because of changing laws and changing church doctrine, they have lost some of their vital similarities. Let me give you a little background from the covenant side of marriage which is important to those who profess to be Christians. Even though the reader may not embrace these beliefs, it's important to briefly share with you the principles upon which covenant beliefs are based. From there we will return again to the legal arena.

Marriage originally was not a *man-made legal* contract. It wasn't even a contract as we understand contracts today. Marriage was and continues to be a union created by God. The very first marital union was the joining of the first two people God created, Adam and Eve. (See the first book of the Old Testament, Genesis, Chapter 2, verses 21-24. The King James Bible is used for all Biblical references.)

Union may seem like a simplistic term, but to the Christian it represents the supernatural, indivisible, permanent joining by God of two people: one man and one woman. It doesn't matter whether the marriage takes place in a church, a judge's chambers, or even in a Las Vegas wedding chapel. It doesn't matter who performs the ceremony—a member of the clergy or even a justice of the peace. God is the one Who *creates* a marriage. It is He Who creates this **indivisible** union. Ecclesiastical and state officials **merely officiate** over the ceremony. They **do not make** the two one. Only God can create that kind of "life."

> The essence of covenant can be summarized in another Biblical term *immutable.*

For Christians, contract terminology is derived from the biblical term *covenant.* The essence of covenant can be summarized in another Biblical term *immutable.* This is used in the New Testament book of the Bible, Hebrews. (See Hebrews 6:13-18 where this term and several other legal ones are used.) Something immutable is absolutely unchangeable; i.e., there is nothing that man can do which can change the effect of what has taken place. That's what happens when a marriage-covenant is created by God. Covenant is the instrument which gives life to what many legally understand is a "marriage-contract."

Specifically with a marriage-covenant, once two people (a man and a woman) **both** for the **first** time, enter into what is legally called a "contract," this marriage-covenant cannot be changed by either spouse, nor by any church official, nor by any governmental authority. There are **no** exceptions. The only "expiration date" is the physical death of one of the parties to that covenant agreement. It is only after the death of one partner that the remaining spouse is then free to enter into another marriage-covenant.

Many may be concerned about the multitudes of spouses who unfortunately are terribly physically abused by their husbands—and in some cases their wives. Should they allow themselves to be so mistreated? There is specific Biblical provision for such abuse. It is given in another book of the Bible, I Corinthians 7:11. The directive here is that the abused spouse can live separately with the option to return to the husband/wife should that become possible; however, during the period of separation, the spouses are still married—still bound by the covenant ("contract") "until death they do part": "But and if she depart [divorce/separate], let her remain unmarried, **or** be reconciled **to her husband** ..."

> There is specific Biblical provision for such abuse.

Man is warned by God not to have anything to do with divorcing (putting apart) two people so joined under the terms of a marriage-covenant. Biblical references to support these beliefs are given in several books of the Bible: Genesis 2:21-24, Malachi 2:14, Mark 10:6-9, Luke 16:18, Romans 7:2, 3, I Corinthians 7:39, et al.

For an in-depth study of covenant-marriage in addition to these Bible references, see Appendix D for publications and/or audio teachings available through Restoration of the Family, Inc.

The source document for God's covenant of marriage is the Bible. The source document for contracts has become the Constitution and the many laws based thereupon. Contracts have legal protections underlying what makes them enforceable. Covenants usually do not have such **legal** protections in our courts of law. They do, however, have Biblical consequences.

> **The source document for contracts has become the Constitution and the many laws based thereupon; that for covenants is the Bible.**

In those instances in which legal protections in general underlie both contracts and covenants, the legal protections are the same. The big dividing line, however, is when we cross over into the area of family law. **The courts have bifurcated the contractual language.** This is what I learned from experience in my six years of "court-ship"—that there is now a huge gulf between contracts and covenants because of man's changing morality that has greatly affected not only the laws of the land in which one lives, but how they are applied. As it regards *due process*, what is being abridged are both procedural and substantive rights.

Some contract language is common to most of us, but as you've seen prior to this chapter, much contract language is confusing to the layman. Part of this is due to the fact that the courts have bifurcated the contractual language in unconventional ways when legally dissolving a "marriage-contract."

What are some basic principles of contracts?

Let's look at this man-made instrument, a contract. A simplified definition of a contract is an enforceable agreement between two or more competent persons embodying an offer by one person to do or not to do a particular thing and an acceptance by another. Certain rights are generally understood regarding contracts:

> **An essential part of free enterprise in our economic system is that <u>the rights created by contracts are protected</u>.** Each party must observe the terms of the contract, and generally **government cannot impair the obligations of a contract.** Economic life would be most uncertain and it <u>would be impossible</u> to plan ahead <u>if</u> we did not have the **assurance** <u>that agreements</u> <u>once made</u> <u>would be</u> **binding**. (14:27)

The government considers marriage to be a legal contract. It, however, does not give contracts pertaining to family law the same rights and privileges that are afforded other similar legal instruments. And the government GREATLY discriminates against the legislative **rights** of many (specifically Defendants)—those who become a party to what it classifies as a "marriage-contract."

No-fault is a national catastrophe.

"No-fault is a national catastrophe. Anything which overturns the order or system of things whereby families are destroyed and the whole of society adversely affected is by definition a catastrophe." (15:1)

This is a quote from J. Shelby Sharpe, an attorney committed to preserving families. He has been a forerunner in the legal arena in the struggle against the destruction of the family unit.

175

Attorney Sharpe has fought for many years against the unconstitutional attack of the government against marriage. His part was not in defense of his marriage but in trying to break through the evil that has permeated our legislative and judicial systems. In his paper, "No-Fault Divorce—A National Catastrophe," Mr. Sharpe spoke of the devastation created by the destruction of more than a million families every year since 1970. This was the year when the Uniform Marriage and Divorce Act was passed by the **National Conference of Commissioners on Uniform State Laws** (a group of tax-supported attorneys [NCCUSL] who formulated the No-fault Law).

Today all fifty states have some form of this statute. [**Attorney Sharpe could find no instance in the statutes when a divorce was denied to the petitioning party, the Plaintiff, under the present guidelines.**]

What the legislative system used as a premise on which to pass such a law was the inevitability of divorce; therefore, the procedures should be changed to minimize the amount of damage to the parties and their children following the divorce. **[This irrational reasoning would be like legalizing murder because it is inevitable that someone will murder another person.]** Tragically, history has shown that the change to a "No-fault" system instead of solving the problems of troubled marriages has only exacerbated the problems like pouring gasoline on a small fire. (15:2)

> **History has shown that the change to a No-fault system instead of solving the problems of troubled marriages has only exacerbated the problems like pouring gasoline on a small fire.**

No-fault Divorce Law mirrors that of Lenin and Stalin's efforts to destroy the family.

Attorney Sharpe gives some insight regarding the direction in which No-fault is and has been taking us. "The No-fault Law in the U.S. mirrors Lenin and Stalin's efforts to destroy the family and restructure it." Mr. Sharpe adds this: "It is significant to note that one of the first things V. I. Lenin did when he came to power in the former Soviet Union after the Revolution of 1917 was to have passed what amounts to our No-fault Divorce statutes. **Lenin, and later Stalin, determined that in order to maintain control of the people it would be necessary to complete-** ly destroy the family and restructure it. Thus, on September 16, 1918, a law was passed whereby one could obtain a divorce by simply mailing or delivering a postcard to the local registrar without the necessity of even notifying the spouse being divorced." (15:3)

> "To maintain control of the people it would be necessary to completely destroy the family and restructure it."

One only needs to look at the increasing number of singles (including some 45% of the workforce) to find that the family unit is quickly disappearing in America. Not only is easy dissolution encouraged, but the judicial system has become so complacent in putting its gavel on marriages that in some instances divorces are being granted without jurisdiction being established; and in others, without the opposing spouse (Defendant/Respondent) even being represented in court.

This is often the case when the Defendant does not have the financial means to hire an attorney and/or may be so emotionally traumatized that s/he does nothing to come against an evil which may be, at the time, too overpowering to address.

As mentioned previously, under the rules of procedure for No-fault (in Florida in 1984), there were only two requirements to be satisfied by the Plaintiff to obtain a legal dissolution: (1) for a corroborating witness to testify that the Plaintiff has lived in the state for six months; (2) for the Plaintiff to state that the marriage is irretrievably broken (no proof, in practice, of which is required). **The former requirement is necessary for the court to have jurisdiction over a divorce action (civil lawsuit).** Does it not seem irrational that all that is needed to dissolve what man deems is a valid contract is for someone to establish the fact that he has lived somewhere for six months and then state that he does not wish to honor the terms of his contract for basically no reason?

For example, considering the overall legal aspects of a contract, would this not be a totally unacceptable justification to dissolve a mortgage contract? **If a contract is a contract, why are the parties to all contracts not given *equal rights and equal protections under the law*?**

The state aids and empowers the Plaintiff by providing his defense—the words to use so that he does not have to come up with any reasoning on his own that will satisfy *just cause* to invalidate his "contract." Anyone can easily memorize the line for his speaking part in this drama before the court: "This marriage is irretrievably broken." This could be (as with me) against a 22-year marriage with children, assets, and sundry kinds of spiritual, physical, emotional, and financial ties.

> **Does it not seem irrational that all that is needed to dissolve what man deems is a valid contract is for someone to establish the fact that he has lived somewhere for six months and then state that he does not wish to honor the terms of his contract for basically no reason?**

178

Many who are reading this book would say that divorce is a good thing. However, if possible, try to get beyond your personal hurts and frustrations. Consider the empirical evidence—the result of divorce—that is so devastating, including the nightmares that many children face. Consider the increase in crime, the psychologically disturbed society we have become, the poverty that divorce has created and—for those of the Christian faith—the fact that God says He HATES divorce and repeatedly commands **not** to "put apart" what He has created. Millions are unwilling to accept this. But does not God know better than we!

The government has an obligation to protect marriage.

Historically, civil laws have been passed to strengthen and preserve the rights surrounding marriage. It was not until recently that our legislative and judicial systems have flagrantly undermined marriage with their promotion of No-fault Divorce. Several court opinions and rulings validate the legal system's history of protecting rather than destroying marriage. This was discussed in Attorney Sharpe's paper on divorce in which he listed several cases where the courts have ruled to protect marriage to the furtherance of society: (15)

1848: In *Sheffield v. Sheffield*, Chief Justice Hemphill observed, "the prospect of easy separation foments the most frivolous quarrels and disgusts into deadly animosities." Hemphill's concluding remarks were that **"when husbands and wives know they cannot end their relationship by mutual consent or for light or frivolous reasons, they become good husbands and wives; for necessity is a powerful master in teaching the duties it imposes."** 3 Tex. 86.

179

1888: The Supreme Court of the United States characterized marriage as "the most important relation in life, and the foundation of the family and of society, without which there would be neither civilization nor progress." *Maynard v. Hill*, 125 U.S. 205, 211.

1913: All of the duties and obligations that have existed at any time between husband and wife existed between those husbands and wives "**before** civil government was formed." The truth is that <u>civil government has grown out of marriage</u> ... from which government became necessary to ... protect the weak, and to conserve the moral forces of society, to the support of religion and free government. *Grigsby v. Reib, 105 Tex. 597, 153 S.W. 1124.*

1941: The government has an obligation to protect marriage: "... the State and society have an interest in keeping intact all such contracts [marriage] and in protecting them to the fullest extent." *Pappas v. Pappas,* 146 S.W.2d 116.

1978: The court reaffirmed this characterization and importance of marriage in 1978 in *Zablocki v. Redhail*, 434 U.S. 374.

The judicial system has redefined the legal rights and responsibilities of husbands and wives.

Attorney Sharpe's research affirms not only that divorce laws were initially designed to protect marriage but that there has now been a complete redefining of legal rights and responsibilities of husbands and wives:

However, **when the divorce laws change, the attitude of the courts toward protecting marriage changes.** This is graphically seen in the language of the opinion in *Cusack v. Cusack*, to wit:

"Until 1969 ... Texas legislation on <u>grounds for divorce</u> remained virtually unchanged for over a hundred years. The adversary nature of divorce litigation remained, and ancient ecclesiastical grounds for separation based upon fault formed the core of substantive divorce law ... It became apparent in the late 1960s that <u>existing grounds for divorce</u> and the <u>defenses</u> thereto were no longer compatible with modern beliefs." 491 S.W.2d 716. **Thus, there is now no judicial protection for a spouse who desires to save a marriage.** (15:6)

Miss Decter, who testified before the Senate Committee on Broken Families (1983), seems to capture the realities of what has happened: "Out of historic error, out of sloth, out of cowardice ... **we are permitting ourselves to become a society that punishes the virtuous.**

> **Man has reversed the basic purpose of our judicial system.**

That punishment is every day being incorporated into laws of the land, written and unwritten.

It is the family—the greatest tribute to, the most brilliant invention of, the human moral capacity—that has lately taken the greatest punishment of all. For one thing, we pretend no longer to be sure what is a family." (6:4, 5)

No-fault Divorce legislation punishes those who are committed to uphold the terms of the contract/covenant to which they swore: to remain faithful to the marital and family rights and responsibilities, to love their spouse until death parts them; to forsake all others, to love and nurture their children, to fight for their families and homes. However, No-fault puts Defendants in a straightjacket making them unable to defend themselves. They are denied *due process* and other constitutional Amendment rights. Two of the many additional egregious denials are: (1)

counsel that effects legal parity with the Plaintiff, (2) preservation of the Marital Communications Privilege.

In a nonjury trial, **children are divided like chattel**, thousands of dollars of properties are taken from A and given to B, and contractual rights and inherent intangibles developed therefrom stripped, destroyed, and whisked away. Defendants (especially women who have been full- or part-time homemakers) are unable to access equal protection and *due process* because of inability to retain qualified legal counsel. (See Amendment Fourteen, page 271.)

Additionally, the **Plaintiff testifies against his spouse** aided and empowered by a state-created unilateral charge (irretrievably broken) against which the Defendant has NO defense. The Marital Communications Privilege, which is often granted in a criminal suit, is used as a lethal weapon by the Plaintiff to sever his legally valid "marriage-contract." This violence is covered under *color* of the act legislators call *dissolution of marriage.*

Marital Communications Privilege:
… permits an accused spouse in a criminal case to **prevent his spouse from testifying against him** …
Hawkins v. United States, 358 U.S. 74 (1958).

"An alternative ground for applying the Marital Communications Privilege is that … intrusion into the marital relationship is wrong and should be prohibited, not because it will have a deleterious effect upon the institution of marriage, but because it offends the importance we place on privacy in our society. A marital privilege built upon this base would be conceptually defensible." (16:329) **Vowing that a marriage is irretrievably broken is**

> **Criminals are given rights those in family law are not—Marital Communications Privilege.**

making a cruel, one-sided judgment on the whole fabric of many years of joys, sorrows, hardships, and victories.

As a result of dissolution, Defendants are denied the right to be recognized socially and legally as married, placing them in a higher tax bracket. The Plaintiff who forces a legal status of "single" upon the Defendant, often almost immediately "restores" to himself the legal status of "married" by "contracting" with another "partner" waiting in the wings.

> All this is only true of one type of contract:
> "MARRIAGE-CONTRACT."

Constitutional protections are designed to safeguard the rights of those entering into valid contracts.

Even though they are in themselves, *lifeless*, contracts like covenants, have something set over them that determines their life and death, their veracity, their guide-lines for performance. This "invisible hand" or overseer for contracts is the Constitution. This unchanging, standard

> The Constitution guarantees that parties to contracts have equal protections.

rule guarantees that parties to all properly executed contracts will be treated alike; i.e., they have the same or equal protections. The purpose of a contract is to assure the parties that the *game rules* will not change and that everyone understands going into the agreement what the expectations will be. Parties to the contract know the exact duration—when it will end—when the terms of this legal instrument are to be satisfied.

The primary protections for our contractual law are based upon the Fourteenth Amendment to the Constitution:

> **No State** shall make or enforce **any law** which shall abridge the privileges or immunities of citizens of the United States, nor shall any State deprive any person of life, liberty, or property without *due process* of law, **nor deny** to any person within its jurisdiction **the equal protection** of the laws.

Ex post facto
is an important constitutional protection.

As mentioned above, to further protect parties to a contract, the Constitution in Article I, Section 10 forbids the states to pass any *ex post facto law* (after the fact). Most state constitutions also contain similar prohibitions. **This is a protection that in family law has been violated in millions of divorce cases.**

The purpose of the *ex post facto* provision is to guarantee that a law will not be passed to invalidate the rights in a contract that has already been legally executed; i.e., the legislature is not to pass a law after the occurrence of a fact or an act that retrospectively changes the legal consequences or relations of such fact or deed.

Black's Law Dictionary gives us the reasoning behind this important protection: "Retrospective laws give a different legal effect from that which it had under the law when it occurred. A law which ... in effect imposes a **penalty** or the **deprivation** of a right which, when done, was lawful; every law which ... alters the situation of a person to his **disadvantage**." (1:520)

Ex post facto, in essence, protects what was done "from the beginning." This is a vital *principle* and protection of contractual law. No later action by man (after the fact) is to alter the original; **it is immutable**. Does this sound familiar to those of you who hold Christian beliefs? (Review Hebrews 6:13-18.)

> **It's not**
> *ex post facto*
> **but as it was**
> **in the**
> **beginning.**

As noted in *Grigsby v. Reib*, **"All marriages come under the law established by God before any civil law."** Many laws based on our Constitution also incorporate vital *principles* God established for what He addresses as covenants. Once God has created a marriage, nothing done later by man undoes this original union. Likewise, no law passed after a like "marriage-contract" has been executed should *impair* or change the obligations of that agreement. Whether we call it legal or Biblical, it's saying the same thing: **Hands off this duly executed instrument!**

> **If a state legislature did enact a genuinely *ex post facto* law, it would be invalid even if it had not been prohibited by the Constitution.**

Dr. Rice, Professor Emeritus at Notre Dame, in his book *50 Questions on the Natural Law* discusses the importance of the *ex post facto* protection as given in *Calder v. Bull*, 3 Dall. at 387-89. "The Supreme Court discussed the natural law issue in *Calder v. Bull*, where it held that the prohibition of *ex post facto* laws, in Article I, Section 10, applied only to penal laws and did not protect property rights from retroactive interference.

Justice Samuel Chase ... stated that if a state legislature did enact a genuinely *ex post facto* law, **it would be invalid** even if it had not been prohibited by the Constitution of the United States or the constitution of the state ...

✔ A law that punished a citizen for an innocent action or, in other words, for an act which, when done, was in violation of no existing law;

✔ **a law that destroys, or impairs, the lawful private contracts of citizens**;

✔ a law that makes a man a judge in his own cause;

✔ or **a law that takes property from A and gives it to B**:

It is against all reason and justice, for a people to entrust a legislature with *such* powers; and, therefore, it cannot be presumed that they have done it. The genius ... of our State Governments, amount to a prohibition of such acts of legislature; and the general principles of law and reason forbid them.... To maintain that our Federal, or State, Legislature possesses such powers, if they had not been expressly restrained would in my opinion be a political heresy, altogether inadmissible in our free republican governments." (17:117-119)

Justice Chase explains: "...There are certain vital principles in our free Republican governments, which will determine and **overrule** an apparent and **flagrant abuse of legislative power**; as to authorize manifest injustice by positive law; or **to take away that security for personal liberty, or private property, for the protection whereof the government was established**. An *act* of the Legislature (for I cannot call it a law) contrary to the great first principles cannot be considered a rightful exercise of legislative authority ..." (17:118)

Man, through the legislative and judicial processes, is given the "right" to pass laws, but **these laws can be skewed by personal biases.** For example, would a constitutional amendment be valid that would "... require the **confiscation without trial or compensation of the property** of members of a particular race or religion or to reinstate slavery ..."? (17:116, 117)

Double jeopardy:
The judicial system classifies marriage as a contract, then "litigates" to dissolve its *created* "marriage-contract."
Is murder too harsh a reality?

What is the reality of dissolution? My personal perception is that it is the murder of a marriage which takes place in a trial without a jury, with no *due process*, with no recognizable defense for the Defendant in the midst of onlooking court officials, with no grieving or remorse by those partaking in the "execution." Some may take offense at the term *murder*, but what does the court say dissolution means? It is the act of terminating a marriage: "The bonds of marriage are forever severed/cut apart/dissolved."

Additionally, in a family lawsuit, the Defendant can leave the "death chamber" with accompanying punitive charges including thousands of dollars of financial indebtedness to attorneys, be stripped "naked" of his/her marital status, divested of rights to an intact family with its many former associations—friends and relatives who cause fractures as they take sides. The family home is often sold and joint businesses and retirement whisked away. Lifetime family resources are up for the highest bidder—he who can afford the best legal defense. All this, and it's not considered a criminal act! **In any other arena these atrocities would be considered criminal, but because they are done under color of law —No-fault—they are protected and encouraged!**

> **In any other arena these acts would be considered criminal acts.**

> **Resolution becomes lies, deceit, anger, hostility, and divisions ...**

Doors are opened for children to become pawns of manipulation with many in their adult years turning to model the Plaintiff's behavior as succeeding generations, in increasing numbers, head for the guillotine of the divorce court.

Children are deprived of learning from parents to come together (as one) and work out differences; to forgive; to go *together* to God to bring resolution through the kind of love that circumstances

187

cannot destroy. Instead, resolution is replaced with lies, deceit, anger, hostility, and divisions that set family members, friends, and relatives against one another.

Many who have been legally charged to protect contracts and marriage have forgotten their *function.* Attorney Sharpe wrote that the Fort Worth Court of Civil Appeals, writing in 1941 in *Pappas v. Pappas* on the obligation of government to marriage, decreed:

> **... the State and society have an interest in keeping intact all such contracts [marriage] and in protecting them to the fullest extent.** (15:5)

> There are acts which the Federal, or State, Legislature cannot do, without exceeding their authority ... which will [be a] flagrant abuse of legislative power ... to take away that security for personal liberty, or private property, for the **protection** whereof the government was established. (17:118)

A party to a contract knows the duration.

Two important aspects of any contract are its obligations and duration. Unlike parties of a marriage-*covenant*, parties to a "marriage-*contract*" are not privy to its duration. The husband and wife are also unclear about their obligations to sustain this governmental "contract."

In *The Economics of Divorce* by Lenore J. Weitzman, Weitzman reported that 100 percent of the respondents to a survey indicated they believed their marriage would be a lifelong partnership in which they would share all acquired property and income, in all tangible and intangible aspects: "Whereas the traditional law sought to deliver a system of moral justice and which rewarded the 'good' spouse and punished the 'bad' one, the *No-fault Law ignores the spouse's moral history* ..." (4:1249, 1186)

> **100% believed their marriage would be a lifelong partnership in which they would share all acquired property and income, in all tangible and intangible aspects.**

It's the fourth quarter and someone changes the rules without telling all the team members.

Those who enter into a marriage-covenant (or as the courts define it, "contract") expect the terms and rules will remain the same throughout the life of the agreement. **There is an assumed, unprotected *right* to the benefits that should be an inseparable part of the *continuation* of the "marriage-contract."** This includes not only all tangible and intangible aspects of the marriage, but the "compound interest" that accrues during the lifetime of the parties to the contract. However, as mentioned previously, **the government empowers the Plaintiff to unilaterally have the rules changed**—even during the last quarter of the Defendant's life—and removes most of these rights.

Few, especially women, know the machinations the law has to destroy their financial future. Women usually put their economic well-being in the hands of attorneys. Some attorneys might be more interested in getting the divorce over and collecting a large share of the family assets in professional fees than in fighting against what the wife does not know may be coming down the track:

- ✔ poverty,
- ✔ continual struggles to sustain herself,
- ✔ a drastic change in lifestyle,
- ✔ no retirement,
- ✔ no insurance, and
- ✔ heartaches that cannot be measured on a Richter scale!

Additionally, Defendants may, unintentionally, enable their spouses to cripple their financial future because they are emotionally shell-shocked and unable to see things factually. Thus they become passive in making prudent decisions regarding their future economic well-being.

This book has been written, not by someone who has legal expertise or advice, but by one who has experienced, firsthand, the horrors of being forced into our court system, stripped of dignity, family, and assets; burdened with thousands of dollars of debt, abused and manipulated by the power of legal procedures and seeing both the government and my husband walk away with impunity. This same government also assisted the Plaintiff in transferring some of our family assets, both tangible and intangible, to another "contractual wife."

> **Defendants may, unintentionally, enable their spouses to cripple their financial well-being.**

In Weitzman's book, *The Divorce Revolution*, she gives statistical evidence of these abuses that are so widespread and rampant in our courts. In her ten-year research study on the economics of divorce, she found that **many women are impoverished after a divorce, partially because the court overlooks major assets of the marriage, often ignoring the wife's inequity of professional position, especially if she has chosen not to become the primary breadwinner.**

The husband's **career assets**, including his salary, pension, health insurance, and potential earning power are huge factors in his future economic well-being which are **stripped away from the wife who has been a partner while these assets were accrued.**

Weitzman shows how, today, intangibles are equally as important as the physical assets acquired and accumulated during the marriage.

> The husband's career assets, including his salary, pension, health insurance, and potential earning power are huge factors in <u>his</u> future economic well-being which are stripped away from the wife who has been a partner while these assets were developed.

Dr. Weitzman's book is a must-read for all who receive those dreaded divorce papers. Their lives will be changed forever:

> The wife may abandon or postpone her own education ... to put him through school or help him get established ... she may quit her job to move with him ... she may use her own job skills—skills that would command a salary if she were working for someone else—to help advance his career. (9:129)

Whether the wife types his papers, perhaps during graduate school, or cares for the children while he is developing his career, she is contributing and has become **an indivisible part** of his career. Again, Weitzman points out:

> A career that is developed in the course of a marriage is just like the income that is earned or the real property that is accumulated during the marriage. (9:111, 112)

In America, we have a changing picture of wealth and property. Families no longer have the family farm as accumulated property. Instead, **the ability to earn future income has become a major asset which needs to be divided "equitably" upon divorce.**

Retirement and pensions are large areas of asset accumulation that are often overlooked or avoided during the judicial process. In *Smith v. Lewis*, the California Supreme Court affirmed a malpractice judgment of $100,000 against an attorney who failed to properly represent the wife's best interest in her husband's federal and state military retirement benefits. (9:116)

The ability to earn future income has become a major asset which needs to be divided "equitably" upon divorce.

In the civil suit of *Brumbaugh v. Brumbaugh*, some of the above benefits and others mentioned in Weitzman's book were **"begged of the court," but denied**: "... health insurance, to include major medical and comprehensive, continuance of group life insurance, joint investments and the husband's retirement funds, assessment of the wife's efforts toward the marriage partnership and contributions, direct or indirect, to the husband's accumulations ..." (18:5, 6)

Wetizman cited the fact that **Florida is one of the states that requires consideration be given in support awards for spouse's contributions to a professional degree in property awards.** (9:129) And yet this did not happen in *Brumbaugh v. Brumbaugh*!

Finish the Dissertation, then bring forth the son!
"Ex" the spouse, "ex" the children—nay, nay!

My husband, like many other spouses, earned both his master's and doctorate degrees during the early years of our marriage. I helped to supplement his awarded scholarship when we moved from Michigan to Georgia to attend graduate school by babysitting, sewing for our family and others, and teaching sewing classes in our student housing apartment. I typed my husband's doctoral dissertation. He could not graduate without this being submitted.

Like many young couples beginning their life together, we were short of finances. But also like many other young couples, we pulled together, each helping the other toward a more secure financial future. As we had no money to buy a typewriter nor hire a typist to prepare the manuscript, Doug made arrangements for me to use a typewriter on an upper floor in the mathematics education department at the University of Georgia. I can't remember which floor but there were a LOT of stairs to climb.

Why were the stairs significant? It was because we were anxiously awaiting the birth of our second child. His arrival was to be any day, but we knew unless I finished the paper, Doug could not graduate. These were the days when the University did not have elevators in this building, so I had to huff and puff up the stairs "carrying" our soon-to-be-born, 9-pound 4-ounce blessing.

Getting the dissertation typed was a family project. I packed food for us. We took a cot for our four-year-old daughter to sleep on while I typed into the wee hours of the night. Day after day, night after night, this was the routine until finally it was finished. Our son had been patient, waiting until the manuscript was completed—although he had been jumping rope in my womb for several months! We came home late that final night, praising the LORD that the dissertation was ready for the printing press.

We tucked our sleeping sweet daughter into her bed. Doug went to bed. I stayed up to finish a new wardrobe of clothes that I had started for Shawn's doll so she would have something special to open while I was in the hospital. I wrapped them hurriedly as I was feeling labor pains coming quite regularly. Finished! "Thanks, God, for giving me time to finish the doll clothes!" Time to wake Doug. "It's time to go to the hospital," I announced, as I gently touched his arm to awaken him. Exhausted, but excited, I entered the delivery room and within a few hours we had another blessing from the LORD, our precious son.

Tragically the courts are blind to the fact that there is no equitable distribution which can divide years of faithfulness, partnering with life, the creation and nurturing of the children. **The children, like the tangible and intangible assets acquired during the marriage, cannot be equitably divided.** They are an immutable

The stroke of the guillotine cannot truly divide what is indivisible.

part. The stroke of the guillotine cannot truly divide what is indivisible. The children are not ex-children, the parties to the "marriage-contract" are not "ex," nor are the assets created as a part of the "contract."

They are not *ex post facto*, they are "in facto"!

I have a valid contract and covenant.

As Attorney Sharpe states: "No court should ever be permitted to grant a divorce contrary to the vows of the parties. The parties have the **right** to know the basis upon which their marriage stands. Civil government should support rather than destroy attendant rights pertaining to this voluntary covenant of the parties as to the duration of the marriage and agreed upon grounds for dissolution; e.g. 'until death us do part.'" (15:9)

Sharpe further summarizes the elements of *due process* that No-fault Divorce violates: **"The person sued for divorce can never establish a lack of merit in the suit or a legal bar to it. This is the only claim in an American court where this happens and is the explanation for why one of these claims cannot be defeated."** "No-fault divorce is the only claim recognized in the state courts of the United States where the *due process* clause for protecting a fundamental right, which marriage has been found to be by the United States Supreme Court, is ignored and patently disregarded. In fact, a divorce suit is the only one where the moving party cannot lose, if the parties are married." (See page 277.)

Our government is destroying our societal foundation—the family unit. The legislature loses its focus when it defines marriage as a contract but, in practice, denies constitutional protections and civil rights normally afforded under contractual law. Our judicial system loses its focus when it **litigates** WITHOUT weighing, **equally,** EVIDENCE *against* a "marriage-contract" from **both** parties.

The Trojan Horse has been pulled into our legislative and judicial systems, our homes, and our churches. It's in your hands. Are YOU committed to fight against infringements to our Constitution and its attendant Amendments?

We **cannot** *force* our loved ones to return, but we can continue to fight for our families and remain faithful to our vows. Are YOU committed to that to which you have agreed "for better, for worse, in sickness, in health, for richer, for poorer—until death you do part"?

"... Yet [still] is she thy companion,
and the wife of thy covenant."
Malachi 2:14

Chapter 9

IS IT OVER? HOW COULD I HAVE MISSED ONE OF THE PROCEDURES?

Back in our family home. It was May 1985. What was happening in our lives? My husband no longer had a desire to have control of our home, so I was permitted to return. He had built a new house and taken occupancy during the divorce proceedings.

My friends drove with me back to "Home Drive." Oh, the anticipation in my heart. The excitement of the moment to turn the corner and see our white house with black shutters peering through its surrounding canopy of trees and foliage. I could almost hear the angels singing! Finally. Open the back door and walk in once again. Jorgy, Grace, and I bowed our heads and held hands as we gave thanks and rededicated this home to the LORD.

But ... there were some challenges I had not expected. The house that represented our home had been treated like our marriage—abused, badly beaten. Filthy and with many items damaged or broken, its identity had been obliterated. It had been left for dead as had been our marriage. It had lost its identity. My friend Lois' white glove test for cleanliness never had such a challenge! But ... blessings. She and several other friends came by with their vacuums, cleaning supplies, and tools to help clean and restore the inside, repairing things that were broken. Three days later, we all began to see quite a transformation.

The garage and exterior were in much the same disorder. Owen came by with a trailer to load the debris out of the garage, clear the driveway, and remove the jungle that had grown up around the exterior of the house.

In one of the closets, I found the family picture that I had asked for at our *Supplemental Final Hearing* on May 29, 1985. My husband had testified that it had fallen off the wall and torn. It was quite an unusual tear! My picture had been **cut** out of the center of our family portrait. What a shock to see this. I was not prepared for the sharp arrows that pierced my heart.

It has taken me almost a quarter of a century to objectively reflect upon that "distorted" family picture that I once held in my shaking hands and viewed through tear-filled eyes. Looking back over these many years in the "Schoolmaster's Hand," I now understand some of the good that has come out of my "court-ship" experiences.

Yes, today I "see" with different eyes—eyes that witness how deceived man can be. Perhaps he thinks that he can cut a person out of his life with a pair of scissors or can wave a piece of paper, like a magician, and seemingly make a marriage disappear. Legislators with their power to create laws have given judges the authority to drop a gavel and say, "The bonds of this marriage are dissolved." Snip, snip, as they pronounce death on what is vital to the existence of our society and turn their backs on the aberration they have created as they say, "Case dismissed! I wash my hands of this. No one is at fault."

> **Man thinks that he can wave a piece of paper, like a magician, over a marriage and make it disappear.**

However, our judges, legislators, attorneys, and many others who buy into and promote the destructive belief that divorce is inevitable and proclaim that no one is at fault are themselves "at fault." Even though they try to wash their hands, none are "guiltless" who say, "The marriage between Douglas K. Brumbaugh and Judith A. Brumbaugh

—and the millions of others—is dead, is dissolved because it is irretrievably broken."

Judicial tyranny can happen—even with legal counsel.

Let's review information presented earlier in this book regarding Doug and my jointly owned properties and add some pertinent details. The purpose is to point out that I believe the court showed prejudice not only when I was without legal counsel, but also when I had an attorney. Because of such often-unchecked judicial power, Defendants, some men, but mostly women, are being **stripped of assets and future earning power that are an immutable part of the "marriage-contract."**

I remind the reader of the facts about the **widespread financial disasters engendered by No-fault Divorce and its bias to empower Plaintiffs (male or female) in all aspects of the dissolution**. This is especially exacerbated when the Plaintiff's financial resources greatly outweigh those of the Defendant, enabling him to retain superior legal counsel and defense. Add to this a trial without jury in which the judge makes decisions based upon laws which, at the time of our "legal dissolution," required dissolution of the "marital-contract" when the powerful words, "irretrievably broken" were spoken AND accords him the judicial power to further dismantle the marriage by subjectively distributing the assets and dividing the children—all that has been a part of a bilateral "marriage-contract."

What appears on the surface to be an equitable distribution of the assets rarely is because of **two major undivided assets that are almost always ignored by the courts**: (1) the future earning power of the Plaintiff, that earning power which was developed and nurtured with the help of his spouse and (2) his potential ability to disguise his true tangible and intangible wealth during the proceedings for the *Trial for Dissolution.*

This latter "hidden" asset is possible partially because the Plaintiff has the element of surprise in the situation. His decision to legally end the marriage is often known only to him for a period of time prior to the filing, allowing him to carefully preplan for his new "single" status.

If there is any doubt about the **inequitable** division of **all** assets, consider the empirical evidence from Weitzman's ten-year, statistically documented study reprinted from the UCLA LAW REVIEW, August 1981: "The Economics of Divorce: Social and Economic Consequences of Property, Alimony and Child Support Awards":

> ... Divorce is a financial catastrophe for most women. In just one year they experience a dramatic decline in income and a calamitous drop in their standard of living. Women and children almost immediately become impoverished. **Men experienced a 42% <u>improvement</u> in the post-divorce standard of living, while women experienced a 73% loss.** (4:1251, 1252)

How does one think this might happen? **Did the Plaintiff suddenly become an overnight entrepreneurial giant while his wife was magically morphed into a major sloth?** No. Consider two additional newspaper reports to help you glean some of the actions of our courts that do not give "equal justice for all."

> **Did the Plaintiff suddenly become an overnight entrepreneurial giant while his wife morphed into a sloth?**

The first concerns the 32-year "marriage-contract" of an Orlando couple that was dissolved by the state. Five children had been birthed from their union. The couple together had built a very successful business and acquired an upper income family home with many other tangible and intangible assets. "**After this divorce, Mrs. Wescott has gone from prosperity to misfortune** ... [The court] issued a 1981 divorce order which awarded the husband custody of two minor children, the home, and the family business."

The wife accumulated over $100,000 in attorney fees. Apparently, she eventually was awarded the home but had to sell it because of the attorney fees and/or had to sell it to divide the family assets as indicated by the subheading of the newspaper article: "**Judge orders woman to sell couple's house.**" "**... divorce laws allow judges to make rulings that leave many women in financial ruin.**" And this is considered *due process*!

It's not difficult to see the potentially disadvantaged position females (and some males) may face under the gavel of a judge who has almost unrestrained "discretion" to make **subjective decisions concerning the "division"** of the children and family assets.

> **Legislators have given judges almost unrestrained, unchecked power to make subjective decisions concerning the marriage.**

Admittedly, there ARE judges who do not take advantage of their powerfully vague and subjective discretionary gavel—a part of the No-fault Law passed by the state legislatures, but there are many who do so as is apparent by the post-divorce statistics.

Another newspaper article, "Divorcees forced onto the dole," gives more examples of our nation's judicial injustices perpetrated under color of the No-fault Divorce Law. "'Why are we forced to live on taxpayers' money, when our **husbands may be multi-millionaires?**' asked Sinnikka Lawless, a **mother** with two children at home forced to **live on a pittance** in a divorce settlement."

In 1985, Mrs. Lawless spent $14,000 on five lawyers. Initially, she was given $200 a week for two children plus $75 weekly alimony and mortgage payments by her husband, a dentist, who was reportedly earning $60,000. He appealed, and a judge slashed her payments from $275 to $160, and made HER pay the mortgage!

"'This was done without a hearing, without any testimony in a five minute meeting in the judge's chambers with the attorneys,' she recalls. At the time, she was earning $114 a week." [The reality of divorce proceedings is that many vital decisions may be made **between the judge and the attorneys behind closed doors**.]

"So she went bankrupt. 'My heat and electricity were cut off,' she says. 'I had to go on food stamps, get Medicaid, and energy assistance.'"

Examples could fill volumes with such abuses that have resulted from the inequities running rampant in our courts as a part of the nonjury trials for dissolutions.

Financially poor; yet spiritually nourished: A crate of corn and 70 dollars!

What was happening in my personal life? The focus became: Money, money, where am I going to get funds to keep going? I hardly have enough to put gas in my car. Where am I to get money for filing fees? My freezer was empty except for some ice cube trays. I had been taking bread sandwiches to work. One day while at work a friend asked as we were eating lunch: "What kind of sandwich do you have today?" "Oh it's just something I put together," I replied. "What do you have?" and I quickly moved on to a business matter for the day. What I had was a bread sandwich with nothing between the slices.

On another occasion a friend invited me over for supper. She lived in a gorgeous home and had all the accoutrements for which one could ask. The table was so attractively set with china and silver. I asked what I could do to help prepare the meal and what it was that smelled so wonderful.

The hostess told me that I could fill the glasses with ice from the freezer. When I opened the freezer door, I almost had a cardiac arrest! There was so much food, it almost fell out when I reached in to get the ice. I had lost sight of what a full refrigerator looked like! She told me that we were having Welsh Rarebit. I thought, "Oh yum, some kind of cooked rabbit." This old country girl didn't know it was a gourmet dish that had no rabbit content! I was glad I hadn't vocalized my thoughts before this wonderful delicacy was served.

> **When I opened the freezer door, I almost had a cardiac arrest! The "rabbit" was Welsh!**

I'm sure I enjoyed the meal much more than she—and in a lot of different ways totally unknown to her!

Now back to my real world. On my way home from work one afternoon, I saw a sign for sweet corn. Corn on the cob is one of my favorite "delicacies." My flesh was tempted to stop to buy a dozen ears, but I also knew that the gauge on my gas tank was demanding that it get "fed" before I drove too many more miles. I arrived home not having made either of the above purchases. "Okay, God, what do I do?"

I can remember exactly where I was standing when I was, once again, about to challenge God with the "impossible"! I was in front of the kitchen sink looking out the window.

"Now God, you know that I don't have any food in the refrigerator. You know that I have $5. I need gas for my car and food for my stomach. I know you showed me the sweet corn on my way home, and you know how I love corn on the cob. However, if I buy the corn, then I won't have money to put gas in my car. If I buy the gas, I will have nothing to eat."

> I was having a pity party and "drinking in depression," not with drugs or alcohol, but with negative thoughts!

I had shared these needs with no one else. At that almost EXACT moment there came a knock on my back door. It was my friend Sylvia from across the street. Many days she came by and pulled me out of bed when I was having a pity party and "drinking in depression," not with drugs or alcohol, but with negative thoughts!

I could not believe my eyes. Guess what she was holding? **An entire crate of corn!** Not only that but she said that her sister had given her $70 to give to me. Can you believe that? I was concerned about distributing $5 between gas for my car and a dozen ears of corn. God sent a whole crate of corn and $70.

YUM. Corn for breakfast, corn for lunch, corn for supper!! Yes, my "needs" were being met in new ways that I had not known before!

Another *Supplemental Final Hearing* brought together many "maladministrations"!

Let's return to *Brumbaugh v. Brumbaugh* for a recap. There had been many hearings and depositions which, as time passed, began to hint at some significant differences regarding my husband's income. These discrepancies also appeared to involve some real estate transactions on his part dealing with our jointly held properties. These were not made a part of the "equitable distribution" of assets for the *Supplemental Final Hearing*, May 29, 1985.

This was the hearing where my long-awaited *Motion for Rehearing* concerning our marriage was finally to be **heard**. Our marriage had been **illegally** dissolved April 18, 1984, by a court not having jurisdiction, as the requirement for the necessary corroborating witness had not been met. The April 18 illegal decision became part of the *Final*

Judgment entered June 11, 1984. This judgment included the fraudulent statement: **"Court having taken testimony of a corroborating witness as to residency ..."**

Secondly, my constitutional right to appeal the April 18 dissolution had been brokered by Judge Fuller ON THAT DAY. This date is important because of what I had to agree to do in order to "buy" my constitutional right to appeal the legal dissolution of our marriage. This right to appeal would be earned at the expense of my vacating our home and dismissing my lawyer. Over the course of the next year, I fulfilled **my** part of the verbal contract which caused me extreme emotional pain. May 29, 1985, the day of the *Supplemental Final Hearing* arrived. It was to be the answer to my prayers—the dissolution overturned.

Honorably fulfilling my obligation to our "contract" was so painful in execution that it brought me to the point of not wanting to live. All of the vitality which had sustained me for twelve months rapidly drained from my very being as Judge Fuller uttered the words, "I will not hear the *Motion for Rehearing*." He gave no reason which added to what I perceived was cruel and unusual punishment.

Entering into the aforementioned "contract" resulted in unforeseen fallouts. The consequences of the court-ordered "eviction" from our home were tremendous. This was **not** merely a **structure** to me. This home, once occupied by a closely-knit loving family of four; then by our daughter, our son, and me (abandoned by our father/husband); and then by only our daughter and myself; would now no longer be a part of my life. This change brought with it one of the most excruciating prices I had to pay in my effort to preserve our marriage and our family unit—the estrangement that developed between our children and me once this physical transition took place.

I believe it is important for any spouse who might be forced into an unwanted divorce to be aware of the fact that some spouses initiating such a legal action may have battle plans difficult to assess. They, free from the emotional trauma they've inflicted upon their wife/husband, usually have the clear-headedness needed to strategize. This could include their maneuvering to have a minor child live with them which could give advantages to the Plaintiff—not paying child support and being awarded possession of the home. (**Review page 22, December 28, 1982.**) Even more enlightening, however, is what I discovered twenty years after my court encounters: **the court tries to keep the minor child in the marital home.** This, of course, makes sense if its purpose is to limit the trauma of the child. If, however, the Plaintiff gaining possession of the home will place a wedge between the children and their mother (who in most cases is a Defendant who cannot afford court intercession) then the Courts of Equity which are to adjudicate "equitably" are falling dismally short of their duty.

The Defendant spouse who wants what's best for the children, and may even want to appease her husband hoping for a return to their former life, may readily agree to any request by the father. BEWARE of the possible consequences of such a decision. Under extreme pressure and inwardly sobbing from the inevitable consequences of moving out of our home and away from our children, had I not REFUSED TO AGREE to the divorce decree, our home, I now realize, could have been forever lost to me.

Both children had been with me since the day Doug officially moved out on July 30, 1982 until he suddenly announced to me that he was taking Mike to live with him a couple of months prior to what was to be our *Final Dissolution Hearing* on April 18, 1984. Could other judicial officers at the appellate level not see from my now perspective that some of these court decisions, although legal, may have been "colored" by some hidden details? This is especially puzzling because, according to *Black's Law Dictionary*, a Court of Equity/in Chancery is meant to "render the administration of justice more complete, by affording relief where the courts of law are incompetent to give it ..." (Study page 263.)

Mike had the normal desire of a son to be with his dad. Any time that Doug wanted Mike, there was never any refusal on my part—even when Doug came by with his female friend and the children and their friends to get the boat out of our garage to take them water skiing! Painful? YES! But, **we** cannot change people. I didn't make a scene—I turned around with my broken heart as they drove away and wept. My family ... fractured ... gone.

My court-ordered "eviction" months later resulted in a physical separation from our children that produced an intensely painful estrangement that was pure torture. Along with the confusion brought about by the never-ending question of "Who's right, Dad or Mom?" came a truly bizarre occurrence which greatly exacerbated the already tense atmosphere. For no known reason, once my husband took occupancy of our home, he would no longer allow me to enter it. It also seemed strange to me when someone shared that the judge had ordered Doug to change the locks on the doors and bar the windows. I didn't recall such an order, but the locks were changed and holes were drilled in some of the windows. HUGE carpenter nails were inserted to secure the windows and sliding glass doors. I discovered this was "real" when I moved back into our home. I still have two of the nails! Just what do you think would go on in a child's mind as he saw Dad nailing the windows shut to keep Mom out!! Certainly I wanted to see our children; I loved them more than life itself. Would I force my way in to see them? NEVER! The divorce initiated by my husband would not have my help in adding to the misery he'd already created.

Contact with the children become increasingly fractured and tense. I recall at Christmas that first year, exchanging gifts in the back seat of my car and for our daughter's birthday taking her angel food cake to the back door and not being allowed in to share this with her. Doug didn't inform me of school events. It was embarrassing to have to call the school to find when these were scheduled. I would go for months without having personal time with the children —and rarely any overnights. These experiences continued until I didn't see how I could bear them. But our children were always in my prayers, their welfare utmost in my thoughts, and I worked constantly to be a part of their lives.

What happened with our children is echoed in the sadness of the voices I've heard over the past 20 years each time a hurting spouse has called Restoration of the Family for advice and prayer. The similarity in our personal nightmares enables me to offer them needed empathy.

Again I speak a warning to those of you who may find yourself in an unwanted divorce. As we know, many women do end up raising children alone and on a much lower economic level. **BUT** women who have raised their children alone frequently encounter additional heartaches. Once their daughters, and especially their sons, reach the late teen years they often choose to leave to live with their fathers. Why? It *could* be, in part, that Dad is the one who often has the financial resources to buy the teens designer clothes, cars, take them on vacations, and provide recreational activities. What teen wouldn't enjoy such luxuries?

Moms, please don't beat yourself up if and when this happens. Sons, as do many daughters, prefer at times to be with their fathers. That's a desire that God put into them. And that's why God has the best plan: **This most perfect system of joint custody was invented by God and called marriage.** (Review page 41.) If Dad has financial advantages, children—just as do adults—tend to navigate in the direction of abundance, fun, and permissiveness. But remember, as with your brokenheartedness, your children's forced decision to choose between you and your spouse is tearing them apart—even if they mask it so well that you cannot discern it. Sadly, they become pawns of adult irresponsibility, selfishness, and a court system that is not designed, in practice, to be a Court of Equity/in Chancery.

Imagine the confusion that must have taken place in their minds when they were put in the position of having to choose one parent over the other. **That's like asking someone which arm they'd rather have amputated. Or which eye they'd rather have gouged out.** Obviously, the answer would be, "Neither one!" (See page 78.)

Both of our adult children now live great distances from me. Communicating with them regularly via e-mail and phone brings me great joy. The visits that do occur and the closeness that envelops me at these times help to erase the painful loss of those teen years.

The section that I have just shared with the reader is being inserted after a prolonged and tear-filled, emotional struggle within myself. Readers of this book's drafts have urged me to include more about my family members. I have steadfastly resisted, knowing that our children have suffered more than enough for their parents' legal divorce. What I've shared is but a minute portion of what occurred. I do so only to be of help and encouragement to those who, like me, might find themselves leading a life they could never have imagined as they took their vow of love and commitment—"for better for worse, until death us do part."

Unbelievably, a meaningful coincidence occurred as I was inserting this painful section over which I have wrestled. Our son, now a mature, married, young man, called and with a tear-filled broken voice shared with me that he was on the way to the airport to leave on one of his many mission trips out of the country. He was taking with him hundreds of dollars of needed items he and his wife Jennifer had purchased for the people he would be helping. This included many pairs of eyeglasses. Mike told of some of the experiences of the shopping trip, including miraculously putting in the shopping cart enough to use all but three CENTS of the money he had. How special it was to have him share this with me. I talked about the fact that he would be helping the people to see in a dual way: spiritually and physically! Mike could barely utter, "Yes, Mom, that's true." Our children—Shawn, Mike and Jennifer— are such blessings!

So Moms AND Dads, children DO grow up, mature, and see things as they are (as do some spouses who become sidetracked "in their youth"). Your children love both of you. (I know that I have perhaps short-changed some Dads that have experienced some of these things. You, too, equally feel such pain. Please forgive me, but 95 percent of the people with whom I deal regarding the children have been Moms.)

Legal gymnastics—are you prepared?

Through this series of legal gymnastics I endured what I considered to have been an egregious violation of my human rights and denial of equal justice guaranteed under the First Amendment, et al. Just as with the Colonists who had sustained numerous assaults from the King of England, thus birthing the Declaration of Independence which listed said abuses, we should not be experiencing them again today, but "… in every stage of these oppressions … [I, too,] … was answered only by repeated injury."

DISSOLUTION OF THE MARRIAGE and MOTION FOR REHEARING—the rights of the Defendant ignored in both issues.

Did I, at the time of writing my *Motion for Rehearing,* know how to express *legally* what could have been written to preserve what could have given someone criminally charged equal representation and protection of the laws?

Hardly, when, at that time, I was confused on the difference between a Plaintiff and a Defendant! And certainly didn't know specifics about constitutional issues! Against the court's series of legal gymnastics, not even Representative John Bingham's Fourteenth Amendment for **equal protection of the laws** could reach down to a housewife wanting to preserve the institution of marriage. (Bingham: 12:63)

Life, Liberty, and Property?

A Notice of Appeal regarding the May 29, 1985 *Supplemental Final Hearing* had been prepared prior to the hearing. It was filed with the Fifth District Court of Appeal immediately following the trial. Attorney Durant had also filed, on May 17, 1985, a Lis Pendens against all properties owned by Doug and me to protect our jointly owned assets from being transferred.

A *Motion to Stay* was also filed on my behalf by Attorney Durant. This was to:

... enjoin any of the parties to this action from transferring, disposing, selling, assigning, or in any other way, attempting or encumbering any of the jointly held real property of the parties disposed of by this Court in its Supplemental Final Judgment dated the 29th of May, 1985. In support of this Motion the Wife would show unto the Court that she has contemporaneously herewith filed her Notice of Appeal ... The Wife has taken an appeal from this Court's Supplemental Final Judgment challenging the legal correctness of the award to the Husband of the real property awarded to him by this Court.

The property listed in the *Order to Stay* referred to real property that was still jointly and legally owned by Douglas and Judith Brumbaugh: the family home, an attached lot, and our commercial property. (See page 211.)

> *"It is thereupon ORDERED AND ADJUDGED That said Motion to Stay is hereby granted and neither DOUGLAS K. BRUMBAUGH nor JUDITH A. BRUMBAUGH shall in any manner or way sell, dispose of, pledge, assign, transfer, or attempt to divest themselves of any of their interest to the following described parcels of real property."* **The legal description of our home and attached lot plus our commercial property were listed.**

Judge Fuller honored this Motion to keep either of the parties from transferring real property. Below is part of the *Order to Stay* issued by the court. Carefully read the *Order to Stay*. It appears on the surface as if Judge Fuller was finally giving the Defendant in this case some constitutional equal rights/protections. However, two major facts greatly skewed such an erroneous conclusion and show why I was left with the inescapable perception that oppression continued. As you read the *Order to Stay,* notice the stipulations I was required to meet:

> ORDER TO STAY
>
> This order shall become effective upon the filing and posting of a good and sufficient supersedeas bond by the Wife in the principal amount of **$17,000.00** on or before the **24th day of June, 1985**, conditioned to pay all costs and damages sustained by the Husband, DOUGLAS BRUMBAUGH, as a result of the Wife taking her appeal in this action from this court's *Supplemental Final Judgment* and the appellate court not reversing the property distribution, but not upon reversal as to any other matters in this appeal.

Incredible, but true!

There are two unbelievable hurdles involved in Judge Fuller's *Order to Stay*. Firstly, the amount. Where would I acquire $17,000 necessary to post the bond? It was legal! But ... ludicrous to require me to pay what to me was a huge sum. The court had empirical evidence that I did not have the financial ability to come up with even $1700. I recently was informed that when a bond is posted, the insurance company only requires the person posting the bond to come up with ten percent. At this time, my finances were so bleak that I was taking bread sandwiches to work and had nothing but ice cubes in the freezer!

I again felt I was being required to buy my right for legal action. But even beyond that, consider the dates. The amount was due on the same day the order was signed, June 24, 1985. How could I respond to something I had not yet received! Had I been a criminal, perhaps I would have been protected by the Eighth Amendment:

Excessive bail shall not be required, nor excessive fines imposed ... nor cruel and unusual punishments inflicted. (Amendment Eight)

It was continually being reinforced in my mind that the State of Florida was sending a mixed message concerning the purpose of No-fault. It was **saying** the purpose of No-fault is to "preserve the integrity of marriage and to safeguard meaningful family relationships." **But, I felt that the purpose of the law had become, in my case, one of formalities and procedures, manipulation and control, destruction and annihilation. A law seemingly nondiscriminatory on its face may be grossly discriminatory in its practical application: This is No-fault.**

Continuing with the review of what I perceived to be questionable activities dealing with our jointly held properties, it was later discovered that, at the time the *Order to*

Stay was signed (**June 24**, 1985), the court had not been informed by the Plaintiff that he had quietly contracted to trade our still jointly owned vacant lot in partial payment for a property on which he had commissioned his personal friend (a realtor and builder) to construct a house.

It was on **April 9, 1985** that Doug signed a legally binding contract to purchase a house and lot from his friend Toby. This was evidenced by the legal agreement signed by Doug and Toby and, sadly, they involved our minor son, Mike, by having him sign as a witness on this contract. In a Warranty Deed prepared by Attorney Klinger, the lot attached to our home property was transferred from Douglas K. Brumbaugh to Toby Finacher on June 11, 1985.

On **June 14**, 1985, Attorney Klinger prepared and executed a mortgage on the completed house. This was the mortgage which was applied for prior to the May 29 hearing for which my husband submitted in writing his financial status that **differed from the assets** distributed in the *Supplemental Final Hearing* on May 29, 1985. He wrote the following as part of the loan application:

> *Judy has resisted the divorce on a religious basis. She will accept a separation but not a divorce. **She has repeatedly stated that she will sign no property settlement and thus refuses to sign the court mandate.** Hopefully the session on 5/14/85 will settle the issue. I am currently working on two books as an independent consultant ... I will be paid $10,000 upon completion. The second is an 8th grade text ... Contractual arrangements are still being discussed. But I will be paid at least $30 per hour for my work.* (See pages 101 and 102.)

It seemed clear to me that my husband used **our** jointly owned property as his personal asset—as part of the purchase price for a lot and house without my knowledge.

213

During a former trial regarding property distribution when the **attorneys were presenting to the court** who would receive what assets, who would be given our commercial property, and who would retain the house with the lot, Judge Fuller asked the following question:

> JUDGE FULLER: "What you're telling me, basically, is that the home property would include the lot or not include the lot?
> ATTORNEY SIMON: "Would include the lot, either way."

However, during the May 29 hearing, the lot was severed from our home and given to Doug. The reason why: It was needed because of the pending real estate contract using our jointly held lot as a trade that had been made with it **prior** to this hearing.

More motions continued from Attorney Simon. The fear that I lived in was ever building from all these legal court-related activities. On July 10, 1985, he filed a *Motion for Indirect Contempt* which added to the threatening environment in which I felt I was being encased.

Comes now the Former Husband, Douglas K. Brumbaugh, by and through his undersigned attorney, and moves to hold the Former Wife in contempt of this Court, and would show:

1. On May 17, 1985, the Former Wife filed a Lis Pendens against all properties owned by the parties which was the subject of an equitable distribution of the assets.
2. On June 4, 1985, the Court discharged and dissolved the Lis Pendens.

---

3. On May 31, 1985, the Former Wife caused to be filed a Motion for Stay based upon a supersedeas bond being filed.

4. On June 24, 1985, the Court granted the Motion for Stay and the Order was conditioned upon the Former Wife posting a supersedeas bond in the amount of $17,000.

5. The Former Wife did not post a supersedeas bond, and therefore the order granting the stay has become moot.

6. The Former Wife then, in an attempt to avoid this Court's order which granted the Motion to Stay, but which required the posting of a supersedeas bond, submitted a document entitled, "Public Notice of Appeal" Filed on Following Property: "to Bowles Realty [my husband was trying to sell our commercial building to this firm] and the law firm of Klinger and Friends, Esquires" [the law firm which made the property transfers for my husband]. The reason for the Former Wife filing said document was apparently to create a cloud on the title of the properties ...

7. The attached "Public Notice of Appeal" attempts to avoid the failure to post a supersedeas bond, and to do so without color of law.

WHEREFORE, it is respectfully requested that this Court find the Former wife in contempt, require the Former Wife to submit to the Court any papers she intends to distribute as related to the Court's rules ...

It appeared that my husband did not have clear title to dispose of our real property which continued to be jointly held. Attorney Simon several months later—on **August 22, 1985**—filed a *Motion to Appoint Special Master to Sign Deeds to Real Property:*

> *1. This Court entered a Supplemental Final Judgment of Dissolution of Marriage dated May 29, 1985.*
> *2. The Supplemental Final Judgment contained provisions requiring the Former Wife to transfer certain properties to the Former Husband and the Former Husband to transfer certain properties to the Former Wife.*
> *3. The Former Wife has refused to execute a conveyance transferring her interest in the properties awarded to the Former Husband.*
> *4. The Former Husband is in the process of attempting to sell one of the parcels of property. However, because a notice of appeal has been filed by the Former Wife, and because the Former Wife has prepared a document called **Notice of Appeal** and submitted the document to prospective purchasers of the property, the Former Husband has been unable to sell the property awarded to him.*
> *5. Some title companies will not write title insurance because of the Notice of Appeal that is currently filed, even though there is no stay order or supersedeas bond precluding the transfer of the properties.*
> *6. The real properties in question are as follows: (the home property with lot and commercial building were listed.)*
> *Wherefore, it is respectfully requested that a special master be appointed to execute a Quit-claim deed,*

nunc pro tunc, as of the date of the Supplemental *Final Judgment of Dissolution of Marriage* ...

Almost a year later ...

May 8, 1986, Attorney Simon, my husband's attorney, wrote the letter reproduced in part below to my attorney. Attorney Durant had also on **May 8,** 1986, met with me and told me that he would no longer be representing me as of May 8, 1986. Note what I perceived to be an underlying legal threat in the bolded sentence. It did just that—frightened me and caused me to worry about what he was going to do since I had no intentions of signing over our family assets.

May 8, 1986

Sid Durant, Esq.
448 S. Uturn Street
Mayberry, FL

RE: Brumbaugh

Dear Mr. Durant:

... Enclosed are two Quit-claim deeds to be executed by Judith Brumbaugh. Please have Mrs. Brumbaugh execute the aforementioned deeds in recordable form ...

*In the event Mrs. Brumbaugh fails to execute the documents referred to above, please let me know and **I will determine what procedure to follow next, and my client's position** ...*
Billy Simon

Attorney Durant sent me two letters dated May 9, 1986. One is reproduced on page 218 regarding the Quit-claim deeds. The other was his letter confirming the fact that he would no longer represent me.

Dear Judy:

I enclose herewith copy of letter dated May 8, 1986 along with Quit-claim deeds I have received from Attorney Billy Simon for you to sign. This is for you to decide what to do with ... I understand you have filed a Motion for Rehearing in the Fifth District Court of Appeal. I would request that you do give me a copy of that Motion for Rehearing.

Sincerely,
Attorney Durant

The two Quit-claim deeds were for the lot adjoining our home property and for our commercial property. Notice this was a **year after** the real estate transactions had been executed by a second attorney that Doug had hired for this purpose, Attorney Klinger. I signed neither deed.

I didn't (and don't) agree with the government judicially stealing (from a layman's perception) our marital properties, but most of all, for putting the gavel down on our 22-year marriage—and without jurisdiction to do so.

My husband's attorney tried to stop the appeal.

Let's return to my appeal that had been filed with the Fifth District Court. My husband and his attorney appeared to me to utilize procedural extremes to hinder the appeal and to put up a steady stream of roadblocks both to discourage and prevent me from further fighting to preserve our marriage. Attorney Simon filed a *Motion to Dismiss* the appeal. The brief being attacked was one that Attorney Durant (with my assistance in research and typing) had prepared before he withdrew from my case.

On page 219 and 220 are some of the reasons Attorney Simon wrote in defense of having my Appeal denied. My brief was to preserve our family and its contractual rights, including our marital properties.

The Appellee, DOUGLAS K. BRUMBAUGH by and through his undersigned attorney, moves to strike the brief of the Appellant for failure to comply with Rule 9.210, Florida Rules of Appellate Procedure, and would show:

AS TO STYLE AND CONTENT

A. Facts:

1. The Appellant has served her initial brief in this matter on the 26th day of July, 1985. The Appellant's brief contains **margins repeatedly extending to less than one inch**, in violation of Rule 9.210 (a)(2), Florida Rules of Appellate Procedure.

2. The Appellant's **brief is fifty-five pages**, not including the cover page which is in violation of Rule 9.210(a)(5), Florida Rules of Appellate Procedure.

3. The Appellant's brief contains a document **entitled "Index" and not Table of Contents** and does not list the issues presented for review with reference to the pages in the brief, in violation of Rule 9.210(b)(1), Florida Rules of Appellate Procedure.

4. The Appellant's brief contains a Table of Citations, **but does not list the cases alphabetically**, in violation of Rule 9.210(b)(2).

5. [Doug's attorney did not list the numeral 5.]

6. The Appellant's brief contains a list of cases, but does not state the pages of the brief on which each citation appears which is in violation of Rule 9.210(b)(2).

7. The Appellant's brief does not contain a summary of argument and therefore, is in violation of Rule 9.210(b)(4), Florida Rules of Appellate procedure.

8   The Appellant's brief contains statements in its Statement of the Facts without reference to the appropriate pages of the record or transcript as required by Rule 9.210(b)(3). For example, Appellant included a Statement of the Facts and indicated that the Husband was earning $55,000-$60,000 and it is also referred to in the second issue on appeal. Nowhere in the Statement of Facts or in the argument presented is there any reference to the record on appeal or the transcript, indicating that the Husband/Appellee is earning $55,000-$60,000 per year.

B. Argument:

9. In view of the extensive violation of Rule 9.210, Florida Rules of Appellate Procedure, which governs style and contents of briefs, it is respectfully submitted that Appellant's initial brief should be stricken.

10. Furthermore, Appellant should be required to refer to the appropriate pages of the record or transcript for each factual statement alleged.

The Fifth District Court of Appeal denied my husband's *Motion to Strike* my appeal. It appeared, to me, a layman, that Mr. Simon had filed a frivolous Motion, creating more expense for the Defendant and showing that the **focus in a divorce suit is definitely not for the benefit of the family**.

My friend Sharon who had helped with the Bill to amend the No-fault Law continued to assist me as she could. A letter to her verified the fact that the above Motion on my husband's behalf was denied.

Dear Sharon:

Just a quickie. Hope you received my letter okay and the money. Could you please check with

220

your lawyer and get a copy of that case which was denied in Pinellas County? We received notice from the Appellate Court today that Doug's Motion to Dismiss our appeal has been denied. Pray for victory in a reversal ...

The mailman brought the news.

For the next several years, I was busy filing briefs in the Fifth District Court of Appeal, the Florida Supreme Court, and the United States Supreme Court, as well as dealing with issues in the Circuit Court's numerous hearings regarding our marriage and our *Trial for Dissolution.* There were also ongoing issues with my husband.

> **I was filing briefs in four courts as well as dealing with issues with my husband personally.**

A strict chronology will not be possible from here, as I must fast forward and look back with briefs and letters as my guide. My lack of legal training was becoming more of an impediment as I continued to try to advance up the judicial ladder to the top rung, the United States Supreme Court.

I felt that many acts of injustice continued to occur. One such from August 11, 1986 reared its ugly head. This was from the hearing where Attorney Durant was allowed to withdraw from my case and Judge Fuller struck all of the motions I had filed *pro se.* They represented countless hours of research, preparation, filings, stress, and anxiety.

> **This was from the Fifth District Court. It would not hear my Appeal because I had missed one of the legal "barricades" to equal access to our courts.**

Because of all the pending court actions, my daily routine was overshadowed by a fearful watch for the afternoon mail. Trips to the mailbox often brought denials to the many motions I had written and filed. One day brought a denial of very serious ramifications. This was from the Fifth District Court. It would not hear my Appeal because I had missed one of the legal "barricades" to equal access to our courts. Even though my brief was properly filed and within the time limit, the Fifth District Court stated that I did not file a paper called *Designation of Record*. This is how an Appellate Court determines an appeal. They review the record in order to decide whether the Appellant's position is correct or not. It was my understanding that failure to file this form meant my case would be dead, and I could not get beyond this court to try to legally preserve our marriage. What a heartbreak, daily stress, and emotional trauma. The notice I received from the Fifth District Court of Appeal with its devastating order is reproduced below:

IN THE DISTRICT COURT OF APPEAL OF
THE STATE OF FLORIDA
FIFTH DISTRICT

Judith A. Brumbaugh, Appellant,
Douglas K. Brumbaugh, Appellee   Case No. 86-1294
Date: November 21, 1986

BY ORDER OF THE COURT:

ORDERED, *sua sponte* [voluntarily], that Appellant shall file with this Court and show cause, on or before fifteen days from the date hereof, why the above-styled appeal should not be **dismissed for failure to file a record-on-appeal** in the cause.

Frank J. Habershaw, Clerk

Once I recovered emotionally, I began to think. "I know I researched and discovered that the Attorney of Record files an order, *Designation of Record*, to have the records forwarded." I recall the confused, nerve-wracking experience of preparing and filing, **by the required deadline,** this important legal document to request the clerk of the lower court to transmit the record of my case to the Fifth District Court. Once filed, I assumed all the legal loopholes had been satisfied. Not true! The pressure was on once again.

Back to the courthouse ... More research.

I found it. (See abbreviated form on page 224.) The

> **Judge Fuller had not honored the order to forward my court records.**

request had been properly filed for the records to be forwarded **and** in a timely matter. The proper Certificate of Service had been served to my husband's attorney. It was Judge Fuller who had not honored my request to forward my court records. Review the events that happened with Attorney Durant's withdrawal as my legal counsel. Because he quit, I had no legal representation and was again forced to act as my own attorney. Judge Fuller, during this time, refused to give me access to the court. After he signed the Order to allow Attorney Durant to withdraw, he struck my previously filed motions.

Unbelievable! Judge Fuller had voided all legal papers I had filed during the time when I had AGAIN been forced to act for myself. This was starting on May 8, 1986 when Attorney Durant notified me that he would not do any more work for me. At the hearing on August 11 when Fuller said that he was striking all my motions, I didn't realize what his order meant and how it would affect all the legal papers I had filled. Now I found, once again, the **powerful effect of the strike of the gavel against my marriage!**

But ... my correctly filed *Designation of Record* wasn't all I found when I researched my records. I could not believe what was missing from the court record.

Designation of Record filed to forward my case to the Fifth District Court of Appeal

---

IN THE CIRCUIT COURT IN AND
FOR SEMINOLE COUNTY, FLORIDA

IN RE: THE MARRIAGE OF
JUDITH A. BRUMBAUGH
WIFE, DEFENDANT, APPELLANT

                                CASE NO. 82-3055-CA-04-E
V.   *DESIGNATION OF RECORD*

DOUGLAS K. BRUMBAUGH
HUSBAND, PLAINTIFF, APPELLEE

AMENDED DIRECTIONS TO CLERK

DEFENDANT, WIFE, APPELLANT, ACTING for self, the undersigned layperson notifies the Clerk of Court, with Direction to the Clerk, for *Designation of Record*, to prepare and submit the record on appeal, of the above-styled cause, to the Fifth District Court of Appeal, pursuant to appellate rules …

ITEMS WANTED ON DOCKET:
1. Order of April 29, 1986, regards set aside of *Final Judgment of Dissolution of Marriage*, etc.
2. And subsequent pleadings, placed upon docket, explanation of all pleadings, after April 29, 1986, including the order of April 29, 1986.

                            Respectfully submitted,
                            Judith A. Brumbaugh, Acting for self
                            Counsel for Appellant, Layperson

I HEREBY CERTIFY true copy of above furnished by U.S. mail this July 24, 1986 to Billy Simon, Esquire, Attorney for Husband, 355 Wrong Street Orlando, FL by

                            Judith A. Brumbaugh, Acting for self
                            Counsel for Appellant, Layperson

MY TESTIMONY WAS MISSING. How could this be—my evidence at the trial for the legal dissolution of our marriage. It was part of my testimony defending our marriage—titled, "Marriage Not Irretrievably Broken." (See pages 53 and 54.) A written copy of it had been handed to the court clerk to be entered as **evidence** and as my defense of our marriage during the trial. The *Open Court Sheet* from April 18, 1984 verifies these facts.

Parties present and sworn [Douglas Brumbaugh, Petitioner v. Judy Brumbaugh, Respondent] at 3:09 p.m. Petitioner Witness No 1—Douglas Brumbaugh testified at 3:10 p.m. Respondent witness No 1— Judy Brumbaugh testified at 3:19 p.m. ***Entered in evidence as Respondent Exhibit 1 statement prepared by wife*** *... The Court finds marriage irretrievably broken and granted dissolution.*

Disappearing evidence/testimony from the court records seems like a serious offense. But even beyond that, you may have missed a very important issue in this trial to dissolve a twenty-two year marriage. First, as a review, the Florida legislature has stated that one of the purposes of the No-fault Law is:

... to preserve the integrity of marriage and to safeguard meaningful family relationships.

The dissolution under No-fault is based upon the testimony of only one spouse who states that the marriage is irretrievably broken. The Plaintiff's testimony, his opinion, is used as evidence to "convict" the Defendant while the Defendant's testimony is totally ignored for purposes of whom is "awarded" the favored "verdict"/judgment. The Plaintiff's testimony (conclusions) becomes the **evidence** to convince the court that the Defendant is "guilty."

I remind the reader again to contrast this nonjury dissolution trial with one for a criminal offense where the court's decision would be based on facts presented—and **heard**—by **both** sides with an impartial jury to hear the case and render a verdict. Review the trial proceedings for *Brumbaugh v. Brumbaugh*, typical of "equity" trials which impair the obligation of "marriage-contracts." Keep in mind the **legal definition of litigate—any controversy that must be decided upon evidence!** (1:841)

According to the *Open Court Sheet*, Doug's testimony BEGAN at 3:10 p.m. My testimony began at 3:19 p.m. His testimony—**LESS THAN NINE MINUTES.** Our 22-year marriage was "il"legally "dissolved"—dissolution granted—on the basis of my husband's stated opinion that took a matter of a few minutes. His evidence: "Our marriage is irretrievably broken." **With these "magical" words, the court took (usurped) control of our children and our family assets** distributing them subjectively as the presiding judge deemed was equitable.

Back to the strike of the gavel on August 11.

One of the documents which I filed *pro se* that Judge Fuller later struck was my *Directions to the Clerk* to forward my *Record on Appeal*. As mentioned above, it had to be filed within the given time frame or the case would likely die. It was my understanding that there were no "grace" periods. The deadline for this filing was between the time when Attorney Durant notified me he had quit and several months later when he officially withdrew.

On page 227 is the letter from David Berrien's office, Clerk of the Circuit Court, written to the Fifth District Court of Appeal. This was in response to my questioning what had happened after I had notified the Fifth District Court of Appeal that I had properly filed the paperwork to have the record forwarded. It was the lower court who had not honored the request I filed.

December 2, 1986

TO: Fifth District Court of Appeal

In reference to Mrs. Brumbaugh's concern about the Notice of Appeal filed in our office on July 8, 1986, please be advised that Judge Fuller entered an Order on August 11, 1986 striking all pleadings filed by Mrs. Brumbaugh prior to August 11, 1986. Therefore the Record on Appeal was not prepared by this office.

David N. Berrien

Should I have been confused?

Let's review what seems to be a parallel scenario—at least to a layperson. It was April 18, 1984 when this same Judge, Mr. Fuller, had given me the option of accepting his legal dissolution of our marriage or agreeing to vacate our home and dismiss my attorney in order to contest his decision. He gave me time to confer with my attorney before replying to his "verbal contract." I turned to my attorney: "If I don't do this will this be over today? Does it 'end' my marriage?" He said, "Yes, you need to sign." I could not do that—to agree that man could dissolve something that God says cannot be dissolved and of which I should not be a part. Thus, I agreed to Fuller's terms. (See pages 56-59.)

Attorney Grier met with me outside the courtroom patiently waiting for me to stop sobbing about the Judge's decision to bring down the gavel and the subsequent deal to contest. Grier explained the fact that I would be receiving papers to which I should respond and explained that he could do no more work for me since I had agreed to dismiss him. Thus, within a few weeks, I filed my first Motion *pro se*—that hand-written one that carried me through to the United States Supreme Court.

A similar situation occurred with Attorney Durant. In addition to notifying me that he would not be representing me, he gave me all of the records for our case and followed with a letter confirming the fact that he was no longer my attorney. Again, there were motions and orders that needed to be filed which I proceeded to research and complete.

With Grier, no one told me that it was not proper procedure to represent myself (*pro se*). In fact, I didn't even know what *pro se* meant! All I knew was that I was a "layperson acting for self." Judge Fuller never struck my first *Motion for Rehearing*, even though when I filed it, Attorney Grier, like Durant, had not legally withdrawn as my counsel. In fact, at a subsequent hearing, July 25, 1984, Judge Fuller recognized my Motion that I had prepared and filed while Grier was legally the Attorney of Record. According to the Court Transcript, Judge Fuller said: "We do have this document [my Motion] filed, raising the questions with regard to the divorce itself."

Thus, because of all the court actions which were blocking me from what I felt should have been a United States citizen's rights, I concluded that there was some type of collusion to hinder me from making my Appeal. Only those involved truly know the intent of their hearts. Regardless, I had been caught in the barrage of legal protocol. Part of the brief I submitted to the Fifth District Court of Appeal regarding this matter is below:

Fifth District Court of Appeal

Case No. 86-1294
Reply to show cause Order of
November 21, 1986

JUDITH A. BRUMBAUGH, APPELLANT,
V.
DOUGLAS K. BRUMBAUGH, APPELLEE

Appellant replies to the show cause order of this court of November 21, 1986, and shows cause why her appeal

should not be dismissed for failure to file a record of appeal to the court.

Comes now, Appellant, Judith A. Brumbaugh, and replies to the show cause order of November 21, 1986, and shows cause why her appeal should not be dismissed for failure to file a record on appeal to the cause, and shows:
1. See Exhibit 1 (2 pages) letter of December 2, 1986, and Open Court Order from Trial Court Clerk David N. Berrien wherein he states he did not prepare a record on appeal due to the orders of the Trial Court Judge Fuller.
2. See Exhibit 2, Designation of Record, submitted to the trial court clerk July 24, 1986, of this cause. Note this pleading clocked in by Clerk of Court who admits that this pleading was docketed into cause by the appellant.
3. See Exhibit 3, copy of order of November 21, 1986, to which this pleading is being addressed as a reply thereto.
4. Appellant states she has made all the pleadings required of her to the trial court and to this court wherefore this cause should not be dismissed for failure to file a record on appeal to the cause as the order of November 21, 1986, implies.

With lots of tears and the payment of $135 to record and properly process everything, the lower court was ordered to forward my papers to the Fifth District Court of Appeal. Back on track again.

Has there been enough judicial abuse?

Judge Fuller's conduct seemed to hold me responsible for my lack of understanding concerning procedures which are required to be followed when an attorney withdraws from representation in a case. How would a layman have any idea of these judicial requirements? Certainly, my bar-approved attorney didn't explain them to me. This was on the two specific occasions when he advised me that he was no longer representing me: in his office and in a follow-up letter.

The foregoing was included in a petition I wrote requesting a Writ of Certiorari which was docketed before the United States Supreme Court in 1987:

> *The fact that after her lawyer, Attorney Durant, quit her, he did not plead to the Court for permission to quit her as her Attorney, does not abrogate the right of Judith of her* **constitutional right to act for herself**; *and especially without the Court first establishing the fact whether Judith does or does not have counsel, and whether she does or does not have the right to represent herself ...*

> *The Court, clearly, without Due Process of Law, without Rule to Show Cause, clearly* **denied Defendant right of access to court, right to act for self, right to appeal**, *et al.*

> **The courts shall be open to every person for redress of any injury and justice shall be administered without sale, denial, or delay.**

> *The State further violated the Defendant's rights when Judge Fuller struck pleadings from the case and the Clerk of Courts did not forward pleadings as instructed in Designation of Record, both under in forma pauperis, and in a second Designation with fees paid—violations of basic human, constitutional, and civil rights perpetrated against this Petitioner-Defendant.*

> *Re: Amend. to FRCP 1.611 Sup. Ct. of Fla, Case No. 62,147, Dec. 8, 1983: "And any person*

whether an attorney or not, or whether within the exceptions mentioned above or not, **may conduct his own cause in any court of this state."*

This is supported additionally re: Constitution of the State of Fla., Art. 1, Sec. 21 Access to Courts—the courts shall be open to every person for* **redress of any injury** *and justice shall be administered without sale, denial, or delay ...; Art. 1, Sec. 9, Due Process of Law requires the Court to not deny any person of this right, by Due Process of law, example Rule to Show Cause ...;*

... the duty rests on all courts, state and national, to protect and enforce every right granted or secured by the Constitution of the United States, whenever such rights are involved in any proceeding before the court and the right is duly claimed or asserted ... Montgomery v. State, 55 Fla. 97,45 So. 879 (1908). (19)

Jonathan showed up again.

The man previously mentioned that had given me legal advice came to my assistance again. My goal of overturning Judge Fuller's legal dissolution of our marriage continued to eat away at my meager finances. Jonathan, my "legal knight," informed me that because of my financial status I should be able to proceed without having to pay fees, and I should check into this possibility. Research revealed that this could be done.

> **How did a financially secure middle-class homemaker and mother sink to the status of a legal pauper? Could the courts of Florida have anything to do with this?**

I filed financial papers to obtain permission to proceed to defend myself and to have court-filing fees waived. From my financial affidavits, the Fifth District Court of Appeal determined that I was "indigent" (poverty-stricken) and gave me leave to proceed *IN FORMA PAUPERIS*.

How did a financially secure middle-class home-maker and mother sink to the status of a legal pauper? Could the courts of Florida have anything to do with this? But ... this meant I could proceed from here without paying court costs and could continue to represent myself. Even though it was embarrassing to be classified *in forma pauperis*, the good side of this huge drop in my standard of living became a blessing when I received this letter:

DISTRICT COURT OF APPEAL
Fifth District 300 South Beach Street
Daytona Beach, Florida 32014

Ms. Judith A. Brumbaugh
RE: Brumbaugh v. Brumbaugh

Appeal No. 85-841

Dear Ms. Brumbaugh,

In response to your "Affidavit" received by this Court, please be aware that there are no additional court fees or charges to pursue your appeal to the Florida Supreme Court. Inasmuch as the appellate court filing fee has already been paid, if the Supreme Court accepts discretionary jurisdiction to review the April 29, 1986 Decision of this Court, the record will be transmitted without further cost.

Sincerely,
Frank J. Habershaw, Clerk

The Fifth District Court of Appeal did not reverse the lower court's decisions, but they gave me the right to move forward to the Florida State Supreme Court.

… if the [Florida] Supreme Court accepts discretionary jurisdiction to review the April 29, 1986 Decision of this Court, the record will be transmitted without further cost.

More learning experiences. Each judicial level has its own set of rules and procedures that I had to learn in order to file my briefs. I also had to find out where to file and how to find the information on how to file. I didn't know what questions to ask or where to go to find the answers. Along with acquiring this plethora of new knowledge came other responsibilities, including a deluge of paper work, numerous filings and certificates of service to satisfy requirements to appeal to the Florida Supreme Court. It was and still is totally confusing to me.

> **Each judicial level has its own set of rules and procedures that I had to learn in order to file my briefs.**

Regretfully, the Florida Supreme Court, like the Fifth District Court of Appeal, did not reverse the lower court's rulings. But as I learned from Frank Habershaw's letter (Fifth District Court of Appeal), the court's denial did not kill my case.

> **I didn't know what questions to ask or where to go to find the answers.**

The **denial** meant that the lower court's decisions which included the nonjurisdictional dissolution of our marriage that I had been trying to overturn would stand. The "**did not kill**" aspect meant that I could continue my pursuit. I could go forward trying to have them overturned at a higher level.

233

Attorney Durant reenters the scene.

Attorney Durant, on October 16, 1986, served me with a civil lawsuit for the money that I owed him. My heart pounded as I read the summons. I was being sued AGAIN and this time, my home was again threatened. Was I now going to lose my home and be in the street again? He advised me that I needed to mortgage my home to get the funds ASAP. On the bottom of the summons which I still have, I had written the following information:

I went to Barnett Bank to borrow against the house to pay this. They would not give me a mortgage nor equity loan as they said **I didn't have clear title to same.**

It's puzzling to me that my husband could find an attorney to legally transfer part of our home property (the adjoining lot) and our commercial building to other parties, but I could not borrow against our home on which I was making mortgage payments. As will be discussed in Chapter 10, I later discovered that it appears that the only assets that are protected after the dissolution of a marriage are commercial ones. **There, however, (at least in my case) was no similar protection for the children and other tangible and intangible assets. What a jaded value system**. The legislature has given us avenues to protect our commercial properties but not the marriage, children, and personal assets.

> **My husband could find an attorney to legally transfer part of our home property (the adjoining lot) and our commercial building to other parties, but I could not borrow against our home.**

Financial pressure continued to build. Attorney Durant was demanding to be paid and advised me to sell our home.

It's a blur now as to how I gathered the funds to pay his debt and avert the lawsuit, but I did. Several friends said,

> "You will never get out from under all these legal fees. File and get this burden off your back."

"You will never get out from under all these legal fees. File and get this burden off your back." I made an appointment with a bankruptcy attorney. He explained how this would be good for me and drew up the papers for me to sign. However, after thinking this over, I did not feel that I could do this. The debt had been incurred for a good cause—our family. I would pay it if it took me the rest of my life.

Of course, I still also owed money to Attorney Grier. On April 18, 1984, after our *Trial for Dissolution*, Attorney Grier and I met outside the courtroom. He said that I had wiped him out emotionally with my testimony and my resolve to fight for our family.

We discussed the huge debt that I still owed him. With tears in his eyes, he compassionately told me not to feel pressured to pay him but to remit a small amount each month. Thus, I continued to pay Attorney Grier every month from the time that Judge Fuller told me that Grier could no longer represent me.

For twenty years, every month, I made a payment to his office.

**The debt had been incurred
for a good cause—our family.
I would pay it if it took me the rest of my life.**

235

Chapter 10

MORE CHALLENGES:
THE U.S. SUPREME COURT WAS NOT
"USER FRIENDLY"!

While all this filing was taking place with the Fifth District Court of Appeal, I had also been learning some peculiarities of the United States Supreme Court. And reader, please remember that I am still my own attorney. The filings to the United States Supreme Court, as far as I can trace, appear to have begun in 1986.

> **It was time to plead to reverse the decree against our marriage and test the unconstitutionality of No-fault.**

The first part of the goal had been reached—to keep my case alive by getting through the minefields of the lower court, the Fifth District Court, and the Florida Supreme Court. Now it was time to begin to address the highest court in our land—to plead to reverse the decree against our marriage and to test the unconstitutionality of the No-fault Law. I was coming girded with battle scars (empirical proof from a layman's point of view) of unconstitutional practices running rampant in the lower courts. These denied me legal access and violated the Constitution. **Would the issues raised** in my *Motion for Rehearing* ever be heard? Getting this far, however, did give me some renewed hope that the issues addressed in my motions would finally be addressed.

I had been told that few attorneys reach this level and also had been notified by attorneys Grier and Durant that they were not qualified to handle a constitutional battle at the level of the United States Supreme Court. So realistically what were my chances? STATISTICALLY IMPROBABLE? Yes. I was a homemaker, a legally unskilled layperson struggling against unbelievable odds. However, I could not focus on this seemingly impossible mountain and the battles I had been and still was facing in the lower courts. I needed to continue to pursue the vision that I had been given and pray that wisdom, help, and understanding would come my way.

> **I was a legally unskilled lay person struggling against unbelievable odds.**

At least now I had been officially declared to be a legally "poor person"—*in forma pauperis*, so filing fees were waived. Also, no more attorney fees were accruing because Judge Fuller had allowed Attorney Durant to withdraw from my case forcing me, once again, to act as my own attorney.

Next step. How do I find how to appeal to the U.S. Supreme Court? Where do I find the rules? Not at Barnes and Noble! I learned there was a Supreme Court Rule book that included instructions that had to be followed. After several phone calls, I finally got the address to order a copy. Pressure was increasing as my time to file was speedily slipping by. Anxiously, I was waiting for the book to arrive. Finally it did. Read the text. Decipher its meaning. As I feared, the new language and procedures were not clear to me.

Tick-tock. Again the TIME-bomb was ticking. The fear of a late filing was creating unbelievable stress. Penetrating this living nightmare was my ever-present broken heart. I longed for my husband to see that because of our separation and not being of one accord, he had created a distorted family image. This skewed picture of our marriage greatly grieved me because it gave a wrong picture of commitment not only to others, but especially to our children. So often **children and others learn what they live.** And, how embarrassing to be made a part of such an offense against God.

> Our being separated gives a skewed picture of marriage ... especially to our children.

Despite dealing with these emotions, I had to decipher the *Rules of the Supreme Court of the United States* if I were to continue my quest. Back to the library and *Black's Law Dictionary.* Study, study. Look at more case law.

More typing on my typewriter. Why can't I get a whole page done without messing up? That clock never stops ticking. Pressure, pressure! Finally, after hours of research and study, days of typing and retyping, my brief was ready to take to the post office. Be sure to properly "serve" Doug's attorney. Make copies. Cross all the t's. Dot all the i's. Keep a record of what is filed and where.

> Cross all the t's. Dot all the i's. Keep a record of what is filed and where.

The guidelines were very specific. According to the United States Supreme Court a petition must contain:

- questions presented for review. Questions are to be short and concise. Only the questions set forth in the petition or fairly included therein will be considered by the Court;
- a list of parties to proceeding;
- table of contents and authorities;
- concise statement of the grounds on which the jurisdiction of this Court is invoked;

- the constitutional provisions, statutes, etc. which the case involves;
- a concise statement of the case ... (20:21-24)

These were the issues I was asking the Court to consider in one of my petitions for a Writ of Certiorari:

1. *Whether Final Decree entered June 11, 1984 is void for lack of jurisdiction and for fraud.*
2. *Whether void judgments may be motioned and vacated at any time.*
3. *Whether post-decretal order entered May 29, 1985 is void:*
   a. *For jurisdictional defects.*
   b. *For unlawful property settlement.*
   c. *For abuse of due process.*
4. *Whether above orders of June 11, 1984 and May 29, 1985 afford sister states and State of Florida "Full Faith and Credit."*
5. *Whether above decrees are void for lack of due process, abuse of process, abuse of discretion, denial of access to courts, violation of civil rights/discrimination, et al.*
6. *Whether the rights of an indigent, legally unskilled, have been violated giving rise to vacation of decrees and awarding of damages.*
7. *Whether Petitioner-Defendant has right to trial by jury.*

Petition filed. July, 1986: Docketed.

What does this letter mean from the United States Supreme Court? I think it's good! **"The petition for a Writ of Certiorari in the above entitled case was docketed in this Court on July 28, 1986 as No. 86-5161 ..."** Now what do I do? Wait, I guess.

October 16, 1986: The mailbox! Another letter—from the U.S. Supreme Court. Could it be possible? Are they going to **hear** the issues raised in my petition? With shaking hands, I nervously opened the letter. Oh, no, here we go again. I've been there done that—before! Another denial:

"... **The Petition for a Writ of Certiorari is denied.** Justice Scalia took no part in the consideration or decision of this petition."

File another *Motion for Rehearing.* Another letter in the mailbox:

SUPREME COURT OF THE UNITED STATES
OFFICE OF THE CLERK
WASHINGTON, D.C. 20543
November 4, 1986

> RE: *Judith A. Brumbaugh v.*
> *Douglas K. Brumbaugh*

No. 86-5161
Dear Mrs. Brumbaugh:
The petition for Rehearing in the above-entitled case was received on November 3, 1986 and is herewith returned as out of time. Pursuant to Rule 51 of the Rules of this Court, a Petition for rehearing must be submitted within 25 days after the decision of the Court. As the petition for a Writ of Certiorari was denied on October 6, 1986, the petition for a Writ of Certiorari was due on or before October 31, 1986.

Very truly yours,
Joseph F. Spaniol, Jr., Clerk

Once again, what do I do? Study the Supreme Court rulebook. My response is given below:

November 6, 1986

Mr. Joseph F. Spaniol, Jr. Clerk
Supreme Court of the United States
Office of the Clerk
Washington, D.C. 20543

Dear Mr. Spaniol:

*Enclosed is my Motion for Rehearing which **I am resubmitting** according to Rule 28.2. You returned my motion as you stated that it was out of time. As per your letter, the due date was on or before October 31, 1986.*

According to Rule 28.2: "To be timely filed, a document must be received by the Clerk within the time specified for filing, Except that any document shall be deemed timely if it has been deposited in a United States Post Office or mailbox, with firstclass postage prepaid and properly addressed to the clerk of the court within the time allowed for filing."

My petition for Motion for Rehearing was filed on Friday, October 31 at the post office in Oviedo, Florida which was within the time limit set by the Court.

Pursuant to Rule 28.2, I pray to the Clerk of this United States Supreme Court to enter my petition for Motion for Rehearing as it was duly filed according to the rules set forth within the time limit.

Respectfully submitted,
Judith A. Brumbaugh

Enclosure: Petition for Motion for Rehearing
P.S. I am also attaching a copy of my registered receipt from October 31.

Another one of those dreaded trips to my mailbox. Another letter from the U.S. Supreme Court.

> *November 12, 1986*
> *Dear Mrs. Brumbaugh:*
>   *In response to your letter of November 6, 1986, a document is deemed timely filed upon mailing **only if an affidavit of an attorney who is a member of the Bar of this Court is received** pursuant to Rule 28.2 of the Rules of this Court. Your petition for Rehearing is herewith returned.*
> > *Very truly yours,*
> > *Joseph F. Spaniol, Jr., Clerk*

I now wonder if the convicted felon, Gideon, received such a denial when he appealed from his prison cell. (Review page 115.) More research. My response to the above letter:

> *November 15, 1986*
>
> *Dear Clerk Spaniol:*
>   *In response to your letter of November 12, 1986, **I am resubmitting** my petition for Motion for Rehearing and ask that you reconsider its receipt for the following reasoning:*
>
> > *The United States Supreme Court, according to Rule 46, **permits a layperson to proceed in forma pauperis.** My case has been received by this United States Supreme Court under this rule. Those filing under **in forma pauperis** are exempted from certain requirements such as providing multiple copies, etc. as states in Rule 651, and more specifically regarding Rule 46, **are exempted from requirements of legal counsel.***

*For an "ordinary person" to interpret the "plain meaning of the words" **is it not contradictory to permit me to act for myself and then to require that legal counsel be obtained as a requirement to fulfill a rule of the court?** I have followed Rule 28.2 and gone one step further to validate the proper submission of the petition in a timely manner by sending it registered mail with a returned receipt. Your office signed and returned the Registered Return Receipt, Post Office Form 3811. Therefore, I pray upon this Office of the Clerk, to properly enter my petition for Motion for Rehearing.*

> *Respectfully submitted,*
> *Judith A. Brumbaugh*

Enclosure: Petition for Motion for Rehearing
Previous correspondence including registered receipt validating submission of my Petition "in timely manner."

Another letter in the mailbox!

Dear Mrs. Brumbaugh:

Your petition for Rehearing again received November 19, 1986 is herewith returned for the reasons stated in my letters of November 4 and November 12, 1986. There is no exception provided for pro se litigants to the Rule 28.2 mailing provision, which requires an affidavit by a member of the Bar of this Court.

> *Very truly yours,*
> *Joseph F. Spaniol, Jr., Clerk*

All of this judicial hassle reminded me of how those who were brought before the high court of the land several thousands of years ago and deemed guilty were taken out and stoned by the judicial officials of the day! This is what I felt the United States Supreme Court was doing to me through their rules and procedures. They were modeling with their rules what had happened in the lower courts. I was being denied access to the courts. I felt I was being denied the right to act for myself. There was no *due*

process, no equal rights, no equal protection. **I was being thrown out of court and judicially stoned for technical reasons.** I was found "guilty" without being heard. I didn't "qualify" for a trial by jury because my cause was one to defend a family dissolution! Every attempt to be heard had been rejected again and again.

They stoned me without a trial!

While going down for the umpteenth time, my husband was again busy trying to sell another of our joint assets, our commercial building. Something apparently happened with the sale he had negotiated previously.

Commercial property is protected from seizure in a divorce trial.

In my research, I came across a case that ruled that the court could not divide commercial property without an agreement between the parties or a partition to do so. This is a **protection** for commercial properties **not afforded**—at least not in my case—other aspects of the "marriage-contract"; i.e., children, home, etc.

The legislature, instead of passing marriage laws which have the effect of "preserving the integrity of marriage and safeguarding meaningful family relationships," appears to have a higher regard for commercial properties.

It has charged judicial officers of the court with the responsibility to protect commercial properties but to invalidate (impair) the "contract" under which such properties were acquired—the "marriage-contract"—**which should legally hold together the family and assets.** Instead, the government divides and destroys families while preserving commercial property in the absence of additional stipulations, one of which is that the parties agree to that division!

> **They divide and destroy families, but preserve commercial property in the absence of additional stipulations, one of which is that the parties agree to that division!**

A court in dissolution proceedings has no authority to award to a former husband his former wife's joint interest in a business and the property upon which it is located unless the parties agree to this division or the former husband properly pleads for partition. *Wilbur v. Wilbur*, 299 So.2d 99 (Fla. 3d Dist. 1974)

I felt that awarding our commercial property solely to my husband was yet another violation of my constitutional rights by the lower court—judicial theft—from the viewpoint of a layman! Because my husband did not want to honor his marriage vows, why should I pay the price of losing our assets? Neither of the requirements discussed in *Wilbur v. Wilbur* had been satisfied in *Brumbaugh v. Brumbaugh* as far as my understanding and which the Circuit Court Docket (the document where brief entries of all proceedings relating to a given case are recorded) seems to validate. I did not agree that our marriage, our family, nor any of our assets should be divided and/or reassigned.

We had been able to purchase our commercial building because—as always—we had worked and saved **together**.

245

At the time that this business opportunity arose (to purchase the commercial building), I had temporarily been working outside our home and my extra income contributed to our ability to make the required down payment. We had purchased this property for three reasons:

1. For a business investment with the attendant financial write-offs
2. For help in financing our children's college educations
3. For our retirement income.

During my appeal, I discovered that someone was again in the process of purchasing our commercial property. It was necessary to notify the purchaser that this property was involved in litigation before the United States Supreme Court.

I needed to find the legal procedure to follow in order to file a legal paper to prevent the transfer of our family assets to others. By calling the courthouse, I found it could be done via the legal document called a Lis Pendens.

The form was created from information I gathered. Next: where, when, and how to file it. It was to be filed in the courthouse with copies to be delivered to the proposed buyer as well as Attorney Simon, and my husband. See the abbreviated form on page 247.

Prior to the sale of our commercial building, I made an appointment to talk with Attorney Klinger, the lawyer who had been handling Doug's property transfers.

I told her that I didn't feel there was a clear title on our jointly owned commercial property because of my appeal and that I had no intention of signing off on it or any other of our jointly held properties.

In spite of the Lis Pendens and my talking with Attorney Klinger, the property was sold with Klinger transferring it without my signature.

IN RE: THE MARRIAGE OF
DOUGLAS K. BRUMBAUGH, HUSBAND
AND
JUDITH A. BRUMBAUGH, WIFE

LIS PENDENS
NOTICE OF LIS PENDENS

To Douglas K. Brumbaugh and all others whom it may concern ... property listed below ... is involved in litigation re: 18th Circuit Court ... and United States Supreme Court case filed May 13, 1987...

ALL PERSONS ARE CALLED UPON TO TAKE NOTICE HEREOF. Dated this 26th day of May, 1987.

Judith A. Brumbaugh
Attorney for Self, Layperson

CERTIFICATE OF SERVICE

I hereby certify that a true copy of LIS PENDENS was delivered to Harry Walker, 12334 Kilmore Drive Orlando, FL, and a copy to Attorney Billy Simon, 355 Wrong Street Orlando, FL and a copy mailed by certified mail to Douglas K. Brumbaugh 403 New Street.

Judith A. Brumbaugh
Attorney for Self, Layperson

(Names of parties above, other than wife and husband, are changed as well as addresses on this abbreviated form.)

Lis Pendens filed to notify all interested parties that a case was pending before the United States Supreme Court regarding this property

Laws of confiscation violate
the principle of equality.

Dr. Rice, in his book *50 Questions on the Natural Law*, discusses the Nazi period in Germany and **how property judicially stolen was returned to its rightful owners**:

> Whenever the conflict between an enacted law and true justice reaches unendurable proportions, the enacted law must yield to justice, and be considered a "lawless law" ...

> **After the war, the German courts recognized the claims of Jews to the restoration of their property ...**

> "These laws of confiscation, though clothed in the formal rules . . . of a law, . . . [are] an extremely grave **violation** of the suprapositive principle **of equality before the law** as well as of the suprapositive **guarantee of property**. **The equality principle is the foundation of any legal order and must remain inviolable**. . . . These [provisions] were and are by reason of their **unjust content** and their violation of the basic demands of any legal order **null and void**; this law could not, even at and during the time of the Nazi regime, *produce any legitimate legal effect*." (17:24, 25)

And yet our government in a different but related way takes control of our properties under color of law in our divorce courts!

DUE PROCESS IS DUE.

I continued to file briefs until another petition for a Writ of Certiorari was finally docketed. I received the letter on page 249.

SUPREME COURT OF THE UNITED STATES
OFFICE OF THE CLERK
WASHINGTON, D.C. 20543

May 21, 1987

H 9925
PO Box 244, Ste E-43
Collegeville, PA 19425

Dear Mrs. Brumbaugh:

> RE: Judith A. Brumbaugh,
> v. Douglas K. Brumbaugh
> No. 86-6907

The petition for a Writ of Certiorari in the above entitled case was docketed in this Court on May 16, 1987 as No. 86-6907.

A form is enclosed for notifying opposing counsel the case was docketed.

Very truly yours,
Joseph F. Spaniol, Jr., Clerk
Edward C. Schade, Assistant

To have my petition docketed means that the court had acknowledged it as being timely filed and in proper form. What an unbelievable process it had been once again! My hope was renewed that the issues I felt were wrongly judged would be heard.

I mailed the form to notify Doug's attorney that our case had again been docketed before the United States Supreme Court. Attorney Simon sent a notice to the Supreme Court asking for procedures and directions how to become qualified to practice before them with a copy to me.

One of the issues I addressed in this brief was a defense of *due process.* It summarized some of the insidious roadblocks the government appears to put up for anyone trying to defend herself in our courts of law without hiring an attorney: A section from my brief regarding this is written below:

> *Due process, et al., as experienced by this defendant, wife, an incompetent (defined as not legally educated or qualified for the task), and as an indigent, in today's judicial system has been like the legislature passing statutes and establishing precedent law that a defendant can defend her marriage, family, properties, etc., **if** she will prevail in a 12-round bout with Mohammad Ali!* *The promoters of the "fight," the judges, and the referee all full well know that Mohammad will ... [win] ... and said opponent will carry the scars of that defeat the rest of her life!*
>
> *A corresponding amount of fear has accompanied this defendant each time she works on a motion, goes into court, etc., as if she entered the ring with Mohammad Ali. (19:18)*

A defendant can defend her marriage, family, properties, etc., if she will prevail in a 12-round bout with Mohammad Ali!

Additionally, recall that in Chapter 5, it was shown that there was no corroborating witness at the *Trial for Dissolution* to give jurisdiction for Judge Fuller to legally dissolve our marriage and a subsequent fraudulent *Final Judgment* was entered: "... The Court having taken testimony of a corroborating witness as to residency..." From a layn,an's point of view, it would seem that without dissolution, **there would be no legal authority to legally adjudicate a person's property interests**:

> ... *because the trial* **court did not have jurisdiction to adjudicate the husband's property rights** *that portion of the Final Judgment awarding the husband's property rights to the wife was null and void ... the void portion of the Final Judgment did not transfer title of the property to the wife ... Whigham v. Whigham, 464 So.2d 674.* **Circuit Court, which did not have personal jurisdiction of defendant husband in divorce proceeding, and no jurisdiction to award to wife husband's interest in land located in Florida and owned by parties by entireties.** *Webb v. Webb, Fla. App. 156 So.2d 698. The Supreme Court approved a chart which indicates* **that there is no time limitation for challenging a void judgment** *under Rule 1.540(b). Florida courts before and after the adoption of Florida Rule of Civil Procedure 1.540(b) have stated that a* **void judgment may be attacked at any time** *because such judgment creates no binding obligation upon the parties, is legally ineffective, and is a nullity.*

Judicially taking properties away from others claiming rightful ownership is very common in a divorce lawsuit even though in most other situations it's unlawful to do so. Again, I emphasize, under color of law and in the absence of *due process*, IN PRACTICE, properties are reassigned and the state transfers ownership. This is done with or without the agreement of both parties to the "marriage-contract" that the court has made void; i.e., the court unconstitutionally impairs the obligations of the "contract" and then distributes the "spoils." The impairment is in direct violation of Article I, Section 10 of the United States Constitution. Additionally:

> The courts have stated that in the absence of an agreement between the parties or appropriate pleadings a chancellor is without authority to effect what might be a property settlement between the parties to a divorce action … (*Harder v. Harder,* Fla. 264 So.2d 476)

There are millions of Defendants in divorce cases who never obtain justice, especially those financially disadvantaged. The abuses of the system are many against this **class** of indigents including the failure to provide some means to ensure **quality** legal counsel for those who cannot afford it—as can be done in criminal cases—and the absence of offering financial parity between the Plaintiff and Defendant when the Defendant is financially disadvantaged. Does this not seem to be such a tragic contrast to a once-convicted felon, Mr. Gideon, for whom our government provided, not only a highly qualified attorney for his defense (FREE), but one who shortly thereafter became a United States Supreme Court Justice: Justice Abe Fortas?

One lesser-known practice which I found to be discriminatory is that of the court not offering information that would aid the Defendant in traversing the minefield of legal language, procedures, and timetables. Recall in Chapter 6 the discussion of the *Simplified Dissolution Packet* offered those not objecting to the state's impairment of their "marriage-contract." Those **agreeing to a dissolution (uncontested) are rewarded** by qualifying for the Florida Bar-prepared packet and avoid the potential judicial prohibition of access to court and sundry blockades which are a part of the court system. And, of course, they are not burdened with thousands of dollars of legal fees.

Those qualifying for the *Simplified Dissolution* are unlike indigent Defendants (and many who are not indigent) who can be denied, in practice, their right to petition the government for a redress of grievances and the constitutional right for appeals and rehearings. These acts/omissions by the government greatly disadvantage such Defendants. As has been shown previously in this book, those who may be in jeopardy of being incarcerated are asked the following questions and given the following rights:

1. Do you understand that you have the right to have a lawyer appointed on your behalf?
2. Do you have enough money to hire a lawyer?
3. Would you like the court to hire an attorney for you?
4. You have a right to appeal.
5. You have 21 days to appeal any court decision.
6. If you plead guilty, you give up your right to appeal.

Because I have experienced and witnessed many instances of what I perceived to be abuses discussed throughout this book, I find it difficult to reconcile what is stated in the Florida Constitution and what in reality happens:

The Florida Constitution and those of many other states avow that "All natural persons are **equal** before the law and have inalienable rights, among which are the right to enjoy and **defend** ... and to acquire, possess, and **protect property** ... *No person shall be deprived of life, liberty, or property* without *due process* of law ... **The courts shall be open to**

> **We have rights ...but we aren't equal before the law.**

every person ... and justice shall be administered without sale, denial ..."

Yes, we have rights, but exercising these rights, once a person becomes embroiled in the idiosyncrasies of our complex judicial system, proves that we are NOT equal before the law in safeguarding our families and properties.

As I continued my "court-ship," I continually found the courts are NOT open to every person and justice is not administered with equality.

An unexpected call gave me hope again.

An unexpected phone call early one morning. The person on the other end identified himself. He was a professor at a law university and had heard of my legal battle after many years of "court-ship." He was calling regarding my Appeal that I had filed with the United States Supreme Court.

> My appeal had finally reached the United States Supreme Court ... "Are you sure?" he asked.

"This is Professor Rice from the Law School of Notre Dame." I was shocked that he had called. How did he know? "I understand you feel that your case has been docketed before the U.S. Supreme Court. Are you sure of this?" he asked. "There are few attorneys who reach that level."

> *Amicus curiae*, I didn't know what this meant—but was thankful.

"Yes Sir, I have the paper from them." "Tell me what it says." My answer confirmed that *Brumbaugh v. Brumbaugh* had been docketed. Dr. Rice asked that I send some of my papers to him for review. "We would like to file a brief, *Amicus curiae* [friend of the court], if your case is heard." I didn't know what this meant—but was thankful. I only knew that it was a blessing to have someone offer help. I was so excited for this incredible breakthrough. How do I find what to send? Papers are strewn all over the house. What is important? What is not? "God, please help." I gathered what I thought I should send and took them to the post office. Below are portions of my cover letter:

Dear Professor Rice:

May the Lord bless you for your willingness to take a look at my papers. I have been praying, fasting (crying!) since all of this attack on my family started. The pain of it all is indescribable; the injustices in our Nation's court system are unbelievable; and the price on ensuing generations of these ungodly acts is immeasurable.

Enclosed are four sets of papers. The first is the notification that my case has been docketed. The second is a group of what I think are Final Orders. The third includes the last Motion I have filed to the Supreme Court of the State of Florida, with Motion to Dismiss to Strike attached.

I would imagine that my husband's lawyer will be filing some type of Motion to Dismiss to the United States Supreme Court. He has asked them for directions to become qualified to act before the United States Supreme Court ...

Respectfully submitted,
Mrs. Judith A. Brumbaugh

I continued filing some additional briefs, some of which were returned because I didn't follow the correct procedure. On pages 256 and 257 are Supreme Court documents. The first is the letter included on page 249 confirming the docketing for a second Writ of Certiorari, May 21, 1987. That on page 257 is one of the cover sheets for a brief which I filed in support of my Appeal.

255

SUPREME COURT OF THE UNITED STATES
OFFICE OF THE CLERK
WASHINGTON. D. C. 20543

May 21, 1987

H 9925
PO Box 244, Ste E-43
Collegeville, PA 19425

Re: Judith A. Brumbaugh,
     v. Douglas K. Brumbaugh
     No. 86-6907

Dear Mr.

The petition for a writ of certiorari in the
above entitled case was docketed in this Court on
May 16, 1987 as No. 86-6907.

A form is enclosed for notifying opposing
counsel that the case was docketed.

Very truly yours,

Joseph F. Spaniol, Jr., Clerk

Edward C. Schade
Assistant

Notification from the United States Supreme Court that a <u>second</u> petition for a Writ of Certiorari had been docketed

NO. 86-6907

IN THE
SUPREME COURT OF THE UNITED STATES
TERM, 1987

RE: IN THE MARRIAGE OF
JUDITH A. BRUMBAUGH,

PETITIONER, DEFENDANT

V.

DOUGLAS K. BRUMBAUGH,

RESPONDENT, PLAINTIFF

MOTION TO VACATE AND/OR SET ASIDE FINAL JUDGMENT OF CIRCUIT
COURT OF THE EIGHTEENTH JUDICIAL CIRCUIT IN AND FOR SEMINOLE
COUNTY OF JUNE 11, 1984 AND POST-DECRETAL SUPPLEMENTAL FINAL
JUDGMENT, MAY 29, 1985 PER FRCP 1.540(B)(4);RULE 60(B)(4);U.S.
SUPREME COURT RULE 53, ETAL
COMPANION TO U.S.SUPREME COURT CASE # 86-6907

SUBMITTED BY:
JUDITH A. BRUMBAUGH, PETITIONER,DEFENDANT
DRIVE   FLORIDA
PHONE
ATTORNEY FOR PETITIONER, DEFENDANT
LAY PERSON, ACTING FOR SELF

ATTORNEY FOR RESPONDENT: RESPONDENT:

**Cover sheet for one of the briefs filed in
support of second Writ of Certiorari
docketed before the United States
Supreme Court**

I also continued to write others soliciting help in this system that gives judicial privileges to criminals and those who **agree to a dissolution**, but discriminately requires those, such as this author, who may be indigent and legally not trained for such a task, to follow their rules of procedure. Below and on page 259 are two other letters that were written to try to find legal help:

COMMOM CAUSE
Dear Mr. Jones:
I appreciate your talking briefly with me on the phone this morning. Enclosed is a copy of the most recent Petition I have filed on my own behalf—a Motion for Rehearing submitted to the United States Supreme Court regarding my previous petition for Writ of Certiorari which was denied. I have been harassed by the legal system, have been placed deeply in debt, have been placed in a state of poverty ... by nexus actions of the state officials under "color of law."

I am praying that your organization will provide legal help to stop these unconstitutional acts of the State of Florida by either helping me at the United States Supreme Court (at which level I have also had pleadings rejected because they didn't follow proper procedure—but as a layman, I know not how to correct); or in filing a separate suit in the Federal Court.

Thank you so much for any consideration and help that you may be able to give to me. I anxiously await to hear from you with a positive response.
Judith A. Brumbaugh
P.S. At your request, I will forward to you the original petition for Writ of Certiorari which has documented proof from court records of above abuses.

Dear Judge Bork:

I am one of the scores who has been involved in a divorce litigation against my will. I hold a belief that my marriage is "until death us do part," and to not let man put apart what God has put together.

After a twenty-five year marriage, I, this week, brought home a pay check for two weeks for $111 and await tomorrow's mail to receive my "tempo-rary" rehabilitative $35 a week alimony, [*See below] while my husband with a doctorate earned while we were married has his salary, retirement, insurance benefits, our commercial building, etc. I have no money to pay you.

I still have legal bills which I am trying to pay. I can only pray that you will extend your hand; that is, legal expertise. I thank you in advance for anything that you may be able to do.

Sincerely,

Judith A. Brumbaugh

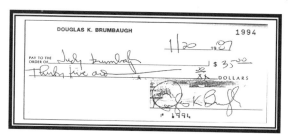

*Even though I had a master's degree in Clothing and Textiles and was working on an MBA, my earning power was limited because of the age of the Clothing and Textiles degree, but more so because my priorities did not include establishing a professional career outside our home and climbing the corporate ladder but to fight for my family. My family was more important than worrying about the demeaning salary and substandard level of living I had been forced into for the past several years.

**But even so, my prayer is that the loving, caring man
that I married will one day return.**

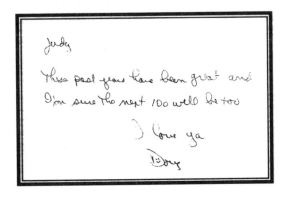

More motions and petitions to the U.S. Supreme Court.
As with the lower courts, there were rejections because I
did not properly follow FRCP (Federal Rules of Civil Procedure). But I continued ... Another trip to the dreaded
mailbox. Today ... Another letter from the Supreme Court.

SUPREME COURT OF THE UNITED STATES
OFFICE OF THE CLERK
WASHINGTON, D.C. 20543
November 16, 1987

Mrs. Judith A. Brumbaugh
  RE: Judith A. Brumbaugh
    v. Douglas K. Brumbaugh
    No. 86-6907
Dear Mrs. Brumbaugh:
  *The court today entered the following order in
the above entitled case.*
  The petition for rehearing is denied.

> *Very truly yours,*
> *Joseph F. Spaniol, Jr., Clerk*

PETITION FOR REHEARING—DENIED. So says the highest court in this country. For six years I had fought to preserve our marriage. Our country's laws guarantee equal access—to be **heard** by all who petition the courts. The cause I had so faithfully championed, however, was destined not to be heard. *My constitutional right to petition the government for a redress of grievances was denied.*

The Court of Equity under which families are legally dissolved could not be permeated. This is a court which seemingly is designed so that justice would be administered "... *according to fairness as contrasted with the strictly formulated rules of common law.*" (1:321) After reading this entire book, is it not ironic that this Court of Equity simply does not only **not** do that for which it was created, it actually prevents it from being done—at least from my perspective?

As stated in my first *Motion for Rehearing:* "No-fault divorce is in violation of my First and Fourteenth Amendment rights and is not in the best interest of our children."

Would the reader like to guess what could have happened in *Brumbaugh v. Brumbaugh* had the judicial privileges extended under a court of law as in the criminal case *Gideon v. Wainwright* been extended to me, the defendant—and at no charge? Defended by an attorney who a year later became Supreme Court Justice Abe Fortas!

"God, WHY?"
Perhaps one day I will know.

Photo taken by Ann Nixon

Author, Mrs. Judith Brumbaugh, with her Bible and (symbolic) sword to fight for her family against the Trojan Horse, No-fault Divorce. Will you join in the pursuit to establish, restore, and strengthen covenant-marriages?

Post log

Court of Equity/Court in Chancery

Classification of court under which legal dissolutions of marriages are heard

Florida Statutes: Title VI Civil practice and procedure. Chapter 61: Dissolution of Marriage, Support, Custody; 61.011 Dissolution in chancery; 61.052 Dissolution of marriage

"Courts of chancery (equity courts) **have been abolished** by all states that have adopted Rules of Civil Procedure. Court ... which administers justice and decides controversies in accordance with rules, principles, and precedents of equity. Justice **administered according to fairness as contrasted with the strictly formulated rules of common law** ... denotes the spirit and habit of fairness, justness and right ... *Gilles v. Department of Human Resources Development*, 11 Cal. 3d 313, 113 cal.Rptr. 374,380, 521 P.2d 110.

The object of which is to render the administration of justice more complete, by affording relief where the courts of law are incompetent to give it, or to give it with effect, or by exercising certain branches of jurisdiction independently of them." (1:321, 322, 484)

"**Court of law**: Any duly constituted tribunal administering the laws of the state or nation; •n a narrower sense, a court proceeding according to the course of the common law and governed by its rules and principles, as contrasted with a 'court of equity.'" (1:323)

Bibliography

Bibliographical references are given in parentheses with two numerals such as (1:291). The first numeral (1) refers to the numbered reference in the bibliography; the numeral following the colon refers to the page in that reference (291).

1. Henry Campbell Black, M.S., *Black's Law Dictionary*, West Publishing Co., St. Paul, Minnesota, 1979.
2. Robin Denaro, *The Daily Telegram*, "Always and Forever: Woman founds ministry on belief that marriage is an unbreakable bond," June 16, 1994.
3. *Brumbaugh v. Brumbaugh, Final Judgment*, June 11, 1984.
4. Lenore J. Weitzman, *The Economics of Divorce: Social and Economic Consequences of Property, Alimony and Child Support Awards*, Reprinted from UCLA Law Review, Volume 28, Number 6, August 1981.
5. Judith Brumbaugh, Fran Austin, Brief to President Reagan, "An Appeal to the President of the United States," Unpublished paper, July 4, 1984.
6. *Broken Families*, Hearings before the Subcommittee on Family and Human Services, United States Senate: Oversight on the breakdown of the traditional family unit, focusing on the causes and implications for society and the role of government in helping prevent the breakup of families, Part 2, September 22 and October 4, 1983.
7. *Broken Families*, Hearings before the Subcommittee on Family and Human Services, United States Senate: Oversight on the breakdown of the traditional family unit, focusing on the causes and implications for society and the role of government in helping prevent the breakup of families, Part 1, March 22 and 24, 1983.
8. Liz Mathieux, "Everybody Meet Judy Brumbaugh! "FTU Wife Tailors Doctor – Husband's Threads," *The Sanford Herald*, September 30, 1974.

9. Lenore J. Weitzman, *The Divorce Revolution: The Unexpected Social and Economic Consequences for Women and Children in America*, The Free Press, 1985.
10. Edwin Lindop, *The Bill of Rights and Landmark Cases*, Franklin Watts, New York, 1989.
11. United Press International, "Langley proposes tougher divorce law," *The Orlando Sentinel*, March 15, 1985.
12. *1791-1991 The Bill of Rights and Beyond*, The United States Commission on the Bicentennial.
13. J. M. O'Neill, *Religion and Education Under the Constitution*, DaCapo Press, New York, 1972.
14. Ronald Anderson, and Walter A. Kumpf, *Business Law Principles and Cases*, South-Western Publishing Co., Cincinnati, 1958.
15. J. Shelby Sharpe, "No-fault Divorce—A National Catastrophe," Unpublished paper.
16. Daniel W. Shuman, "Decisionmaking under conditions of uncertainty," Judicature, Volume 67, Number 7, February 1984.
17. Rice, Charles E., *50 Questions on the Natural Law: What it is & Why we need it*, Ignatius Press, San Francisco, 1999.
18. *Brumbaugh v. Brumbaugh, Answer to Petition for Dissolution of Marriage*, March 4, 1983.
19. *Brumbaugh v. Brumbaugh, In the Supreme Court of the United States, Companion Case Sup. Ct. U.S. 86-6907.*
20. *Rules of the Supreme Court of the United States*, 1 First Street, N.E., Washington, DC 20543, 1980.

APPENDIX A
Legal Terms

Adjudicate	To rule upon judicially
Amicus curiae	A person with strong interest on a subject matter of an action who files a brief on behalf of a party; commonly filed in appeals concerning matters of a broad public interest
Appeal	A proceeding undertaken to have a decision reconsidered by bringing it to a higher authority
Appellate court	A court having jurisdiction or appeal and review; one to which causes are removable by appeal, certiorari, error or report; not a trial court
Arbitrary	Done without adequate determining principle, depending on will alone, tyrannical; failure to exercise honest judgment
Bifurcate	To divide into branches or parts; to separate
Bill of attainder	Extinction of civil rights with forfeiture of properties
Brief	Written statement prepared by the counsel arguing a case in court; contains summary of facts of case, pertinent laws, argument of how law applies to facts supporting position
Circuit Court	Courts whose jurisdiction extends over several counties; usually have general original jurisdiction
Color of Law	The appearance of semblance; without substance of a legal right; implies power made possible because wrongdoer is "clothed" with the authority of the state
Constitutional	Consistent with the Constitution
Contract	An agreement between two or more competent parties creating obligations that are enforceable or otherwise recognizable at law; set of promises, for breach of which the law gives a remedy, or the performance of which the law in some way recognizes as a duty
Corroborating witness	A person not a party to the lawsuit who affirms Plaintiff's residency without which court does not have jurisdiction
Covenant	A Biblical agreement created by God the terms of which are immutable; i.e., actions of man do not change the obliga- tions; God sets the terms as with marriage-covenant until the physical death of one of the parties
Defendant	Party against whom a charge is brought in a civil or criminal proceeding
Deposition	A discovery device—statements taken under oath outside the courtroom, usually in one of the attorney's offices, to obtain information for evidence to be used by the court in a civil action or criminal prosecution
Derogation	Partial repeal or abolishing of a law; acts which limit or impair its utility and force (such as those in the Constitution)
Dissolution	Act to dissolve; termination

Docket	Brief entries of proceedings of all important acts done in each case from its inception to its conclusion
Due Process	Rules and principles for our legal system for the enforcement and protection of private rights. It gives the right to be heard regarding issues of life, liberty, or property; rights are not only to be heard but also enforced and protected
Due Process: Procedural	Aspect of *due process* in which a person is guaranteed fair procedures
Due Process: Substantive	Aspect of *due process* which protects a person's property from unfair governmental interference or taking
Duly	In proper form; according to law in both form and substance
Ex post facto	After the fact; law passed after occurrence of an act which retrospectively changes the legal consequences of such fact. Article I, Section 10 of U.S. Constitution: States are forbidden to pass any *ex post facto* law; law which changes the rules; law which imposes a penalty or deprivation of a right which, when done was lawful; law which alters the situation of a person to his disadvantage: *Wilensky v. Fields*, Fla., 267 So.2d 1, 5
Hearing	Proceeding with definite issues of fact or of law to be tried in which witnesses are heard and parties proceeded against have right to be heard
Immutability	Unchangeable; exempt from change; impossible to negate
Impunity	Exemption or protection from penalty or punishment
Inalienable	Rights which are not capable of being surrendered or transferred without the consent of the one possessing such rights
Incompetent	Lack of ability, esp. legal, to discharge the required duty
Indigent	One who is needy and poor; refers to one's financial status
In forma pauperis	A pauper; describes permission given to indigent to proceed without liability for court fees or costs; such will not be deprived of his rights to litigate and appeal
Judicial	Belonging to the office of a judge; involving the exercise of judgment or discretion; administration of justice
Jurisdiction	Right and power of a court to adjudicate concerning the subject matter in a given case; power and authority of a court to hear and determine a judicial proceeding
Jurisprudence	Method of ascertaining the principles on which legal rules are based
Legislative	Making or giving laws; function of law-making
Lis pendens	A pending suit; notice filed on public records for purpose of warning all persons that the title to certain property is in litigation, and that they are in danger of being bound by an adverse judgment; notice is for purpose of preserving rights pending litigation
Litigate	To seek relief in a court of law; to carry on a suit; any controversy **that must be decided upon evidence**

Magna Carta	Charter regarded as foundation of English constitutional liberty; includes provisions for preserving personal liberties
No-fault Law	Type of divorce in which marriage can be ended on mere allegation that it has "irretrievably broken" down or there are "irreconcilable differences." Under such statutory ground for dissolution, fault on the part of either spouse need not be shown or proved
Notice of Appearance	Giving notice to the court for the purpose of coming into court as party to a suit
Opinion	Statement by a judge or court of the decision reached in regard to a cause tried or argued before them, expounding the law as applied to the case, and detailing reasons upon which the judgment is based
Petition	Formal written request addressed to some governmental authority; right of people to petition for redress of grievance is guaranteed by the First Amendment, U.S. Constitution
Plaintiff	Party who brings a civil suit in a court of law
Pleading	Formal allegations by the parties of their respective claims and defenses
Quit-claim deed	Giving up one's claim or title; Deed that is intended to pass any title, interest, or claim
Record on Appeal	Official documentation of all proceedings in court; history of the proceedings on the trial of the action below; record furnished to the appellate court: pleadings, objections to evidence, rulings, charges, transcripts of examination of witnesses, docket entries
Redress	Satisfaction for an injury or damages sustained
Rehearing	Second consideration of cause; to call court's attention to error, omission, or oversight in first consideration
Retrospective	Law which affects acts or facts occurring before it came into force; gives different legal effect from that which it had under the law when it occurred
Supersedeas	Writ containing command to stay proceedings; suspension of power of trial court to issue an execution on judgment appealed from
Tyrannical	Act in which a sovereign or ruler uses power unjustly and arbitrarily, to the oppression of his subjects
Usurp	To seize by force, and without right of another's rights; unlawful seizure or assumption of sovereign power; assumption of government or supreme power by force or illegally, in derogation of the Constitution and of rights of the lawful rules
Writ of certiorari	Device for requesting review by higher court in cases where such court has discretionary right to accept or reject appeal

APPENDIX B
Constitutional Issues

This Appendix is designed to accompany Chapter 8, page 164 et al., and to give a summary of some of the many violations our current No-fault Law imposes upon Defendants forced into court because of a civil action known as a divorce. Most cases from which these violated principles have been drawn are not given. This is not meant as a research paper on such but to alarm enough people that something will be done to bring about change. We don't need another superficial governmental study to determine the already existing plethora of empirical evidence that No-fault is working tyrannically as an agent to destroy families.

Starting on page 270 is a table of important constitutional Amendments with which the reader needs to familiarize himself before proceeding to the second table which follows the first. The latter, "Principles From Constitutional Amendments Used to Reverse Lower Court Decisions," is not specific to No-fault, but the principles bear careful consideration to rights abridged under the vague, discriminatory No-fault Law which violates many principles of *due process*, equal protection, and equal rights under the law. This has been reinforced not only through personal experience but by my ministering to both men and women who also have been victims of this **law which is vague, discriminatory in practice, and repugnant to the Constitution**, <u>and thus should be struck down</u>—voided.

Again, I want to clearly state that this information is presented from the viewpoint of a **layman not trained in legal matters**. It is from **facts and opinions** gained through six years of "court-ship" and twenty-two years of living out the ravages of what began with an unconstitutional court decision April 18, 1984—i.e., executed without the court having jurisdiction: "This marriage is dissolved."

Amendments to the Constitution

The Constitution is to secure the most fundamental
and surest guarantee of our freedom:
equal justice under the law.
Some of the Amendment and/or Article blocks
contain additional help (in smaller print) for the reader.

Article I, Section 10	No state shall ... pass any bill of attainder [extinction of civil rights with forfeiture of properties], **ex *post facto* law, or law impairing the obligation of contracts** ...
Amend. 1	Congress shall make **no law** respecting an establishment of religion, **or prohibiting the free exercise thereof** ... [or to hinder people] to petition the Government for a **redress [satisfaction for an injury or damages sustained] of grievances.**
Amend. 4	The right of the people to be **secure** in their persons, houses, papers, and effects, **against** unreasonable searches and **seizure** There is an indivisible association between liberty and property. The right to acquire and hold property is fundamental because it secures life and liberty as well. It's necessary to secure rights against illegal searches and seizures. Government cannot take property without proceeding against citizens according to laws and procedures **known (person with reasonable research) and applicable to person in question. LAW MUST BE REASONABLE.**
Amend. 5	No person shall be held to answer for capital, or otherwise infamous crime, unless on ... indictment of a Grand Jury ... **No person ... shall be deprived of life, liberty, or property, without *due process* of law.** Rights to **legal counsel** are extended to suspects in custody as well (*Miranda v. Arizona).* Guarantees public trial before an impartial jury. Guarantees every defendant shall be **informed of the charges against him or her and have assistance of a lawyer**.
Amend. 6	In all criminal prosecutions, the accused shall enjoy the right to a speedy and public trial, by an **impartial jury** ... **to be informed of the nature and cause of the accusation**; to be confronted with the witnesses in his favor, and to have the **Assistance of Counsel for his defense**. 1963 U.S. Supreme Court ruled that a state had to provide **counsel for indigents** accused of a serious crime; Supreme

	Court has deemed that Law is a very complex subject and the average person needs the assistance of counsel in most lawsuits ... **if defendant is too poor to hire an attorney he cannot have equal treatment under the law** if he or she is involved in a trial without the aid of a trained, experienced member of the legal profession. (*Gideon v. Wainwright*)
Amend. 7	In Suits at common law, where the value in controversy shall exceed twenty dollars [$20], **the right of trial by jury shall be preserved** (IN CIVIL CASES). Civil law pertains to disputes between private parties and between private parties and the government that do not involve criminal offenses. "In controversies respecting property, and in suits between man and man ... the ancient trial by jury is one of the greatest securities to the rights of the people, and to remain sacred and inviolable." George Mason (12:49)
Amend. 8	Excessive bail shall not be required**, nor excessive fines imposed ... nor cruel and unusual punishments inflicted.**
Amend. 14, Section 1	No State shall make or enforce any law which shall abridge the privileges or immunities of citizens of the United States; nor shall any State deprive any person of **life, liberty, or property, without** *due process* **of law**; nor deny to any person within its jurisdiction the *equal protection* **of the laws**.
Amend. 14 (Additional help)	Extends to states many of limitations that apply to Federal Government concerning individual rights. Makes Bill of Rights binding on states. **Personal rights and liberties are protected by the** *due process* **clause of Fourteenth Amendment from impairment by the states.** Supreme Court has made many rulings that incorporate **First Amendment clauses into the Fourteenth. 1961 incorporated criminal law protections in the 5th and 6th into the 14th, including right to counsel and right against self-incrimination.** (12:68) Properties cannot be taken from corporations as well as private citizens without *due process* of law. Corporations (a legal person) claim protection against state regulations designed to control working hours and conditions. Attempts of States to regulate them (hours and working conditions) abridged "*due process*" clause. (12:67) RE: Equal protection clause of 14th: *Plessy v. Ferguson:* Justice John Harlan of Kentucky. "Our Constitution is color-blind, and neither knows **nor tolerates classes among citizens**.": Justice John Harlan (12:69)

EQUALITY FOR ALL AMERICANS. The "separate but equal" doctrine was dealt a death blow when the Supreme Court ruled that "separate but equal" segregated educational facilities were inherently "unequal" and unconstitutional. *Brown v. Board of Education*, 1954. The 14th Amendment has now been interpreted to protect other rights against state infringement: *Gitlow v. New York*, 1925. (12:68) Also, in the criminal case, *Gitlow v. New York*, Supreme Court decreed **1st Amendment protection** was extended to state actions by 14th Amendment. (10:57).

Principles From Constitutional Amendments Used to Reverse Lower Court Decisions (in cases other than those for dissolution)

Expectations must be clear.

Due process requires civil and criminal enactments and regulations promulgated whereby it is sufficiently clear that persons who are affected can **gain a reasonably clear idea of what the law requires of them**. (In No-fault there is no way a Defendant can know that; i.e., there is no clear picture of what a person has to do to continue the "marriage-contract.")

Laws are not to be vague.

A state that forbids or requires the doing of an act in terms so vague that men of common intelligence must necessarily guess at its meaning and differ as to its application **violates the first essential of *due process*.** (Defendants in No-fault do not know the terms under which they may defend their "marriage-contract.")

It is a basic principle of *due process* that **an enactment is void for vagueness.** If prohibitions are not clearly defined, a clear and precise enactment may nevertheless be overbroad in its reach if it prohibits constitutionally protected conduct.

(To legally dissolve a marriage under No-fault, the judge must determine, **in light of his personal subjective <u>feelings</u>**, about the marriage and whether there is a reasonable possibility of reconciliation. This calls for a prediction that must be largely a guess based on the self-serving testimony of usually one of the parties, the Plaintiff: "Is it irretrievably broken?")

Laws are not to be discriminatory.

A law non-discriminatory on its face may be grossly discriminatory in its practical applications. (Empirical evidence has shown that the state's objective has been to destroy marriages by its absence statistically of protecting the Defendant's right to continue the "marriage-contract.")

Subjective opinions are not to determine legality of an act.
The legality or illegality of an act cannot be made to be dependent upon the uncertain advice of one man's opinions or against another's; **thereby, impairing life and liberty on the basis of another person's SUBJECTIVE judgment.** (This is done in No-fault with the denial of trial by jury of one's peers. Instead, the judge is forced to act as God in making his subjective judgment of guilt or innocence— something impossible for the judge to do; i.e., to remedy a fair and impartial judgment on the basis of subjective judgment. Defendant can lose home and other properties, future earnings, right to live with children, old age security, medical coverage and inheritance rights without clearly defined **fault**.)

Specifics of law must be clearly stated.
Primary purpose of a constitutional requirement of specificity is to give sufficient notice that an act has been made criminal **before** it is done. If a criminal provision either forbids or requires the doing of an act in terms so vague that men **of common intelligence must necessarily guess at its meaning** and differ as to its application, it violates the first essential of *due process* of law. (No-fault Defendants are not given such notice.)

Criminal acts must be so defined before a crime is committed.
One's act must be determined as a crime attendant with specific sanctions **before it is committed.** (Under No-fault, Defendant is subject to an offense which isn't spelled out in the "contract." The specifics were "for better, for worse ... until death we do part." Yet, the "marriage-contract" is subject to be broken by the state for no crime or violation of the contract. This violates the constitutional *ex post facto* and impairment of contract protections.)

Parties must be informed.
Due process requires that the citizenry be specifically informed of their rights and responsibilities and the legal prohibitions with which they must abide. *Due process* requirements of the US Constitution require rules which will prevent a vindictive prosecutor from punishing a Defendant for doing some things the law allows the Defendant to do. (These rights are violated under No-fault.)

Representation not to be hindered by economic status.
Under *due process*, there could be no equal justice when the kind of trial a man gets is determined by the amount of money he has. (In No-fault the Defendants, often being women without adequate funding, do not have financial resources nor ability to borrow funds to be "equal" with Plaintiff's resources to defend herself. This hinders the right to equal protection.)

Equal protection can apply to legal representation.
The Fourteenth Amendment prohibits any state from taking action which would deny to any person within its jurisdiction **equal**

protection of the law. Equal protection of the law has been applied to allow for reasonable differences and to make up for the differences between the sexes. (The Court in giving equal protection to the Defendant [more often a female] should allow for the difference in financial ability to afford equal defense. Defendants in a No-fault suit are not afforded same [equal] protection, to defend against the contract being legally dissolved, that is afforded Plaintiffs.)

Legislature isn't to confer special benefits.

The Legislature cannot unreasonably **impose a particular benefit** or concur a **special right** or privilege upon a portion of the people. (Under No-fault, the legislature gives Plaintiffs [majority sect] the automatic **right** and "**cause**" [irretrievably broken] to a dissolution. The Legislature gives rights to one class, the Plaintiffs, in detriment to a "dissenting" Defendant [minority sect]. Likewise, the Florida Bar makes available to a "sect," those not contesting a divorce [uncontested], "easy and affordable access to Florida's courts" through its state's *"Simplified Dissolution Packet."*)

Benefits inherent in contract should be protected.

State, by impairing obligations of the "marriage-contract," especially when against wishes of Defendants, forces Defendants to give up their **benefits inherent within the contract**. These are meant to be an inseparable part of the **continuation** of the contract.

It isn't in best interest of government to dissolve more than a million families every year.

The crucial question in equal protection cases is whether there is an appropriate governmental interest suitably furthered by differential treatment. It is not appropriate governmental interest to legally dissolve and/or impair more than a million "marriage-contracts" every year, throwing scores of women and children into poverty with the attendant cost to the taxpayer, the state, as well as AFDC and Medicare. This is against state interest, let alone the unmeasured human cost.

LAWS ARE TO BE VOIDED UNDER THE CONSTITUTION IF THEY ARE SUFFICIENTLY VOID AND VAGUE! (Judiciary Act of 1789, Section 25) "... **the supreme authority in the national judiciary must of necessity be able to determine whether or not the laws of a state violate the Constitution or laws of the United States.**" "**A law repugnant to the Constitution is void**": **Chief Justice John Marshall (13:261, 262)**

APPENDIX C
Attorney Reviews of Book

This book is a very thorough and detailed exposition of your "no-fault" divorce experience. **I believe it could be educational for individuals who are contemplating divorce, because it explains a process they cannot possibly understand until they've been through it.**

I think it may be most helpful to people who want to *initiate* the divorce process because these people typically are very desperate to believe that divorce will set them "free" and give them a "new beginning" and they, very often, *do not want to believe that it will have precisely the opposite effect.*

I often explain to potential clients how horrific the divorce process will be and how unjustly and unfairly the laws can be applied and how indifferent and insensitive the judge (and GAL: guardian ad litem [an attorney who is appointed by the court to represent the best interests of the divorcing parties' minor children], or social worker, etc.) can be. In most cases, after they reflect on the truth and acknowledge the possibility that divorce will not solve their problems, they reconsider their position.

People who read your book will certainly have a new appreciation for the possibility that their divorce will spiral out of control and that they will not get the results they had fantasized about. This could be a real deterrent to people contemplating divorce.

People who are the unfortunate respondents to a divorce action will derive sympathy from your book and may be able to put their own misfortunes in perspective: "Well, at least my divorce isn't as bad as Judith's!" However, having read your account, I hate to say that your experience is not atypical. I wish I could say that your case was an anomaly, but I am all too familiar with situations as bad as yours and, in some instances, even worse.

I think a lot of your observations about the no-fault system are dead-on. In sum, no-fault makes the marriage contract into the only legal contract that can be unilaterally breached and the loser pays. I also liked your analogies between the no-fault divorce system and the criminal justice system. It's true that criminals have more rights and are afforded more *due process* than divorce respondents.

Another caveat to consider: A lot has changed since 1984 and continues to change with respect to No-fault Divorce. There is an undercurrent of dissent among members of the family bench and bar with respect to No-fault Divorce. They realize that the concept did not address the problems it was created to address and, in fact, actually created problems that no one anticipated.

There has been a lot of talk about the future of No-fault Divorce and what may come to replace it. **One suggestion is to bifurcate marriage altogether: to have two "kinds" of marriage**—a civil partnership (which would be sanctioned and recognized by the government and which would be subject to dissolution only under the government's laws) and a religious marriage (which would be sanctioned and recognized according to the tenets of the parties' chosen religion and which could be dissolved pursuant to "laws" established within the church). There has also been talk about making divorce an administrative proceeding (like employment matters) in order to take it out of the civil courts entirely. And, of course, some still like to talk about illegalizing divorce (just like in the good ole' days ☺).

Kelly M. Dodd, Attorney at Law

Judith Brumbaugh is a very courageous woman who has used her personal nightmare to help others.

I feel confident that Judith's struggle to be heard provided the climate and framework for Florida's current dissolution statute which now accords spouses contesting dissolution greater rights and more opportunities to be heard than existed before Judith began her difficult, and lonely, efforts to preserve – and restore – family life as the building block of American society.

Claire Ford, Attorney at Law

The manuscript is excellent. You address the *due process* argument well. I would add that the person sued for divorce can never establish a lack of merit in the suit or a legal bar to it. This is the only claim in an American court where this happens and is the explanation for why one of these claims cannot be defeated.

As an attorney with more than 40 years of experience in litigation involving federal and state constitutional issues, No-fault Divorce is the only claim recognized in the state courts of the United States where the *due process* clause for protecting a fundamental right, which marriage has been found to be by the United States Supreme Court, is ignored and patently disregarded. In fact, a divorce suit is the only one where the moving party cannot lose, if the parties are married.

> No-fault Divorce is the **only claim** recognized in the state courts of the United States **where the *due process*** clause for protecting *a fundamental right,* <u>which marriage has been found to be by the United States Supreme Court,</u> **is ignored and patently disregarded**.

> This is the only claim in an American court where … the person sued … can never establish a lack of merit in the suit or a legal bar to it.

> [No-fault] is the only … suit … where
> the moving party cannot lose …

Any intellectually honest study of the effects of divorce on the individuals involved and society as a whole will disclose that **it is the most devastating event that has ever occurred in American history by any measurement. This book describes those consequences and explains why all No-fault Divorce Laws should be repealed.**

J. Shelby Sharpe, Attorney at Law

277

APPENDIX D
Resources

Publications by Restoration of the Family
To contact, schedule a presentation, or order publications:
www.RestorationOfTheFamily.com or write: Restoration of the Family, Inc., PO Box 621342, Oviedo, FL 32762-1342.

Brumbaugh, Judith, *The Miracle of Marriage,* 2001: Author examines and lays to rest some popular misconceptions about marriage and divorce; text strongly emphasizes, from a Biblical perspective, the permanent nature of marriage.

The Nature of Marriage: Audio CD (MI): Live radio interview recorded in Michigan between Brumbaugh and live audience with call-in questions regarding marriage and divorce.

Why Divorce?: Audio CD (PA): Live radio interview recorded in Pennsylvania between Brumbaugh and live audience with call-in questions regarding marriage and divorce.

RELATED SUGGESTED READINGS
These are **not** available from Restoration of the Family

Jacob, Herbert, *Silent Revolution*, University of Chicago Press, Chicago 60637, 1988: Learn of the underlying, unrealized fallouts of divorce; discover how the nationalizing of No-fault Divorce through efforts of the NCCUSL (National Conference of Commissioners on Uniform State Laws) happened; learn how transferring property in divorce has hidden and latent affects on women and related societal status and economic well-being; how the housekeeping and child care skills utilized gratis during marriage by stay-at-home moms—while vital to the family structure—are not marketable in post-divorce situations and greatly disadvantage a woman forced into the workplace. Jacob shows how children are legally "restructured"; how they have become latchkey children raising themselves; how the now-common practice of joint custody, practically nonexistent before 1975, has been an outgrowth of No-fault Divorce.

Parejko, Judy, *Stolen Vows, The Illusion of No-Fault Divorce and the Rise of the American Divorce Industry,* Instant Publisher, Collerville, Tennessee, 2002: Working as a Family Court Mediator, the author discovered a not-so-subtle pressure to move clients in only one direction—towards a "settlement," so the divorce machinery could keep rolling. Her eventual demise came when she began questioning the underlying assumptions embedded within our system of laws. As a result of her research, she learned how the pretext for the change to No-fault Divorce was to make divorce a "kinder and gentler" process, where judges' roles would simply be to terminate the legal bonds in marriages that were clearly "dead," but instead, the general practice turned into classifying *all* marriages as "irretrievably broken," without question. The nationwide embrace of No-fault Divorce, which was engineered by a little-known quasi-governmental body of lawyers (NCCUSL) with immense influence, has resulted in a lucrative multi-billion-dollar divorce industry.

Reagan, Michael, *Twice Adopted*, Holman Publishers, Nashville, Tennessee, 2004: The tragic "inside" story of a childhood ripped apart by divorce, childhood sexual abuse, and boarding schools. These evils generated a hidden anger in Michael, an individual misunderstood by many, until the compassionate love of his wife opened the door to healing and restoration. This is an insightful revelation of how rebellion against stepmother Nancy Reagan was his way to release the anger that had been fostered by family disorder and sexual abuse. Many informative sections will help parents recognize signs of childhood pornography and abuse. Suggestions to help recognize, prevent, and lessen your child's exposure to them are also included.

Wallerstein, Judith S., *The Unexpected Legacy of Divorce*, Hyperion, New York, 2000: Focuses on the insidious sleeper effects of divorce that show up many years later in children. The information in the book is based upon interviews of children who were victims of court-ordered shared parenting. It shows how it affected their friendship with peers, their coping with two households of differing authorities, their struggles within, their loneliness, their anger and confusion, their having to raise themselves, and their becoming unwitting mediators in conflicts between their battling parents; all of these negative experiences culminated in personal struggles to establish their own families while lacking a "template" of how a successful marriage works.

Weitzman, Lenore J., *The Divorce Revolution: The unexpected social and economic consequences for women and children in America.* The Free Press, New York, 1985 (Available through interlibrary loan): A must read for those served the dreaded divorce papers. Lenore uncovers and focuses on some of the lasting economic and social effects of divorce suffered by women and children. One such consequence is the powerful hold that the initiator of a divorce holds over the spouse and children, especially if the initiator is the breadwinner and is male. The reader learns that many legal rights are unknown to women. They rely on their attorneys who, for whatever reason, do not adequately protect their female clients. Weitzman reveals that divorced women are often impoverished by No-fault because the court fails to acknowledge many of the intangibles created within the marriage that the bread-winning spouse takes with him—his earning power, his career assets, his retirement, his salary.

Index